Why I'm a
MORMON

EDITED BY JOSEPH A. CANNON
WITH SCOTT AND CHERI LOVELESS

ENSIGN
PEAK

Library of Congress Cataloging-in-Publication Data
Why I'm a Mormon / edited by Joseph A. Cannon.
    pages cm
  Includes bibliographical references.
  Summary: Essays by prominent members of The Church of Jesus Christ of Latter-day Saints, explaining why they are members of the church.
    ISBN 978-1-60908-739-5 (hardbound : alk. paper)
    1. Mormons—Biography. 2. Mormons—Doctrines. 3. The Church of Jesus Christ of Latter-day Saints—Biography. 4. The Church of Jesus Christ of Latter-day Saints—Doctrines.
5. The Church of Jesus Christ of Latter-day Saints—Membership. I. Cannon, Joseph A., editor.
    BX8693.W49 2012
    289.3092'2—dc23
    [B]   2011041188

Printed in the United States of America
Worzalla Publishing Co., Stevens Point, WI

10 9 8 7 6 5 4 3 2 1

CONTENTS

CONTENTS

PREFACE

IN THE SUMMER OF 1964 my father took two of my brothers and me to the World's Fair in New York City. (That we got there by riding our bicycles from Los Angeles is another story.) Through an interesting and, to my mind, providential, chain of events, The Church of Jesus Christ of Latter-day Saints managed to obtain one of the prime spots for its spectacular pavilion.

The Church's participation in the World's Fair was thought by many to symbolize an important new step in the growth of the restored Church, its entrance onto an international stage. Even to a young teenager it felt like the beginning of a great transformation in people's perception of the Church, not only by "the world," but by members of the Church itself. There was a growing consciousness that we were indeed becoming the international Church called to our imagination by President David O. McKay.

And yet it would not have been possible to have written a book of this scope and diversity about Latter-day Saints in 1964. It is not that there weren't interesting and notable Mormons then; there just weren't as many of them, and they were mostly concentrated in the Mountain West. It is true that George Romney was then the governor of Michigan. Elder Ezra Taft Benson had served as President Dwight D. Eisenhower's secretary of agriculture from 1953 to 1961. Elder Richard L. Evans, who had a hand in the Church's participation in the World's Fair, was famous as the voice of *Music and the Spoken Word* and would later become the president of the International Rotary Clubs. And, of course, our beloved prophet,

David O. McKay, was listed as one of the top five religious leaders in America in a poll by George Gallup in 1968.

Still, while membership in the Church doubled during President McKay's tenure, in 1964 there were just two and a quarter million Latter-day Saints. A large percentage of them lived within a one-day journey by car from Salt Lake City, Utah. Fewer than two percent of Latter-day Saints lived in Latin America.

Fast forward. Just a few years ago my daughter, Abby, was called to serve in the England London Mission. Shortly after she arrived, we received an e-mail mentioning her wonderful first companion, a young woman from Stockholm, Sweden. In her next e-mail we were treated to a photograph of the companions. Abby's companion was a tall, beautiful African woman who indeed had been born in Stockholm of Nigerian immigrants. As time went on, Abby also had companions from Italy, by way of Australia, Armenia, Romania— oh, and Kansas. Nearly every aspect of this paragraph was unimaginable by Latter-day Saints in 1964.

The stories in this book reflect the tectonic change in the Church since that great coming-out party at the 1964 World's Fair. There are some familiar names in the book, though, hopefully, less familiar stories. There are other less familiar names whose stories take us around the world to places one would have had to have been farsighted indeed to have imagined in 1964. But there are also stories in this book of members who were alive at the time of the World's Fair who moved forward into the world deeply and broadly into professions and activities at a level of success that also would have been difficult to conceive of nearly five decades ago.

As noted, it would have been difficult to have written this book fifty years ago. Today it was difficult enough to write, but for the opposite reason. There are already too many entries. Space constraints prevented the inclusion in this volume of numerous equally compelling stories. Fifty years hence, observers will look back with great astonishment at the growth and development of the Church, and there won't be room in multiple volumes to capture the individual contributions and diversity of members of the Church in that day.

With the humble recognition that all of us fall short of the glory of God, nevertheless, we are not ashamed of the gospel of Jesus Christ. We feel that we can embrace the test, "By their fruits ye shall know them" (Matthew 7:20).

JOSEPH A. CANNON

MATAUMU TOELUPE ALISA

MATAUMU TOELUPE ALISA is an artist who has mastered many media. But he is best known for his large murals in private collections and public buildings across Hawaii, including the Hawaii Judiciary Building and the Hawaii State Convention Center.

Born in 1942 in a *fale* or thatched-roof hut on the island of Upolu, Western Samoa, Mataumu immigrated to Hawaii at age eighteen and enrolled at the Church College of Hawaii (now BYU–Hawaii). He had such a passion for art that he would regularly sneak into the art room after hours and paint all night. Consequently he slept through enough classes to earn academic dismissal. Frustrated, he found his place at the Honolulu Academy of Arts, where he studied before and after his mission to Samoa (1967–1969).

His life and his art were significantly influenced by David Asherman and Juliette May Fraser, artists with whom he did several joint projects. He was inspired by the great murals of Mexico's Renaissance when the trio traveled to Mexico to create a ceramic tile mural.

In 1975, Mataumu completed his first large mural (ten by sixty feet) for Molokai High School. During this project he met Ann

Zukin, an art student from California. They were married in 1976 and have reared five children.

In 1982, the BYU–Hawaii art department requested that Mataumu bring his studio to the Laie campus so students could experience a major work in progress—a mural for the University of Hawaii at Manoa. Through this experience, he was inspired to return to school in 1984 to, as he puts it, "help me to be a better artist and a better patriarch for my family." He received his BFA in 1987 and his MFA from BYU in Provo, Utah, in 1990. By 1997, he was teaching at the university that had once dismissed him. He retired in 2011.

A quiet man with a happy nature, he is always serving. His disarming sense of humor comes in handy when he critiques student work with quips like: "Your trees look like they're from Jurassic Park," or "I think your painting needs a blessing."

Among ceramic muralists, Mataumu Alisa is known for the consistency of his glaze finish in large ceramic murals—something extremely difficult to maintain. His secret? "As I place each batch of tiles into the kiln and fire it up, I offer a prayer to know the right time to turn off the kiln. I invariably feel a gentle whisper, 'Now is the time,' and I offer another prayer of gratitude."

. . .

A N IMPORTANT PART of why I am a Mormon is the way my parents came into the Church. My parents were born at a time when The Church of Jesus Christ of Latter-day Saints was new to Samoa, and its members faced tremendous religious persecution. My father's birth in 1899, after an arranged marriage between a maiden of one village and Chief Seaga Toelupe of Malie, created an alliance between the two villages. Relatives of the maiden who were new members of the Church were named foster parents of the baby. They were serving as a missionary couple, and having this baby helped their work and the Church gain respect and acceptance from other villages and churches.

A year later, my mother was born of a similar arranged marriage. Something incredible happened—an LDS missionary couple related to my mother were granted a request to be foster parents of the baby girl. As was the custom in the Church in those days, these two sets of missionaries, with my parents-to-be, moved from village to village and island to island working to build up the Church. Both couples sent their children to a new Church school in Sauniatu, a beautiful, isolated village built inside the crater of an extinct volcano by early Saints who had been persecuted and expelled from their villages for being Mormons.

My parents met there, married, and were called on a mission of their own to build the Church in Samoa. They would go to a village to live while they taught the gospel. Because Samoans love to sing, my parents would introduce the Church by organizing a choir. Singing in four-part harmony with someone standing in front of the singers waving a stick was a novelty for most of these people. My father wrote songs of the Restoration for the choirs to sing. My mother taught the young men of another faith to play the organ so they could have a choir in their church as well. When the LDS Church was finally established and strong in one village, my parents would be called to preach elsewhere.

I was the last child of two girls and eight boys. Before my sisters and I were born, an influenza outbreak swept through Samoa, killing many people. My father returned from his Church assignments to find that one of his small sons had died and been buried. My mother was holding a second son, fearing he would soon stop breathing. They had previously lost one other son to illness. I later asked my mother what my father said when he came home to such sorrow. She said, "He put his hand on my shoulder and told me I would see my boys again." Father gave the dying two-year-old boy a priesthood blessing. My mother recalled it as a strange blessing that said the boy would live to bury both his father and his mother. This son survived. A third son would die years later.

One day an entourage of chiefs arrived at the village where my parents were serving. They brought a message from my father's natural father, Chief Toelupe. He wanted my father to be the next chief. My father had other brothers. He said he could not serve as chief because he was serving in the Church. The aging chief then did the unthinkable: he sent emissaries to the mission president to have the Church release his son. The mission president wrote a note to my father asking him to pack up and come by the mission home on his way to Malie to be the new chief. He set apart (blessed) my father to be chief of the Toelupe family and to bring them the gospel. He set apart my mother to be a counselor to her husband in this assignment.

According to tradition, the holder of the Toelupe title was expected to be a Protestant. Toelupe ancestors had received Christianity from missionaries of the London Missionary Society (LMS) from England. Since their descendants traditionally maintained an association with the LMS, the Toelupe chief was the patron of the LMS Church in Malie. Another expectation of the holder of the Toelupe title was for the chief to have a chief's tattoo, an intricate, inked design that runs from the chest to below his knees. When Father was introduced into the village, he was widely accepted as *faife'au* (minister of the gospel) and *matai* (chief). Being the minister of the gospel, he decided not to be tattooed. His dual calling as missionary and chief has brought positive changes for good in the village of Malie.

Just in front of our home, the old chief's round meetinghouse sat atop an elevated stone platform. The chiefs, when they met, would gather in a circle wearing their traditional lavalavas, arranged to afford a view of the sacred tattoos. My father would come to the meetings dressed as a missionary, wearing long white pants, a long-sleeved white shirt, and a black bow tie. The meeting always started with a ceremony drinking kava juice to honor ancestors. Surrounding the meetinghouse, to prevent intruders from breaking the sanctity of the meeting, the untitled men of the village stood armed with clubs.

I was two years old and curious. Whenever I heard the clapping for a meeting, I would run out of the house, straight to the chiefs' meetinghouse. My father would tell the armed men to let me come to him. This was unheard of. I would also ask my father for a drink of kava. Standing right next to him, I would drink from the same cup shared by all the chiefs. In Samoan culture, it is very unusual for a child to enter the circle, much less drink from the chiefs' cup. But family was important to my father, and he did not want to exclude us. Finally, an older chief suggested that they bestow a title on me to make it official for me to join the circle of chiefs and drink the kava. My chief title is Inu tu—which means to stand and drink.

Father formed a new branch of the Church at his farm, and there he taught and baptized many Chinese laborers who worked close by. He also organized a choir at a nearby prison. The prisoners were allowed to attend church and sing in the choir. Many of them joined the Church. In Malie, my mother organized the women. They chose a woman president of the village to bring women's and children's problems to the chiefs' council.

My father died at the young age of forty-seven, when I was only three. The day he died, I was under his hospital bed. He told me to be quiet and not let the doctor know that I was there. I remember that the whole village came wailing to touch him as he lay in the village meetinghouse. He was buried beside the road between his village and his farm. The men placed a large stone pointed to heaven at the head of his simple grave. It was impossible for my oldest brothers, away at school and work, to return. At seventeen, the son my father had blessed to live to bury him made all the arrangements for the burial. He was also the one responsible for the burial of my mother when she died at age eighty-nine. Mother announced one morning that she had seen her sons and declared it was time for her to go home. Three days later she died.

Before my father died, he instructed my mother to move our family to the village of Pesega, where the mission home was located, so we could be close to the Church. During our move, a Chinese widower who had been married to our cousin asked my mother to adopt his five children because the government was deporting Chinese laborers. Our now enlarged family lived in a *fale,* a thatched-roof home without walls, where blinds woven from coconut leaves were let down to block wind or rain. We all slept close to each other on the floor on mats made of lauhala leaves.

I learned how to pray by watching my mother. She had great faith. Every night she would kneel and begin her prayer by singing the hymn "O My Father." My adopted little brother, Lafi, and I would fall asleep each holding onto one of her ankles. I remember waking up—sometimes many times during the night—and my mother would still be praying. We woke up in the morning still holding her ankles.

The most beautiful day of my life was the Saturday morning I was baptized. People were all dressed in white standing on the thick green grass within the white wall surrounding our chapel when I went down into the clear, clear water of the outdoor baptismal font. While awaiting the completion of a new Church school, I attended the Marist Brothers School. One day during recess a priest drew a picture of Mary, the mother of Jesus, on the blackboard. I had never seen anyone do that before. I decided then that that was what I really wanted to do.

I began to draw pictures every day. I would draw on any piece of paper I could find. My mother noticed my new interest and provided me with my own blackboard. I used it constantly. In school I was punished frequently because I drew instead of doing schoolwork. They would make me stay after school and pull weeds for an hour, then I would go home and draw some more. When the school needed someone to paint scenery for its popular annual operettas, I had my first opportunity to design and paint on a large scale.

My family moved to Hawaii, where I finished high school as a good art student. In the fall of 1963, I entered the (LDS) Church College of Hawaii. It was the most frustrating time of my life. I was not prepared to take so many classes. The art classes were not long enough. After the first semester, I was dismissed from school and went to work for a year. I returned, but the second time was worse. I hated even the art classes. At night I would sneak out of the dorm and walk on the roof of the school, thinking. I felt there was something else I must do. One night I walked into the auditorium where a group was practicing for a play. I practically begged them to let me paint the scenery. They were pleased with my work, and it was a rewarding experience. When the semester was over, I knew I should be in an art school. I enrolled in the Honolulu Academy of

Arts and enjoyed learning from the internationally known artists the Academy brought to Hawaii.

The following year I was called on a mission to Samoa. My art teachers were not happy with my decision to go, but I knew I should serve a mission. When I returned to the Academy after my mission, my very first project won an award and was purchased by the San Diego Museum of Fine Arts. I sold my class projects faster than I could produce them. To sustain myself, I also worked as a plumber. I was happy with life because each day I was doing something in art.

Soon the Hawaii State Foundation on Culture and the Arts awarded me a commission to create a large ceramic tile mural on the theme of ancient Hawaiian sports for the high school on Molokai. I extended the size of the mural to 600 square feet so I would have more to learn. After three years of education, frustration, and excitement, it was dedicated in 1975. It was the most perfect thing I had ever done.

One day, while I was sitting in my studio, something like a voice spoke to my mind that unless I married, I would make no further progress in my life. Later, during the dedication of my mural in Molokai, I became better acquainted with Ann Sherman Zukin— one of the most important and happy events of my life. After a brief courtship, we were sealed in the Oakland Temple seven years after I returned from my mission. Ann was called to serve in the Relief Society presidency (our Church women's organization), and I served in the Young Men's program. These callings were important factors in our marriage that taught us service, love, compassion, and patience. My desire has become to express in my art the goodness and love of the Lord to all humankind. I hope to perfect my way of communicating through my murals so that every brushstroke expresses my gratitude and brings someone closer to Christ.

Whenever I have questions in my life or need direction, I think of my parents. For me, growing up in the Church in my particular family is a miracle. I didn't have to find the Church; I was given it. My parents were teachers of the gospel. I was taught gospel principles. I watched my parents live them. I grew up knowing that God lives, that Jesus is the Christ. Many times I have had the Spirit testify to me that the Church is true. The Church *is* true. That is why I am a Mormon.

NOLAN ARCHIBALD

NOLAN D. ARCHIBALD is executive chairman of the board of Stanley Black & Decker, Inc., a $12 billion global corporation that markets its products in more than 100 countries. Until the March 2010 merger with Stanley Works, he had served as chief executive officer of The Black & Decker Corporation for twenty-four years, the second-longest-serving CEO of the largest 1,000 companies in the United States that were not family controlled. When first appointed president and chief executive officer in March 1986 at the age of forty-two, he was the youngest CEO of a Fortune 500 Company.

Mr. Archibald is a recipient of the American Marketing Association's Edison Achievement Award for significant and lasting contributions to marketing excellence and product innovation. He has been cited by *Business Week* as one of the top six managers in the United States and by *Fortune Magazine* as one of the country's "ten most wanted" executives. He is currently a member of the boards of directors of Lockheed Martin Corporation, Huntsman Corporation, and Brunswick Corporation and is a member of the President's Leadership Council at Brigham Young University. Past board memberships include: ITT Corporation, the Johns Hopkins University Board of Trustees, and Associates of the Harvard Business School.

Nolan graduated from Dixie State College in Utah, where he was an honor student and an All-American basketball player. He led his team to the National Junior College finals and was recruited by more than fifty major universities in the United States. He later graduated cum laude from Weber State University, where he was Scholar Athlete of the Year in 1968. He was an All-Conference basketball player under Dick Motta and played on Weber State's first team to participate in the NCAA basketball tournament, when only thirty-two teams participated. He was one of fifteen Division I basketball players out of four thousand named an Academic All-American. He earned a master's degree in business administration from the Harvard Business School in 1970.

Following graduation from Harvard, Nolan was invited to try out for the Chicago Bulls in the NBA. He was offered a contract to play with the Pittsburgh Pipers in the ABA. In 1993, the National Association of Basketball Coaches honored him as one of their "Silver Anniversary NCAA All American Basketball Team." He is the only athlete in Weber State's history to receive this honor.

Nolan was born and raised in Ogden, Utah. He is married to the former Margaret Hafen. They are the parents of seven sons and one daughter and have eighteen grandchildren. Nolan has served as a bishop twice and as stake president of the Washington D.C. Stake. He currently serves as an Area Seventy.

· · ·

JESUS CHRIST SAID, "Wherefore by their fruits ye shall know them" (Matthew 7:20). Today there are more than six hundred Christian churches teaching different doctrines, all professing to be the "Church of Jesus Christ." The reason I am a member of The Church of Jesus Christ of Latter-day Saints (a Mormon) is that I believe it is the same church that Christ established in the meridian of time, restored back to the earth through a prophet, Joseph

Smith, in these latter days. Just as Jesus Christ revealed his will in Old and New Testament times to prophets like Moses, Isaiah, Peter, and Paul, so he did to the Prophet Joseph Smith. Why do I believe The Church of Jesus Christ of Latter-day Saints is the Church of Jesus Christ restored by Him through his prophet, Joseph Smith? As Christ said: "ye shall know them by their fruits" (Matthew 7:16).

What are some of the "fruits" of The Church of Jesus Christ of Latter-day Saints? One of the most notable is the Book of Mormon. The Book of Mormon is a thousand-year scriptural history written at about the same time as the Bible. The Book of Mormon contains accounts of multiple wars and histories, visions and prophecies, and doctrines and exhortations of a people who lived here on the American continent. It also contains the account of Jesus Christ appearing to these people following His resurrection in Jerusalem. We have the Old Testament that testifies of Christ, we have the New Testament that testifies of Christ, and we have the Book of Mormon, "Another Testament of Jesus Christ." It is one of the fruits of the Church.

Another fruit is the organization of the Church itself. During Christ's ministry, He organized and established His church, "built upon the foundation of the apostles and prophets, Jesus Christ himself being the chief corner stone" (Ephesians 2:20). Two thousand years later, The Church of Jesus Christ of Latter-day Saints is organized in the same manner as Christ's Church was in the meridian of time. Our current prophet, Thomas S. Monson, was called by Jesus Christ as was Peter of old. And like Peter, who served in a presidency with James and John, President Monson presides over the Church with two counselors. We also have twelve modern-day Apostles who function as did the Apostles of old.

In addition, countless men and women are called to serve in a variety of leadership and pastoral positions who receive no compensation for their service. Like those called at the time of Christ, these members are not taught or trained for the ministry in special seminaries or colleges. Nor are wealth, education, or social position relevant factors to the positions in which they serve. A bishop with little formal education may preside over a ward with many highly educated doctors and lawyers. The organizational structure of the Church is identical to that which Christ established, and is another fruit of The Church of Jesus Christ of Latter-day Saints.

Another fruit is the members themselves. What other organization in the world today "produces" the kind of individuals and families you find in The Church of Jesus Christ of Latter-day Saints? One of our Apostles, Dallin H. Oaks, said, "Of course, our Church does not have a monopoly on good people, but we have a remarkable concentration of them" ("The Gospel in Our Lives," *Ensign*, May 2002, 34–35). What other organization has young men and young women who abstain from tea, coffee, alcohol, tobacco, and illegal drugs; who abstain from sex until marriage; who daily attend early-morning seminary classes; and who read the scriptures regularly?

A well-known fruit is our missionary program. What other organization today has more than fifty thousand young men and women who put their schooling, careers, and personal and family lives on hold to accept an assignment from a prophet to serve for eighteen months to two years as full-time missionaries? They receive no monetary compensation.

Missionary work for these young men and young women is extraordinarily demanding. They are expected to work twelve to fourteen hours a day, six and a half days a week, with no vacation or holidays. Equally remarkable is that older couples accept calls as missionaries or mission presidents, serving up to three years. They too put their careers and families on hold to serve in the missionary program of the Church. Since the restoration of the Church, more than one million individual Latter-day Saints have been set apart as full-time missionaries. This is at a time when many other churches are challenged just to get their young people to attend church.

Another fruit is the Word of Wisdom, the law of health given to the Prophet Joseph Smith one hundred and seventy-five years ago. The Lord told Joseph Smith that tobacco, alcohol, tea, and coffee were not good for us. He also said to eat meat sparingly and that fruits and vegetables and grains were good for us. The Lord further said that "all saints who remember to keep and do these sayings . . . shall receive health in their navel and marrow to their bones; . . . and shall run and not be weary, and shall walk and not faint" (Doctrine and Covenants 89:18, 20). Practicing Mormons have better health and live longer than the national average.

Our church welfare program is another fruit. It teaches its members to develop self-reliance in six areas: education, employment, health, home storage, resource management, and social and emotional strength. When members of our church need some type of temporal assistance, they receive things like food or clothing from the Church. But whenever possible, they work for what they get.

Our welfare program has also helped countless people not of our faith during times of disaster and need. Last year alone, The Church of Jesus Christ of Latter-day Saints sent humanitarian aid to hundreds of projects, giving millions of dollars in aid.

Strong families represent another fruit of LDS Church membership. Members are taught to set one night a week aside as a family home evening devoted to family instruction, activity, fun, and togetherness. We are taught that no other success can compensate for failure in the home, and that the most important work that we will do will be within the walls of our own homes.

Perhaps the most important fruits of The Church of Jesus Christ of Latter-days Saints are its doctrines. Many of our doctrines, although taught in the New Testament, are unique among today's Christian churches. Take the nature of God. What Joseph Smith learned from his first vision and subsequent revelations about God was that the Father and the Son are two separate and distinct beings; that the "oneness" described in the scriptures is one in purpose, one in mind, one in character. We believe "The Father has a body of flesh and bones as tangible as man's; the Son also; but the Holy Ghost has not a body of flesh and bones, but is a personage of Spirit. Were it not so, the Holy Ghost could not dwell in us" (Doctrine and Covenants 130:22).

Another doctrine is the nature of man and the nature of woman, which I think is a profound and unique doctrine taught in The Church of Jesus Christ of Latter-day Saints. We are indeed created in the image of God. We are actual spirit offspring of God. He is literally the Father of our spirits, and human intelligences born of God—both men and women—have, as His children, infinite potential. Family and eternal marriage are central to our exaltation. We believe families can be together forever if we have faith and are obedient to God's laws. This is part of what we call the plan of salvation, which answers life's most profound questions: (1) where we came from, (2) why we're here, and (3) where we're going. I know of no other church that answers these three profound questions.

Modern-day revelation is another profound and unique doctrine of the Church. The heavens are not closed. God reveals His truths to apostles and prophets today just as He did in times of old. If God is the same "yesterday, today, and for ever" (Hebrews 13:8) and spoke to prophets in Old and New Testament times, why would He stop in our day? Does He love us less? Do we not need the same guidance today as His followers did then? Why is it so hard to believe that He would "do nothing, but he revealeth his secret unto his servants the prophets" (Amos 3:7) in Old and New Testament times and not continue to do the same today? As our ninth Article of Faith states, "We believe all that God has revealed, all that He does now reveal, and we believe that He will yet reveal many great and important things pertaining to the Kingdom of God."

Other doctrines we teach are also fruits: "When ye are in the service of your fellow beings ye are only in the service of your God" (Mosiah 2:17); "Adam fell that men might be; and men are, that they might have joy" (2 Nephi 2:25); "This is my work and my glory—to bring to pass the immortality and eternal life of man" (Moses 1:39); "We believe in being honest, true, chaste, benevolent, virtuous, and in doing good to all men" (Articles of Faith 1:13); "The glory of God is intelligence, or, in other words, light and truth" (Doctrine and Covenants 93:36).

These are but a few of the "fruits" of The Church of Jesus Christ of Latter-day Saints and are only part of the basis on which my membership rests. I have accepted the admonition of the last Book of Mormon prophet, Moroni, who invites all the inhabitants of the earth to find out if "these things" are true for themselves.

"And when ye shall receive these things, I would exhort you that ye would ask God, the eternal Father, in the name of Christ, if these things are not true; and if ye shall ask with a sincere heart, with real intent, having faith in Christ, he will manifest the truth of it unto you, by the power of the Holy Ghost.

"And by the power of the Holy Ghost ye may know the truth of all things" (Moroni 10:4–5).

We believe that God answers prayers. We literally believe that if you pray and ask God, He will manifest these truths to you. I have studied these things; I have prayed about these things; and I have received personal revelation that these things are true. This spiritual confirmation, this very personal revelation in answer to prayer, is why I am a member of The Church of Jesus Christ of Latter-day Saints.

DAVID ARCHULETA

DAVID JAMES ARCHULETA was born December 28, 1990, in Miami, Florida, to Jeff, a jazz musician from Utah, and Lupe, a salsa dancer and singer from Honduras. David was exposed to diverse music genres growing up in Utah, from Latin music on his mother's side to jazz music from his father's

collection. He was particularly fond of and inspired by gospel, pop, R&B, and "soulful" music, as well as Broadway musicals.

At ten years old, David won the children's division of the Utah Talent Competition, leading to other television singing appearances. He became the Junior Vocal Champion on *Star Search 2* when he was twelve. In 2007, at sixteen years old, he became one of the youngest finalists on the popular television series *American Idol.* In May 2008 he finished as the runner-up, receiving 44 percent of over 97 million votes.

Barely after *Idol,* David saw massive success straight out of the gate with his first lead single, *Crush,* a catchy pop tune, which charted at No. 2 on the *Billboard Hot 100* and has since sold two million downloads.

David is deeply passionate about helping others, supporting numerous charities such as *Rising Star Outreach, Invisible Children,*

Children's Miracle Network, and *Stand Up to Cancer.* In the aftermath of the 2010 Haiti earthquake, he delved into his Latino roots by lending his voice to the recording of *Somos El Mundo,* a Spanish version of *We Are the World.*

David has toured extensively across the United States, the United Kingdom, and Asia to perform for fans. "It's amazing how one song can change someone's life," he says. "It's been done for me so many times, and I want to give to my fans the same thing those artists have given me."

• • •

I WAS FORTUNATE ENOUGH to be born and raised in The Church of Jesus Christ of Latter-day Saints. But I think everyone realizes there is a time when you really, on your own, become converted to the Church by the Spirit from your own experiences—when you gain your own relationship with Heavenly Father. We all have challenges with our self-identity when we're teenagers, and I guess that is when most people begin to ask their own questions. That was the case for me. Things came up that challenged what my parents had been teaching me, and I had to find out for myself.

I guess I was about twelve years old when I started wondering about things. I never questioned if God existed; that wasn't a problem for me. But one of my challenges was that I didn't understand a lot of things. I always had trouble comprehending things in school. Maybe that is why music is something that I connected so easily and quickly with. I didn't talk very much—I still don't talk very much—but there was something I felt in music that made so much sense to me. I couldn't always explain it to other people, so I just shared how I felt through my music and singing.

For some reason, especially when I was a child, I felt a powerful connection to the songs in church, those moving songs we sang.

I knew God existed because I could feel Him during the music. I could feel His Spirit so strongly through those songs.

During my teenage years in particular, the challenge for me was to know if God cared about me individually. That was what I needed to understand for myself. I thought He had a lot more to worry about than little old me. I was a quiet, shy boy who didn't know what he wanted from life. I didn't have any sense at all of my self-worth, and my shyness made that problem even greater. It complicated things. It seemed as though everyone else was good at sports, or they could play the piano really well, or they were super singers. I loved to sing, but I didn't think I did it very well. So, as much as I loved singing, I didn't think that was what would make me successful in life.

I didn't feel like I had any worth in the eyes of someone as great as God. I was even afraid to pray because I didn't think God would want to hear from me. I *would* pray sometimes, but I just didn't know if He wanted to listen to me. I would attend church and listen because I always felt it was really important to learn about God, but I didn't understand the process of gaining a relationship with God because I didn't think I could. I didn't think I was capable of it. I felt I was so small and insignificant and so lacking in skills or education or talents.

What made that start to change was when I first really started reading my scriptures, when I was around eleven or twelve years of age. At first the scriptures didn't make a lot of sense to me, but then I began reading independently and I started understanding some things. The stories and also the character of the people I was reading about started to really strike me. I was drawn into the scriptures by how much the people seemed to love and look forward to things in life, how much they loved God, how much they loved their families. The optimism they showed for life struck me the most.

As I was reading more and really paying attention to the

Church, I would ask myself questions as to what I was supposed to accomplish, why I was here on earth. When I wondered about my self-worth, I would go into seminary class and get my answers there. Once I was old enough to ask questions and wonder, that was when things started to make more sense.

I think I really started to believe that the Church was true when I was finishing reading the Book of Mormon for the first time. When I read the scriptures, the words about prayer really stood out to me. I could see there were people who truly had conversations with God. After I completely read through the Book of Mormon, I saw Moroni's challenge to pray and ask God yourself. His words were so convincing. Moroni already knew this was true, but he challenged people at the end of the Book of Mormon to ask for themselves if this book was true and see if God would give them an answer. It was humbling to read what he had to say and to take on that challenge. I had to get up enough courage to ask God if this was real and if it was true. And the great thing is that I did learn for myself that the Book of Mormon is true!

The more I prayed, the more I started realizing who God was and understanding that He wasn't just some super ultra Being who acknowledges you only when you do something amazing, but He was someone I could talk to with reverence. Someone who cared about the challenges I had. Someone I could have a relationship with and who would love me, no matter what. That is how I gained my own testimony of the gospel: when I established my relationship with God. I had to pray and do something I wasn't sure about. But once I got over that hump, I knew I could pour out my respect and appreciation to Him, and I knew that I didn't have to be a king or a prophet or a bishop to pray to him. I knew I could praise Him and let Him know my thanks to Him. And when I was able to let Him know that, I could really feel His love. I could feel Him saying, "My son, I love you so much, and I care about you," and I could feel impressions from the Spirit saying, "Here is what you can do." It was just really surprising to feel something back.

Music is a strong element in my testimony because of how present those feelings of the Spirit are when you are singing about things that matter. The feeling is *so* strong.

One of the most memorable prayers that I've ever had answered was when I was in high school. I was confused. I had vocal cord paralysis. I thought that was the answer that I wasn't supposed to do music anymore. But my desire to do music never went away. When *American Idol* came, I was going to school and had a summer job, and I was wondering whether to audition. I didn't want to think about it because I didn't think I was good enough, but something kept urging me to go. The feeling wouldn't leave me alone, and so I decided to pray about it. I felt dumb again because I didn't think that Heavenly Father would care enough about a decision like this. But at the same time, I felt like it was important to pray about it. So I knelt beside my bed and asked Him about this thing that had been on my mind. I asked Him what His opinion was about me auditioning for *American Idol,* if I should quit my job and do it. I immediately got a strong, strong feeling back: "Go and audition. There is something for you to learn." I was really surprised about that. It almost felt as though a big wind rushed over me. That was when I made my decision to go.

During *American Idol,* I saw how my beliefs really came into play because I felt like Heavenly Father had given me that opportunity. I wouldn't be there without Him. So I made sure I gave back to Him because I didn't want to disappoint Him. I knew my relationship with music was closely tied to Him. I knew I had a responsibility to share what I had felt and learned from music. Even though each week on *Idol* was very challenging, I worked hard to pick songs that allowed the feelings of the Spirit to be there and to make sure people understood why I was there. Especially when I sang "Imagine," I was sure I would get voted off the show, but I felt I was doing what Heavenly Father would have wanted me to do.

I couldn't believe the response I got from the people who worked on *American Idol,* and then the judges, and then all the people after that. All I did was sing the songs in a way that was meaningful to me and allowed me to feel that spiritual feeling. People of all ages wrote me letters telling me what they felt. I was shocked by how direct they would be, saying they weren't sure what it was but that they had felt something powerful and strong and beautiful. So many letters were coming in, just hundreds of them. Hardly any of them were, "You are so cute"; most of them were just thank yous and people saying there was something they felt when I sang. Many said they weren't sure what they were feeling, and they asked if I could tell them what it was. I hadn't realized how people who didn't feel the Spirit often didn't know what they were feeling. I knew Heavenly Father really wanted me to be there, He had a purpose for me, and He wanted me to help people feel good and come closer to Him. It was touching for me to have that opportunity.

I guess that was one of the most remarkable things for me, to see how the Lord works. I didn't go on TV and say I was a Mormon. All I did was sing the songs that I felt people would be able to connect to, the same way I've been able to connect to things through the Spirit. I didn't feel like I did this incredible performance there. There was something else that was coming across to people. It is amazing how the Spirit can communicate in that way.

I feel the Spirit when I sing, and I have learned that others can feel the Spirit as well. When I realized that the Spirit was what I was also feeling when I went to church, I learned how to serve other people better. I learned how you can love your family better and get to know God better as you try to live the commandments and be obedient. It is like the Spirit feeds you and helps you little by little. When I connected those two together, I understood that my

Heavenly Father is also the one who allowed me to have music because I feel Him so strongly through it.

I know that the way we can be happy is to know that Heavenly Father loves us, and that happiness comes through having a relationship with Him. That is why I'm a Mormon. And I just want to do whatever I can to help people understand that and seek a relationship with Him for themselves.

ROBERT F. BENNETT

A FORMER UNITED STATES SENATOR from Utah, Robert F. Bennett has earned a reputation among his colleagues, constituents, and clients as a pragmatic problem solver who seeks creative and common-sense solutions. He first entered the political arena in

1962 by managing the senatorial reelection campaign for his father, Wallace F. Bennett, who served as a U.S. senator from 1951 to 1974.

Prior to seeking office himself thirty years later, he held a variety of governmental and business positions, including serving as CEO of Franklin International Institute (now FranklinCovey). While Mr. Bennett managed the firm, it grew from four employees to a listing on the New York Stock Exchange.

After his election in 1992, Mr. Bennett served on the Senate Banking Committee, the Senate Appropriations Committee, and as chairman of the distinguished Joint Economic Committee, where he was at the center of national economic policy discussions. He was also the ranking Republican on the Senate Rules Committee and counsel to Republican leader Mitch McConnell of Kentucky.

Mr. Bennett was at the forefront of health-care reform when he cosponsored the Healthy Americans Act, the first major bipartisan health-care legislation in more than a decade. Widely praised by health-care experts, the bill would have guaranteed quality, affordable, and portable health coverage for every American, cutting health costs by more than $1.2 trillion over the next decade.

Mr. Bennett is a graduate of the University of Utah, where he was student-body president. He and his wife, Joyce, are the parents of six children and grandparents of twenty.

. . .

WHY AM I A MORMON? When some people look at my background, they ask, "How could you *not* be a Mormon? You were born into a Mormon family with progenitors who knew both Joseph Smith and Brigham Young and all of their successors as heads of the Church, one of whom was your own grandfather. Your parents took you to church meetings and socials virtually from birth. You went to school with Mormons, worked with Mormons, dated Mormons, and did all the proper things young Mormons are supposed to do while they are growing up, including serving a mission. You ran for public office in a state where the large majority of voters were Mormons. You are a Mormon simply because it has always been the right social and political thing for you to be—period."

I respectfully disagree with the notion that one cannot break out of the patterns of his early years. I can cite examples of those with similar backgrounds, some in my own family, who have made the decision as adults not to have any further affiliation with Mormonism.

I fully concede that my family and early church training had an important impact on me. When I began a serious study of Mormon doctrine and scripture as a teenager, I was predisposed to believe it. When I took the next step and prayed for confirmation of its truth, it was not difficult for me to hear the "still small voice" that whispered that it was, in fact, from God. Nonetheless, while I acknowledge that my family prepared the way for me to accept it, I maintain that I am a Mormon because I was convinced from my

own experience with prayer, as a young man, that God speaks to us directly when we humble ourselves and properly seek His counsel.

My mission experience reinforced this conviction. I watched people's lives be changed, immeasurably for the better, by their acceptance of the things we were teaching them. I listened to them as they told me how *their* prayers had been answered, often in ways more dramatic than mine had been, as they sought the confirmation that the scriptures promised them. I also saw what happened to people who made the choice to walk away from the Church after having embraced it.

Thus, I remained a Mormon as a young adult because I saw how much good the Church does for its members.

Then came marriage and a family. During our child-rearing years, we lived away from Utah, in areas where our children's friends and teachers were not Mormons. Plenty of good people around us were doing their very best to live good lives without any contact with the Mormon church. As we interacted with them, my wife and I saw how much easier it was for us to deal with our family's challenges than it was for some of them—not because we were better parents than they were, but because we had the help of the support system that the Church provides.

We are seeing that same pattern repeat itself in the lives of our grandchildren. Our daughter told me of a high school teacher in California where our grandson was enrolled who knew all about all of her students: which ones were on drugs, which ones were caught up in messy sexual relationships, and which ones were drinking too much. This teacher told our daughter that our grandson had none of these problems; indeed, she said, "*All* the Mormon kids in my class are just fine."

My career has literally taken me all over the world. I have dealt with a wide variety of people and have often been alone in distant cities on business assignments. Opportunities to cut corners on a deal or to step outside the bounds of one's marriage vow have often been present, and I have seen some of my associates do that. Some of them have questioned me about my refusal to join them. "Aren't you even curious?" one asked me, when watching a prostitute wander through a hotel lobby seeking clients. But my observation of what happens in the lives of those who use "curiosity" as an excuse to cheat on a formal and solemn commitment has reconfirmed to me the wisdom of the prophet who wrote, in the Book of Mormon, "Wickedness never was happiness" (Alma 41:10).

Adherence to Mormon standards of conduct has served me well throughout my life.

One of the characteristics of the Mormon church is its reliance on a "lay priesthood," a system where the leadership of a congregation is chosen from the membership of that congregation, with no prerequisites of education or status. I have had the opportunity of serving three times as a counselor to a bishop and once as the bishop myself. In that role, with support from my own counselors, I presided over a congregation of several hundred people of all ages. I was responsible for choosing which of them would hold the various teaching and administrative positions in the group, for seeking to resolve the complaints and concerns of those who had problems, for encouraging and counseling the youth, for dispersing charity funds to those in need, and occasionally for providing Church discipline and correction when required for those who had fallen into serious transgression. It was a time-consuming, emotionally draining, challenging calling, coming as it did in addition to my own employment and family responsibilities.

I could not have done it without the constant support of the Lord, which was available to me through prayer on my own and in prayerful consultation with my counselors and, if needed, those who presided over me (who also served in a volunteer status). I learned to rely on God, and there were many times when His Spirit was very close.

In recent years, I have again studied the Book of Mormon at length to see how it holds up half a century after the youthful enthusiasm of a twenty-year-old missionary has died down. I have discovered much greater depth, wisdom, and power in it than I did before, giving me a new and deeper understanding of just what a miraculous scriptural treasure it really is. It can pass the test that modern scholars apply to it, and it stands as a support for the Bible in a doubting age.

I am a Mormon because the heft of sound scholarship reaffirms the sweet whisperings of faith.

I am a Mormon because over the course of a lifetime of varied experiences, joys, crises, hardships, and challenges, Mormonism has taught me the vivid truth that God exists and that He loves me. He has heard my prayers and answered them again and again, in every case with what has been best for me (even when I did not see it at the time). He has told me through the teachings of His prophets, living and dead, that a magnificent eternal glory is available to me and to all who will humble themselves enough to seek it in the way He prescribed, which requires simply acknowledging His hand in all things and keeping His commandments.

I am a Mormon because the lessons and blessings of Church service are embedded deep in my soul.

Given these truths, indeed, how could I *not* be a Mormon?

Alex Boyé

Alex Boyé has been entertaining audiences worldwide for over fifteen years. He has had hits in more than fifteen countries and has sold more than half a million CDs. He has performed alongside such groups as Bryan Adams, George Michael, Simon and Garfunkel, MC Hammer, Vanilla Ice, N'SYNC, Jay-Z, The Backstreet Boys, Jordyn Sparks, Missy Elliott, Mary J. Blige, David Archuleta, and The Smashing Pumpkins.

Born and raised in London, England, Alex joined The Church of Jesus Christ of Latter-day Saints as a teenager. He served a mission in Bristol, England. At the suggestion of his mission president, he decided to pursue music as a career.

Alex has performed in many notable venues across the United States, including the MGM Grand in Las Vegas. He has also played a walk-in role in the CBS sitcom *How I Met Your Mother.*

Alex has had music featured in several movie soundtracks, including *Charly, The Dance, Baptists at Our Barbecue, Church Ball,* and *Scout Camp.* He recently performed the hit song "Born to Be a Scout" in front of 100,000 Boy Scouts during the National Boy Scouts of America Jamboree celebrating 100 years of Scouting, an event watched by millions of people worldwide.

More recently, Alex recorded two solos on the Mormon Tabernacle Choir CD *Come, Thou Fount of Every Blessing,* which has garnered rave reviews and reached No. 1 on the Billboard Classical charts. When he performed these songs during the Mormon Tabernacle Choir's Pioneer Day Commemoration concert in the Conference Center, Alex received a standing ovation from LDS Church prophet and President Thomas S. Monson.

Referring to himself as "the token black guy in Utah," Alex says he loves to laugh and that some of the highlights in his life include giving a Book of Mormon to Prince Charles, joining the Mormon Tabernacle Choir, and marrying his wonderful wife, Julie.

• • •

I was born in London, England. My mother and father are Nigerians. They separated shortly after my birth, and my father went back to Nigeria. He sent for me when I was two and I lived there until I was five, when I was sent back to London to be with my mother. By the time I was eleven, my mother decided to go back to Nigeria for a visit. She told me she would be back in three weeks. I didn't see her again for eight years.

It wasn't all bad. She left me at a boarding school, the kind you see in Harry Potter movies but without the magic and the moving scoreboard. During vacation times I lived with my uncle. This went on until I was about sixteen years old. At about this time I began to have serious, recurring nightmares, possibly because I missed my mother. The nightmares were about death. I was often afraid.

I had a little experience with churches. I felt that my mom was spiritual, but her experience was with an African religion. Before I went to boarding school, I went to a church just across the street from where we lived. I really only went so I could learn English better, but it did give me joy. I didn't know why, but it just felt good to be at a church and worship.

I met my first Mormon where I worked during the summer when I was sixteen. It wasn't a very good start. He was my supervisor at a very busy downtown McDonald's. He was always on me. He was a big guy, six foot five, and would often pick me up by the back of my neck. He felt that there was too much fighting among the employees and that our language was bad. He told us it was very important that we get along together.

He also told us that our language reflected who we are and that there was a power in speech that could lift us and make us better people.

I had never heard anything like that. I asked him sarcastically, "Are you one of those God people?" He told me he was a member of The Church of Jesus Christ of Latter-day Saints, otherwise known as the Mormons. I made the mistake of telling him I was not interested in his church. Now I became his project. He figured out a way to bring the gospel into every conversation.

He kept trying to find a way to get me to go to church, mostly by talking about the activities. One day he asked me if I liked American girls. I did not realize that this was a trick question until a few weeks later. When I got home from work one night two formally dressed girls were standing on my doorstep. I could tell by her accent that one of them was an American.

I let them in. I was only being polite. After a few minutes of friendly introductions, they told me who they were and a little bit about Mormon missionaries. They started to teach me some gospel principles. I think they could tell I wasn't paying much attention. The American stopped making her point and said, "Thank you for giving us the chance to be able to teach you about the gospel of Jesus Christ and the fact that He lived, and died, and after three days He was resurrected and lived again. Because of that we will all live again after we die."

I was stunned. My night-mares about death came flooding to mind. "What did you say?"

"We will live again after we die."

"How do you know that we live again after we die? Have you ever died? Do you know anyone who has died and lived again?" She said no. "Then how can you know?" I thought I had her.

All of a sudden she stood up. "I will tell you how I know. I have come thou-

sands of miles from America. I have never been away from home. I left my parents, college, friends, and many other things I love. Of all the things I have left behind, nothing comes close in importance to the message we have to share with you today." I had never heard anyone talk like that before, especially the young people I knew. I could feel her commitment. I felt what I now know to be the Spirit. It really did touch me. I knew that even though she hadn't seen any-one come back from the dead, she knew, and I knew that she knew. Three weeks later I joined the Church.

My testimony was soon challenged. One week after I joined the Church, I was homeless. It was during the summer, and I was liv-ing with my uncle. He had the habit of having me go to the shop and get him groceries, including tea, coffee, and alcohol. He was a gambling man. After shopping, he would have me stop by the local betting agent and place a bet on one of the horses.

A couple of days after I had first attended church as a baptized member, my uncle handed me a shopping list and sent me out. As I was standing in the shop looking at the list, I got thinking, "Wait a minute. All these things are in violation of the Word of Wisdom (our Mormon health code). I can't do this." I turned around and went back to the flat. When I came through the front door, he saw me empty-handed.

"Where is the stuff I sent you out for?" I told him I couldn't do that anymore. "Why?"

"Because I am a member of The Church of Jesus Christ of Latter-day Saints."

I was scared. He was a very intimidating man. He quickly turned and went upstairs. He came down with my suitcase in hand, threw it out the door, looked at me, and said, "Get out."

"What am I going to do? Where am I going to live? You know my mom is in Nigeria. I don't have anybody but you."

"I don't care. Maybe those people from that cult you joined will help you."

This is where my church experience really started. In fact, I didn't have anyone to turn to. The sister missionaries had been transferred. My old supervisor and new friend from McDonald's had left for his mission. As far as I was concerned, every connection I had to the Church was severed. I just walked the streets of London crying my eyes out.

As I was wandering, I remembered a parking lot, a junkyard really, not far from where I lived. There was an old, white, rusted-out van parked there. I slept there that night. I kept crying, lonely and miserable. I was supplicating the Lord, praying to know why this was happening to me. "This is not what I signed up for. Why didn't you leave me where I was? At least I was having fun and enjoying myself." I had expected my new life would be wonderful, filled with new friends and happy experiences. I had heard of the persecution of Joseph Smith and the early members, but thought that was all history, the roots of the Church.

Then something like a miracle happened. One of the things my uncle had thrown in my suitcase was the copy of the scriptures the sisters had given me. While I was feeling so sorry for myself, I had a sudden strong impression. It wasn't a vision or exactly a sound that I heard, but more a voice that I felt. I felt the voice say to me in the most loving way possible, "Would you let me speak now?" The strong sense came clearly to me and said, "Read section 121 of the Doctrine and Covenants." I found the scriptures and turned to section 121 and read about Joseph Smith's suffering and asking why. Of course, I had not read this before or even been aware of it. I hadn't even been too sure what the Doctrine and Covenants was. I also remember reading what I now know as section 122, where the Lord lists all the terrible things that could happen to Joseph Smith.

There I was, in a rusted old van, homeless and with almost no experience in the Church, reading verses I had never heard of before. I was hoping I could get some kind of comfort, but what I got was more than comfort. I had an overwhelming sense that the purpose of life was to be tested. The words I remember most, and which struck me with the most power, were, "The Son of Man hath descended below them all. Art thou greater than he?" (Doctrine and Covenants 122:8).

I felt within myself the question, "Alex, are you greater than Jesus Christ? Do you really want to leave the Church? If Jesus Christ had left the Church, where would you be?" And I felt at that moment that I was going to be part of something great. That experience is something that has always kept me going.

I didn't die that night. I woke up and things just started to happen. Some members of my ward, the Hyde Park Ward, helped me find housing until I could finish school. I was later called to the Bristol Mission.

Early in my mission, I attended a baptismal service. The missionary who was assigned to sing had been transferred, and someone asked if I would sing. I had never sung before in public, but as I began to sing I felt something within me. My whole frame shook. My mission president, Philip C. Pugsley, was there, and from then on he had me sing at conferences, baptisms, and other meetings. I became known as the "singing missionary."

President Pugsley changed my life. On the last day of my mission he said, "I hope you are going to do something in music."

I see music not as a career but as a mission. I want young people to know that there is a war going on. The adversary uses music to damage our thoughts, character, and testimony, but the Lord uses music also—to uplift us and draw us to Him, to strengthen our testimonies.

I am thankful that the Lord found me and drew me into the gospel, and I pray that any talent I have can be used in His service.

Richard Bushman

Richard Lyman Bushman is Gouverneur Morris Professor of History Emeritus at Columbia University in New York City, and more recently visiting Howard W. Hunter Chair of Mormon Studies at Claremont Graduate University in California. He has also taught at Brigham Young University, Boston University, and the University of Delaware. Educated at Harvard College, he earned an A.M. in history and a Ph.D. in the history of American civilization from Harvard University.

Dr. Bushman's first book, *From Puritan to Yankee: Character and the Social Order in Connecticut, 1690-1765* (1967), was awarded the Bancroft Prize. He has also published *Joseph Smith and the Beginnings of Mormonism* (1984), *King and People in Provincial Massachusetts* (1985); *The Refinement of America: Persons, Houses, Cities* (1992); and *Joseph Smith: Rough Stone Rolling* (2005). He has also served as one of the general editors of the Joseph Smith Papers project.

• • •

I CAME TO HARVARD IN 1949 from a Mormon upbringing in Utah and then in Oregon. I was never happier than during my undergraduate years. I began studying physics, migrated to mathematics, and finally, allured by the social sciences, switched to history of science.

My sophomore tutor, I. B. Cohen, the noted historian of science, agreed to tutor me if I would read the books he was reading. Thrilled at the prospect, I spent an hour in his office from time to time talking books. He seemed intrigued by my western and Mormon upbringing. Once he said to me in rather avuncular tones, "You know, there are people around here who think Mormonism is garbage." He meant no harm, I am sure. He felt that to reach full maturity I must grow out of my childhood beliefs as so many others were doing in our secular age.

Many years later, I was interviewed by a National Public Radio correspondent during the bicentennial of the birth of the first Mormon prophet, Joseph Smith. I had published a biography and had come expecting questions about his character and significance. I planned to comment on his investment in city building and his fertile religious imagination and what these mean for us today.

Instead, the interviewer began with Smith's early religious experiences. It was not enough to say that as a boy he was confused about religion and, like others, found answers in a vision. The interviewer pressed me for details about the darkness that overtook Smith before the vision and the appearance of two individuals who identified themselves as God the Father and Jesus Christ, right there in the woods near Smith's home. He wanted to know about the angel Moroni standing in Joseph Smith's room in a pillar of light clothed in a white robe and about Joseph's trip to a hill nearby where he pried up a rock and found in a stone box a pile of gold plates and a "magical" instrument for translating their contents. How did he translate? the interviewer wanted to know. By looking into stones, I had to tell him.

Finally, after extracting all this information, the interviewer came to the punch line: How can someone like you, a retired Columbia

University history professor and author of a number of books, believe all this? I felt tricked, since the question was not about Joseph Smith but about me. Subsequently I realized he probably did not intend to embarrass me but was moved by genuine curiosity. How could an educated, well-informed, modern Mormon accept all the stories that go with Mormon belief?

In his 2007 volume *A Secular Age* Charles Taylor, a retired professor of philosophy from McGill University, says that over the past six or eight centuries, we have moved "from a society where belief in God is unchallenged and indeed, unproblematic, to one in which it is understood to be one option among others, and frequently not the easiest to embrace." This change often leads people with a religious temperament to question their deepest feelings and feel they should give up their faith, "even though they mourn its loss." To give up religion is a devastating loss; it is to relinquish what seems highest and best in life, the source of hope, the ground for moral commitment, the steadying hand in times of turmoil. A world without God is flat, dry, and dreary. Harvard's W.V. Quine said that atheists like himself "have a taste for desert landscapes." But not everyone wants to live in the desert.

As a Mormon, I have a steeper hill to climb in the secular age than most aspiring believers. Taylor has centuries of Catholic philosophical thought to back him up as he braces himself for the shocks of secularism. Mormons have to account for gold plates, an ancient history translated by an uneducated neophyte, angels buzzing in and out, and revelations coming thick and fast. If Protestant and Catholic Christianity are a green New England landscape against Quine's desert, Mormonism is a jungle. How can you possibly populate your religious world with so many broad-leaved trees, looping vines, tropical flowers, and flaming birds, the modern person wants to know. The modern, scientific understanding of reality simply cannot tolerate this kind of self-indulgence.

Yet, the exotic elements of Mormon belief are the very resources we Mormons use to construct our belief in this secular age. Instead of being a burden we secretly wish to slough off, the Book of Mormon—Joseph Smith's translation of the gold plates—is our chief bulwark against unbelief.

During my sophomore year at Harvard, I went through a period of skepticism, possibly spurred by I. B. Cohen's friendly advice. At the time, logical positivism was at its height among undergraduates. Anything that did not begin with the senses was nonsense, leaving out religion altogether. I remember also studying Nietzsche's critique of Christianity as the embodiment of a slave mentality. Christians taught themselves to think like servants, Nietzsche imperiously claimed. Was my attempt at humility simply slavish? I asked myself. Was my God only the illusion of a servile soul?

Such questions came to mind more often than was healthy for someone who had already committed himself to go on a mission for the Church. I was slated to go to New England to serve for two years. What was I to do about my doubts? I arrived in Cambridge in 1951 and, like all incoming missionaries, was interviewed by the mission president. When asked about my testimony, I told him I was not sure I believed in God. There I was, under obligation to teach the Mormon gospel and not sure if I had even the rudiments of religious faith.

The mission president, a retired faculty member from Utah State University, took my confession in stride. He simply handed me a Book of Mormon and asked me to see if I could find an explanation for it, then sent me off to Halifax, Nova Scotia, a long way from his influence. And so I read the Book of Mormon with a new purpose in mind. For three months, I thrashed about in my new role as a missionary, walking the streets of the city looking for people to study Mormonism while turning the Book of Mormon over in my mind. Could Joseph Smith have made it up? Did someone else write it for him? What about the witnesses who held the plates in their hands? Were they coconspirators? Were they pressured to sign the statement?

Somewhere in this period, I read some of the early work of Hugh Nibley, the erudite Mormon Hebrew scholar who devoted his life to defending the veracity of Joseph Smith's writings. Nibley took an approach to the Book of Mormon I had not encountered before. He began with the Book of Mormon stories of Lehi's family leaving Jerusalem in the early sixth century B.C.E. in search of a new promised land and compared that account to ancient historical sources from the period. The family had been directed like Abraham to seek a promised land, eventually coming to the western hemisphere. The book described their journeying down the Arabian Peninsula paralleling the Red Sea, turning eastward toward the southern coast bordering the Indian Ocean, and building a ship before beginning an ocean voyage to the New World.

The account describes Lehi's party coming to a small green oasis on the Arabian coast where they found trees they could work into lumber for the ship. Nibley pointed out that just such green spots do exist along the otherwise barren Arabian coastline, a fact not noted in the Bible and likely unknown to Joseph Smith. In my doubting frame of mind, that was an arresting observation. Nibley's technique was to multiply examples of convergences of this sort between historical scholarship and Book of Mormon details. No one convergence was conclusive, but their accumulation mounted up.

The ultimate outcome of my spiritual searchings, my ruminations about witnesses, and Nibley's scholarship was conviction. When the mission president came to Halifax after a few months, I was able to tell him I believed the Book of Mormon was true. Though I was still a little wobbly, the book had become a rock on which to rebuild my faith. This extravagant volume, partly because it did claim so much and seemed to come out of nowhere, won me over. Starting there, I constructed the rest of my faith in Mormonism—its authority, the scriptural force of Joseph Smith's other revelations, the truth of Christ, the descent of the prophetic office from Joseph Smith to the present Church leadership, and the possibility that any of us can receive revelation if we open our minds and hearts. Thus, the Book of Mormon allowed me to live happily in that jungle of religious beliefs that Mormons inhabit.

Yet Mormon reliance on the Book of Mormon sometimes takes a peculiar form. Mormons I know often say, "I don't see how Joseph Smith could have written the book." They are not saying this compels the conclusion that it is true history and came from heaven; they only assert it is not a work that Joseph Smith, with his limited education, could have concocted on his own. They are saying it is a puzzle. These are Mormons who have read the book over and over, approaching it from every angle. In their experience, it is not a simple text. It is a complex thousand-year history of an ancient civilization. It proposes a geography; contains a numbering system based on eight rather than ten; talks of government, politics, war, theology, economy, prophecy, history, poetry. Layer after layer of meaning unfolds to the careful reader, too much for an uneducated twenty-four-year-old to have invented. And no plausible evidence exists that anyone else wrote it, so where did it come from?

The implication, of course, is that it came from God and actually was written on gold plates, but the believing Mormons I know don't usually put it that way. They say only that Joseph Smith could not have written it. Even Nibley, after a lifetime of arguing for the Book of Mormon, draws back and says none of the historical evidence is conclusive for him. In the end, belief in the Book of Mormon is a matter of faith.

Rather than providing Mormons with rational proof for God and religion, the Book of Mormon seems to keep alive a possibility; it helps prop open the secular frame of mind that we all inhabit with its common sense and mundane explanations for everything. The book is just enough of a wonder that we cannot foreclose completely the possibility of spiritual forces entering the world. The Book of Mormon helps us hold ourselves open to faith, enables us to entertain the possibility of God, even of a God who knows us and will heed our petitions.

I believe most Mormons would acknowledge the truth of the above description, but only as the rational half of the story. For many Mormons, God and the Book of Mormon are not just possibilities but realities, even the most forceful realities in our experience. We believe the book is true. It requires something stronger than a "maybe" to make a commitment to a Mormon life.

Mormonism asks a lot of its people. We tithe our income, give many hours to Church service, abstain from all sorts of worldly pleasures, teach Mormonism to our children, and identify with our Mormon faith even when it is embarrassing. Such things require more certainty than the kind of tepid faith I described above.

Taylor again helps us to understand what is going on. In his Introduction, he refers to the autobiography of one Bede Griffith, who relates an experience on a country walk during his senior year at school. He heard birds singing, saw hawthorn trees in bloom, and suddenly was overwhelmed with their beauty. "I thought that I had never seen such a sight or experienced such sweetness before. If I had been brought suddenly among . . . a choir of angels singing, I could not have been more surprised." A feeling of awe came over Griffith, making him feel "inclined to kneel on the ground . . . and I hardly dared to look on the face of the sky, because it seemed as though it was but a veil before the face of God."

Taylor cites this as a human intimation that "somewhere, in some activity, or condition, lies a fullness, a richness, . . . more what [life] should be." Somewhere life is deeper, more vibrant, more worthwhile. "There may . . . be moments when the deep divisions,

distractions, worries, sadness that seem to drag us down are somehow dissolved, or brought into alignment, so that we feel united,
moving forward, suddenly capable and full of energy." Taylor's
purpose in describing these experiences—and their opposite in
alienation and ennui—is to understand belief and unbelief as "lived
conditions, not just as theories or sets of belief."

Even those with faith sometimes treat religious beliefs merely as
propositions about the world, like scientific statements, as if belief
in God were in the same category as belief that organic evolution
describes the emergence of human life. Taylor is drawing attention
to the fact that religion does something more; it entails a kind of
experience, a sense of fulfillment and wholeness, a heightened consciousness that compels our desire. For me and others, the Book
of Mormon oftentimes serves as an avenue into this sense of fullness and plentitude. It is not just a piece of evidence about religious
propositions, but a key or a doorway into a more abundant life.

Some Mormons speak of their experiences in reading the Book
of Mormon as evidence, as if reading it and praying were a kind of
scientific experiment and the spirit and tears that resulted were the
proof. I see it differently. I think reductions to evidence obscure the
full meaning of the spirit enveloping one as he or she is immersed
in the study of the Book of Mormon. When we have an experience
that convinces us that the Book of Mormon is true, it is much more
than a propositional truth of science or philosophy. It is the truth of
life as in Jesus' saying, "I am the way, the truth, and the life" (John
14:6). What I feel at such times brings me onto a plane of existence
that I rarely live on in ordinary times. It gives me a taste of an existence that usually is beyond my reach.

I think Mormons give themselves to the Mormon life so assidu-
ously because we know there are better ways of living, a greater fullness to be enjoyed, a state of serenity, peace, clarity, unity, power, and
greater joy. We do all that we do in hopes of living that way. While

the high moments may come infrequently, the sense of fullness remains an overarching presence, like the light in the sky just after sundown. We want it for ourselves, our families, and our friends. When that light dims, we struggle to regain it. That is what keeps us, keeps me, on the Mormon path.

The Book of Mormon was my starting point for that kind of discovery. The very wonder of the book helps me to get around the obstacles to belief in our time; it opens the possibility of transcendence. But more than an evidence for God, the book points to something higher. It awakens the hope that even in a secular age, we can realize a fullness of life.

JASON CHAFFETZ

JASON CHAFFETZ was elected to represent Utah's 3rd Congressional District on November 4, 2008, by standing firm on core conservative principles of fiscal discipline, limited government, accountability, and a strong national defense.

Jason was raised in California, Arizona, and Colorado. He moved to Utah in the mid-1980s after being recruited by LaVell Edwards to be a placekicker on the Brigham Young University football team. After completing a successful college football career and earning his degree in communications, he married his wife, Julie, and spent more than sixteen years in the local business community. Jason and Julie have been married for twenty-one years and have three children.

In 1995, Jason's mother passed away after a long battle with cancer. During that time, he was deeply touched by the personal generosity of the Huntsman family and their commitment to fight against cancer. When Jason heard that Jon Huntsman Jr. was mounting a gubernatorial campaign, he arranged a meeting through a mutual friend. Shortly thereafter, Huntsman named Jason his campaign manager.

Jason worked for two years with Governor Jon Huntsman Jr., first as his campaign manager and then as his chief of staff. In 2005, he rejoined the private sector and managed his own company,

Maxtera Utah, a corporate communications and marketing firm, until being elected to represent the people of Utah's 3rd Congressional District in Congress.

. . .

I GREW UP IN CALIFORNIA, ARIZONA, and Colorado, in an agnostic household. We didn't participate in any religion.

One of my very first memories is my first prayer. I was probably five years old or so, but remarkably I can remember it as crystal clear as day. My parents were out of town, and I had a babysitter. A thunderstorm took out all of the lights, and I was scared. I remember crying and my babysitter suggesting that we kneel down and pray. I can still remember that feeling, the warmth and comfort that came over me when I knelt down and said a prayer. I didn't even know what prayer was, but I've always remembered that comfort, and it still touches my heart.

I also had a handful of experiences where I recognized true evil. One time when I was ten years old, my father was out of town. It was at night, my mother was there, and the lights were out. I hadn't fallen asleep yet when the doorbell rang. I went to tell my mom, and she was already huddled in her closet dialing the police department because someone was trying to break into our home. It scared the living daylights out of me. Experiences like that one helped me to understand the contrast between a truly peaceful, good thing versus something that was bad and scary.

As I got older, I began to sense the light of Christ. I started to recognize the existence of something more powerful than simply being alive.

I also remember being in my backyard in a sleeping bag and looking at the stars and thinking, "Where is the end of space?" As you get older, you begin to think through bigger questions. I was starting to realize, "Wow. This earth is so big. There's got to be much more to it than what I'm seeing and what I'm learning at school each day." I increasingly recognized that something more powerful and more beautiful than I had yet been exposed to existed.

When I was a junior in high school I watched my parents, who had been married eighteen years, get divorced. This was difficult. The next year, my father moved to Colorado, so I graduated from high school there, but I toggled between Arizona and Colorado. I had grown up playing soccer, and in California and Arizona, it's warm 365 days of the year, so I played year round. I was a pretty good soccer player. One day I was sitting on a bench in the lunch area—outside, of course, it's Arizona—and my high school vice principal said, "Hey, we'd like some of you guys on the soccer team to try out for the football team." I was the only one who tried out, so I made it.

We were a terrible team. We were 0 and 10. I was such a skinny kid that no other position was going to work for me except kicker. We were already into the third game of the season, and they had me try a fifty-plus-yard field goal. I missed, but it was so close that I started getting recruited by different colleges. I thought, "Wow, I haven't even made one yet, and I'm already getting recruited. What if I actually made one?" I started focusing, and I was tenacious. I thought, "I can do this. I'm going to do this." I turned myself into a good placekicker, good enough to get recruited by BYU even though I wasn't a member of the Mormon church.

I remember meeting with LaVell Edwards and others. They knew I was a decent kicker, but they wanted to know about my grades, and they wanted to know about my lifestyle. I came to BYU in 1985, the year after their national championship, and graduated in December 1989. My junior and senior years were Ty Detmer's freshman and sophomore years, so we scored a lot of touchdowns. I held five records at BYU—I still have two of them. They were all about extra points because we kicked extra points all day long. I was fortunate to be on a team that scored ten touchdowns in a game and allowed the first-string kicker to stay in.

The standards at BYU were not difficult for me, if you don't count having to learn to wear socks to class. I was pretty much leading a Mormon lifestyle anyway. I don't know how, frankly, but somehow I had always stayed away from alcohol and drugs and other types of temptations. Most people at BYU probably assumed that I was a member of The Church of Jesus Christ of Latter-day Saints.

I had known a few Mormons. The Vandeweghe family was very close to my family. Kiki Vandeweghe played for UCLA, and his mother was the first Miss Utah to become Miss America. My impression of Mormons was based on that family. They were a happy, successful family, and we liked them and admired them. When there was discussion about my going to BYU, I looked through that lens, and I had a positive impression. Also, each of my parents was excited and pleased that I was going there.

When I got to BYU, I didn't know anything about the Mormon church. I had to take some religion classes, but when I told my professors that I was not a member of the Church, they indicated that as long as I attended, I would pass. (The classes were pass/fail.) However, my roommate at the time, Jeff Christensen, said to me, "Jason, you don't owe it to anybody else, but you do owe it to yourself to find out what a lot of us at this university have seen and felt. This community has been good to you. Will you please try reading the Book of Mormon, and will you try getting down on your knees to pray? You'll have to do it by yourself. I can't do it for you."

His words really sunk in and touched me. I thought, "Maybe I should do that. They paid for my education. I'm a starting place-kicker on the team. The least I could do is read their book." I didn't follow through until my senior year, but I did read the Book of Mormon and I did pray. I got down on my knees, and I prayed, and I felt that same warmth and comfort that I had felt when I was five years old. It was such an overwhelmingly good and positive emotional feeling that I did it again.

I taught myself how to pray. It was a very personal thing. Nobody explained to me how to do it. In the movies I had seen people say the 23rd Psalm before they ate a meal, but to truly humble my heart and to get down on my knees to ask for help and insight was another matter.

Also, when I opened the Book of Mormon, it didn't read like a novel. I had to learn my way through it. I still study it and learn. It was confusing for a first-timer who didn't know how to pronounce any of the names and didn't have a historical basis or any childhood teachings to lean on. But the more I read, and the more I prayed, the more I recognized the truthfulness of the gospel. I could not deny that getting baptized was the right thing to do.

I didn't want to just call up my parents and say, "Guess what?" So I waited until Christmastime. My parents basically believed: If those are the decisions you want to make, then more power to you. That same December was the last time I played a football game. I kicked in the Holiday Bowl against Penn State. Although we lost, it was a great and memorable game.

When I came back, I told Floyd Johnson, the equipment

manager for the team, that I was ready to get baptized. He said that I had to have the missionary discussions. I said, "But I'm ready to get baptized now." He insisted, so we contacted the Missionary Training Center. Each time I had a discussion, they would send a van full of missionaries. They knew they had a "live one." I would have eight or ten missionaries in my living room, practicing the discussions on me. They were so nervous, I would often say, "It's okay, guys. I'm going to say yes, so just keep going." Then the next discussion would come, and they would send eight or ten different missionaries.

After we had set a date for my baptism, my roommate, Jeff, said to me, "Jason, you should really invite or at least tell LaVell Edwards." I had insisted that the baptism not be a public event. I had seen others who had hundreds of people attend, and that was not my style. But I went to see Coach Edwards and told him I was going to get baptized. He was so excited that he gave me a big bear hug and asked, "When is it?"

I said, "Well, Coach, I'm sorry, but you're not invited." I'm still embarrassed that I told LaVell Edwards that he couldn't come to my baptism.

He said, "Well, will you please go see Rex Lee?" meaning the president of BYU.

So I went to see Rex Lee. Rex was always boisterous. Of course, he was excited as well, and he asked, "When is it?"

I said, "President Lee, with all due respect, I'd rather you not come." Again, I'm still a little embarrassed that I didn't allow him to come.

Just a handful of us were there when I got baptized. Jeff baptized me, the roommate who had challenged me to get down on my knees and humble myself—not easy for a twenty-something-year-old. I was the first member of my family to get baptized, and it's been the best thing in my life.

I look back at all the little turns and twists that took place in my life to get me to that point, and it seems miraculous. It was not mere coincidence. And it was not all rosy. I had challenges, and I was tempted to do stupid things. The history and the background of the Church and the plan of salvation seem somewhat complicated to me. But the gospel is very simple. The simplicity of the gospel, I think, is part of the brilliance of Heavenly Father's plan.

I hope and pray that people will take that private time when no one else is around to pray with an open heart. I hope they will read the Book of Mormon and shed anything they might have seen or heard about the Church that was filtered through another person. I hope they will truly humble themselves to communicate directly with their Heavenly Father.

The response may not be a bolt of lightning, and it may not be immediate, but there eventually will be a warm feeling of goodness that cannot be denied. Then, over the course of time, new and positive experiences will open up in their lives. I want everyone to see what I've been able to see and to feel what I've been able to feel. I want others to know that challenges and difficulties may come, but the gospel of Jesus Christ can give more insight, more comfort, more knowledge, and better ability to deal with life than anything else.

NORM CHOW

NORM CHOW, one of the top offensive coaches in football history, returned to his alma mater, the University of Utah, in January 2011 as the offensive coordinator. He came to Utah from UCLA, where he served as offensive coordinator for three seasons. Before UCLA, Norm was the offensive coordinator for the NFL's Tennessee Titans. He is credited with helping quarterback Vince Young attain 2006 AP Offensive Rookie of the Year and become the first rookie quarterback to play in the Pro Bowl.

Before joining the Titans, Norm spent thirty-two productive years coaching at the collegiate level, enjoying three national titles (BYU, 1984; USC, 2003 and 2004), tutoring three Heisman Trophy winners, participating in twenty-seven bowl games, and earning three Assistant Coach of the Year awards. He also worked with eight NCAA top-thirty career passing efficiency leaders, mentored six first-round NFL draft picks, and worked with one Pro Football Hall of Fame member (Steve Young).

Under Norm's lead, USC's offense (2001–2005) ranked in the top twenty in total offense in his final three seasons, played in three BCS Bowl games, and won two national titles. He spent the 2000 season as the offensive coordinator and quarterback coach at North Carolina State. Previously, Norm spent twenty-seven years

(1973–1999) at Brigham Young University in various positions as an offensive coach. The Cougars posted a 244–91–3 record during his time in Provo, appeared in twenty-two bowls, and saw twenty-one offensive players earn All-America honors. In twelve of his eighteen years as offensive coordinator at BYU, he led the offense to a place in the NCAA's top ten in total offense. Norm began his coaching career as the head coach at Waialua High School in Waialua, Hawaii (1970–1973).

Norm has garnered numerous coaching accolades, including the Broyles Award (2002) as the nation's top assistant coach, National Assistant Coach of the Year (by American Football Foundation, 1999; Athlon, 1993), and NCAA Division 1-A Offensive Coordinator of the Year (*American Football Monthly* 1996, 2002). In 2006, Fox TV's Terry Bradshaw named him the NFL's Top Assistant Coach.

Norm graduated from University of Utah with a bachelor's degree in physical education (1968) and a master's degree in special education (1970), and from BYU with a doctorate in educational psychology (1979). He and his wife of more than forty years, Diane, live in California and Utah. They have three sons, a daughter, and five beautiful grandchildren.

• • •

M Y FIRST GRANDDAUGHTER was born in 2006. As I held that tiny being, her head cradled in my hand, her small fingers wrapped around one of mine, I couldn't help but think of those who had preceded her on this earth.

There were my Chinese grandparents, who traveled to Hawaii to live out the American dream; my Portuguese grandfather, who sailed from the Azores; and my Hawaiian grandmother, with her stern face and kind heart. Then my thoughts turned to my wife's family—her pioneer-stock mother, whose kitchen skills retained a

NORM CHOW

touch of her parents' Denmark; and my wife's father, whose astonishing gardening skills were probably passed on to him by ancestors working in the great gardens of England.

I also thought of my parents and my children and my wife. The small being in my hands was not only a manifestation of all of us, but was also the greatest of blessings from a loving Heavenly Father *to* us. This blessing that brings to light the importance of eternal families is the main reason why I am a Mormon.

The youngest of three boys in a very close-knit family, I was born and raised in Honolulu, Hawaii. My parents were devout Catholics who took us to Mass each Sunday. I'm not sure if I learned much doctrine from these outings, as the priest conducted Mass in Latin in those days. However, I did learn from my mother the importance of regularly attending a religious service.

To this day, my mother prays her rosary each morning. She taught me the importance of religion in one's daily life as a source of strength and inspiration. From my father I learned the values of hard work, discipline, and loyalty. His life's goal was to support us in all of our endeavors, athletic and otherwise, and he showed me by example what a father should be. He never missed a single sporting event that my brothers or I participated in and often volunteered to coach or assist our teams.

I moved to Utah to attend the University of Utah on a football scholarship. Although many members of The Church of Jesus Christ of Latter-day Saints live in Hawaii, and a beautiful temple sits on the North Shore of the island of Oahu, I knew next to nothing about the Mormon church when I arrived in Salt Lake City.

The woman who would become my wife was a lifelong member of the Church who was waiting for a missionary she had dated since high school. I first spotted her in an elementary education class. I knew she had done the homework, and I had not, so I asked to be partnered with her. Somehow, I convinced her to go out with me. As we dated, I took the missionary discussions, but I didn't really consider the Church beyond learning its basics.

We married in 1968, a time when interracial marriage was still frowned upon. But my wife's family were very accepting of me. They also never questioned me about the Church or expected me to be baptized.

Shortly after our marriage, we moved to a small town on the North Shore of Oahu where we both worked as educators, she as a teacher at Haleiwa Elementary and I as a teacher and head football coach at Waialua High School. During our time there, I attended church with my wife. We both accepted callings in the ward (congregation), and most people there thought I was already a member. Three years later, we returned to Utah to start a family. At this time I was finally baptized and became an official member of The Church of Jesus Christ of Latter-day Saints.

I began my career in the sports world as a young graduate assistant coach at Brigham Young University. I had two children and a mortgage that was barely met by my paycheck each month. Through divine providence, a lot of hard work, and some dumb luck, I became successful at my chosen profession. BYU football has been alternately praised and cursed over the years, and I have experienced much of both.

There were times it would have been professionally and financially beneficial to accept job offers that would have taken me far from the madding crowds at what was then Cougar Stadium. Yet, when I drove home at night from my office at the Smith Fieldhouse, I realized that the four most important reasons to stay in Provo, Utah, were sitting at the dinner table with their mother. Provo was where their friends were, where the schools they knew and the teachers they loved were, where it was safe and calm, and, most important, where they were happy. So Provo is where we stayed, if not for me, then for those around the dinner table waiting for me to come home.

Despite this professional sacrifice, my wife and I have been blessed by our decision to stay in Utah where we could give our family a stable upbringing. All of our children are strong Church members. Three have been married in the temple. All of our sons are returned missionaries. More than that, they are good people who recognize and honor the values and teachings of the Church—hard work, dedication to family, obedience, and kindness to others.

Of course, I am a Mormon for many reasons. But foremost in my mind are the promises made to Church members regarding family if we live worthily. I am blessed with a beautiful wife who is the backbone of our family, and with four children and five grandchildren. I cannot look at these people as we gather for family events or holidays and not be grateful for the plan of salvation and the promise of eternal family given to us by our Heavenly Father and Jesus Christ. As a father, providing for and caring about my wife and children come before anything else in my life.

Our families here on earth are not yet ours. Heavenly Father has given them to us here to see how we will treat them. If we are faithful and act worthily, they will be given to us forever. I am a Mormon so that I can continue to live with those I love for all eternity; so that I might be reunited one day with the father whose example taught me how to raise my own children; and so that I might one day thank those who preceded me here on earth for the choices they made that enabled me to become the person I am.

I am a Mormon because I want that chance—to be with my family forever.

CLAYTON M. CHRISTENSEN

CLAYTON M. CHRISTENSEN is the architect of and foremost authority on "disruptive innovation," the process by which a product or service first takes root in simple applications at the bottom of a market and then moves "up market" until it displaces established competitors. His research has been ap-plied to national economies, start-up and *Fortune 50* companies, and early and late stage investing.

His seminal book on the subject, *The Innovator's Dilemma* (1997), received the Global Business Book Award for the Best Business Book of the Year (1997), was a *New York Times* bestseller, and is sold in more than twenty-five countries. Professor Christensen is also a five-time recipient of the McKinsey Award for the *Harvard Business Review*'s best article.

Focusing his innovation lens on both education and health care, Professor Christensen examines why schools struggle in *Disrupting Class,* which has received several prestigious awards. *The Innovator's Prescription* (2009) examines how to fix the problems facing health care. It has been given the James Madison and the Circle Awards in Medicine. To better apply his frameworks to the social sector, Professor Christensen founded Innosight Institute, a nonprofit think tank, and three other successful companies.

Clayton Christensen was born in Salt Lake City, Utah, in

1952. He graduated with highest honors in economics from Brigham Young University (1975), received an M.Phil. in applied econometrics and the economics of less-developed countries from Oxford (1977) as a Rhodes Scholar, and received an MBA with High Distinction from the Harvard Business School (1979), graduating as a George F. Baker Scholar. He was awarded his DBA from the Harvard Business School in 1992 and holds five honorary doctorates and an honorary chaired professorship at the Tsinghua University in Taiwan. He served as a White House fellow (1982–1983) as an assistant to U.S. Transportation Secretaries Drew Lewis and Elizabeth Dole. He is currently the Kim B. Clark Professor of Business Administration at the Harvard Business School.

Professor Christensen is committed to family, church, and community. He was an elected member of the Belmont Town Council for eight years and has served the Boy Scouts of America for twenty-five years as a Scoutmaster, Cubmaster, den leader, and troop and pack committee chairman. He served as a missionary for The Church of Jesus Christ of Latter-day Saints in the Republic of Korea (1971–1973). He and his wife, Christine, live in Massachusetts. They are the parents of five children and have five grandchildren.

• • •

As I have progressed through my life, my commitment to The Church of Jesus Christ of Latter-day Saints has deepened for two reasons. The first is my reason for *belonging* to the Church as an organized institution: because of the way the Church is organized, it puts opportunities to help others in my path every day. It facilitates my efforts—and in some instances almost compels me—to *practice* Christianity, not just believe in it. The second is my reason for *believing* that the doctrines taught in the Church are true. As I have studied the Bible and the Book of Mormon, I have come to know through the power of the Spirit of God that these books contain the fullness of the gospel of Jesus Christ. My conviction has deepened as I have continued to study these books and have tried to do the will of my Father in Heaven.

Why do I choose to belong to The Church of Jesus Christ of Latter-day Saints as an organized religion, rather than just attempt as an individual to live a good life? It is because the Church helps me understand and practice the essence of Christianity. The mechanism by which the organization achieves this is to have no professional clergy. We don't hire ministers or priests to teach and care for us. This forces us to teach and care for each other—and, in my view, this is the core of Christian living as Christ taught it. I actually have come to feel badly for my friends who belong to faiths in which professional clergy are employed because they don't know how much joy they miss when they "outsource" the teaching and care of the members of their church to specially trained professionals.

Several years ago I read a story in a news magazine about flooding in several western states that resulted from the rapid spring melting of a heavy accumulation of snow. One photo showed thousands of Mormon citizens in Salt Lake City who had been mobilized with only a few hours' notice through a call from their local Church leaders. They were shown filling sandbags that would channel the flow of runoff water. The article marveled at the command-and-control precision—almost military in character—through which the LDS Church was able to put its people onto the front lines of this civil crisis. Another photo in an article the next week showed a thirty-something resident of a town along a flooding stream in another state, sitting in a lawn chair reading while National Guardsmen filled sandbags nearby. The author of the article attributed what he saw to the "organizational efficiency" of the LDS Church, but he completely missed the point. Thousands of people instinctively showed up and went to work *because they do this sort of thing all the time, week after week, in more than a hundred countries around the world, as part of being Mormon.* This was not an unusual event—just another week in the life of a typical Mormon.

To illustrate, let me review some of the things that I was able to do in the normal course of being a member of this church in a recent year. Because graduate students and young families move into and out of apartments with regularity in the Boston area, a list gets passed around at church every few weeks asking for men to show up the next Saturday to help some family load or unload their rented moving truck. My children and I signed up every time, and we worked shoulder to shoulder with five to fifteen other men and their children for two or three hours, helping the family move. At least once each month, and more often when needed, I visited by assignment an elderly Hispanic couple—a woman who was in poor health and her husband, who was struggling to overcome his addiction to alcohol. They lived in a dilapidated apartment in a rough part of the city. Over the course of the year the men in our congregation replastered, rewired, painted, and recarpeted their apartment. We contributed money to fly their grown children, who were struggling financially and living in other parts of the country, to a special family reunion we helped them organize in Washington, D.C. Every Sunday for two hours, I cared for about fourteen children aged eighteen to thirty-six months in the church's nursery so that their parents could attend Sunday School class in peace. My wife, Christine, was similarly engaged. In the assignment she had at that time, when she learned that a mother had a new baby or someone was otherwise ill, with just a few phone calls she would enlist people to appear on their doorstep for a day, a week, or even months. They would bring meals ready to eat or hands ready to clean the home and do the family's laundry.

The important point about the prior paragraph is that our experience was *not* unusual. *Everyone* in the congregation was similarly engaged, not just accepting assignments to help but also seeking opportunities to help. We gave often and received often. For example, a short time later our family had outgrown our small home, so we found a larger one and put the word out that we would appreciate any help in loading and unloading our rented moving truck. Among those who showed up that morning was Mitt Romney, who had just completed his unsuccessful campaign for the U.S. Senate in Massachusetts. Mitt had a broken collarbone, but for two hours he traipsed between our home and the truck, carrying out whatever he could manage with his one good arm. That spirit is just in the air in the Mormon church, week after week, year after year. The strong help the weak, and the weak help the strong. It creates an extraordinary spirit of mutual love because, as we work to help others who are in need, our love and respect for those we help intensifies. It does not occur to any of us even to wonder, on any given occasion, who is weak and who is strong.

My children have been raised not just by their parents but also by an entire community of remarkable people. One of the world's foremost materials scientists, the dean of the Harvard Business School, a podiatrist, and the executive vice president of American Express Corporation were our sons' Scoutmasters. These men of substance and position selflessly taught our boys first aid and citizenship and camped with them in the snow. Each of our children during their high school years went to "early morning seminary": scripture study classes that met in the home of a Church member every school morning from 6:30 until 7:15. The women who taught these classes had degrees not in religion or theology but in art, law, nursing, and literature. They spent many hours a week preparing and searching for a way to help the sleepy high school students each morning learn an element of the gospel more deeply, and to send them off to school with a firmer resolve to do what is right. Christine and I haven't raised our children alone. A whole community of selfless Christians has contributed to helping them become faithful, competent adults. Whenever we have thanked these men and women for what they have done for us, without exception they have expressed gratitude for having the chance to help—because *they* grew as they served.

Because we employ no professional preachers in our church, regular members—women and men, children and grandparents—give every sermon or lesson. This means that we have the chance to learn from *everyone*—people in all walks of life who are struggling in their own ways to follow God. I have found, in fact, that some of the most profound things I have learned about the gospel of Jesus Christ were taught by people from whom, if judged by the standards of the world, one would not have expected such profundities to come. For example, about a decade ago I was serving as the bishop, or lay minister, of a congregation of college students in the Boston area. We had assigned a college sophomore to give a sermon about repentance in our service on a particular Sunday. I still remember his key point: "We often view repentance as a slow process. It isn't. Change is instantaneous. It is *not* changing that takes so much time." I had been struggling to overcome a particular bad habit, and I resolved that I would change my behavior right then and there—that I would quit "not changing." Where else but in this church could a young, inexperienced student have taught a bishop such a profound lesson?

I believe very strongly that these Mormons I have described are *not* more loving or more selfless or more competent than many, many individuals in other faiths. What is different, however, is that we live and serve within a context that causes us to *use* those attributes—to serve, rather than to be served. And as we use them, they become an even more powerful part of us.

One of the curses that afflicts successful, prosperous people—many of whom have extraordinary talents and good hearts—is that they tend to live and work among similarly successful, prosperous people. They thereby become isolated from those who need their help. What I appreciate about the Mormon church as an infrastructure for Christian living is that it puts me in touch with people I can help. I told a friend once, "If you truly want to live your life as Christ taught, then start coming to the Mormon church. You don't even have to believe what we believe. But if you want to practice Christianity, *this* is where the state-of-the-art is practiced."

This is why I choose to *belong* to The Church of Jesus Christ of Latter-day Saints.

The second topic I want to address is why I *believe* in the doctrines of the Church. I was born into a wonderful Mormon family, and as I grew up I found few reasons to disbelieve the teachings of the Church. My parents had deep faith in its precepts, and their example and encouragement were powerful—I believed in my parents, and I knew that they believed the gospel of Jesus Christ. It was not until I was twenty-four years old, however, that I came to know these things for myself.

I had been given a Rhodes scholarship to study at Oxford University in England. After I had lived there for a few weeks, far away from the supportive environment in which I had been raised, it became clear that adhering to Mormonism in that environment was going to be *very* inconvenient. In fact, doing the sorts of things I described in the first part of this essay within the Mormon congregation in Oxford would preclude my participation in many of the things that had made Oxford such a rich experience for prior recipients of my scholarship. I decided, as a result, that the time had come for me to learn for certain and for *myself* whether Mormonism was true.

I had read the Book of Mormon before—seven times, to be exact. But in each of those instances I had read it by assignment from my parents or a teacher, and my objective in reading it had been mostly to finish the book. This time, however, my objective was to find out if it was a true book or a fabrication. Accordingly, I reserved the time from eleven o'clock until midnight, every night, to read the Book of Mormon next to the fireplace in my chilly room at the Queen's College. I began each of those sessions by kneeling in verbal prayer. I told God, every night, that I was reading this to know if it was His truth. I told Him that I *needed* an answer to this question—because if it was not true I did not want to waste my time with this church and would search for something else. But if it *was* true, then I promised that I would devote my life to following its teachings and to helping others do the same.

I then would sit in the chair and read a page in the Book of Mormon. I would stop at the bottom of the page and think about it. I would ask myself what the material on that page meant for the way I needed to conduct my life. I would then get on my knees and pray aloud again, asking the Lord to tell me if the book was true. I would then get back in the chair, turn the page, and repeat the process again and again for the remainder of the hour. I did this every evening.

After I had done this for several weeks, one evening in October 1975, as I sat in the chair and opened the book following my prayer, I felt a marvelous spirit come into the room and envelop my body. I had never before felt such an intense feeling of peace and love. I started to cry and did not want to stop. I knew then, from a source of understanding more powerful than anything I had ever felt in my life, that the book I was holding in my hands was true. It was hard to see through the tears. But as I opened it and began again to read, I saw in the words of the book a clarity and magnitude of God's plan for us that I had never conceived before. The spirit stayed with me for that entire hour. And each night thereafter, as I prayed and then sat in that chair with the Book of Mormon, that same spirit returned. It changed my heart and my life forever.

I love to go back to Oxford. As the beautiful, historic home of the world's oldest university, the town is filled with students and tourists. To me, however, it is a sacred place. It was there that I learned that the fundamental message of the Book of Mormon is in fact true—that Jesus is the Christ, the Son of the Living God. It was there that I learned that God is indeed my Father in Heaven. I am His son. He loves me, and He even knows my name. And I learned that Joseph Smith, the man who translated the Book of Mormon and organized The Church of Jesus Christ of Latter-day Saints, was a prophet of God in the same sense that Peter and Moses were prophets. I love to return to Oxford to remember the beautiful, powerful spirit that came to my heart in that room in the Queen's College and conveyed these messages to me.

During my adult life I have been blessed to witness or participate in many miracles—events that the scriptures term "gifts of the Spirit." I have healed the sick by the power of God. I have spoken with the gift of tongues. I have been blessed to see visions of eternity; and events in my future that have been important for me to foresee have been revealed to me. These truly have been gifts and great blessings in my life. But when I assess the collective impact that they have had on my faith, my heart, and my motivation to follow Jesus Christ, they pale in significance and power to those evenings I spent with the Book of Mormon in Oxford.

This happened to me a quarter of a century ago. I am grateful to be able to say that in the years since, I have continued systematically to study the Book of Mormon and Bible to understand even more deeply what God expects of me and my family while on this earth. I have spent thousands of hours doing my best to share what I am learning with others and to serve others in the way that Christ wants. And I am grateful to say that, from time to time, that same spirit that permeated my heart in Oxford has returned, reconfirming that the path I am trying so hard to follow is in fact the one that God my Father and His Son Jesus Christ want me to pursue. It has brought me deep happiness. This is why I belong, and why I believe. It has been a wonderful search for happiness and for the truth.

KIM B. CLARK

KIM B. CLARK became the fifteenth president of Brigham Young University–Idaho in August 2005. During his tenure at BYU–Idaho, President Clark has focused his efforts on three overarching objectives: (1) substantially raising the quality of every aspect of a student's learning experience, (2) serv-ing more students, and (3) lowering the relative cost of education. In addition, he has helped develop a consistent model for learning across campus, a complete rethinking of general education, and an innovative approach for online learning.

President Clark was born in Salt Lake City, Utah, and raised in Spokane, Washington. After serving as a missionary in Germany, he married his wife, Sue, in 1971. He earned bachelor's, master's, and doctorate degrees in economics from Harvard University.

In 1978, President Clark became a member of the faculty at the Harvard Business School and was named the school's dean in 1995. He served in that capacity until he became president of BYU–Idaho. While at Harvard, President Clark oversaw an increase in faculty and expanded the school's range of research. Under his leadership, the school's endowment more than tripled, providing a solid foundation for attracting the best students and faculty as well as increasing the Harvard Business School's global presence. During his tenure as dean, several new facilities were also added, totaling more than 325,000 square feet, including housing, a new student center, class-rooms, and an expanded library/academic center.

President Clark has authored one book, *Armor: Divine Protection in a Darkening World,* and coauthored several others, including *Design Rules: The Power of Modularity; The Product Development Challenge: Competing through Speed, Quality, and Creativity;* and *Leading Product Development: The Senior Manager's Guide to Creating and Shaping the Enterprise.*

In addition to serving as president of BYU–Idaho, Kim B. Clark also serves as a member of the Fifth Quorum of Seventy in The Church of Jesus Christ of Latter-day Saints. President Clark and his wife reside in Rexburg, Idaho, and have seven children and sixteen grandchildren.

• • •

FIRST OF ALL, I LOVE THE GOSPEL of Jesus Christ and The Church of Jesus Christ of Latter-day Saints because of my heritage. This feeling goes deep, since in my family I have many pioneers. I grew up in a home where I learned about my family's legacy of faith, and as I have grown older, I have come to appreciate more and more the power of the stories I learned when I was a little boy.

Sometimes people say, "You are a Mormon because you grew up in it. It's the only thing you know." I do love the Church because I grew up in it. But as I have grown, my family's stories have taken on greater meaning because the lessons of those stories have played out in my own life. I have come to understand that the stories of the Mormon pioneers are also my story, and I appreciate the connection that I have to them.

My great-great-grandfather Edward Bunker heard about the Church in his early twenties, in about 1843. He made his way west from where he was working in Connecticut to Nauvoo, Illinois, where he joined the Church after the martyrdom of the Prophet Joseph Smith. Edward Bunker crossed the plains five times in his life. He joined the Mormon Battalion. He went on a mission to England. He was a handcart captain. He was also called by Brigham Young to settle in Santa Clara, Utah, and he eventually established a town called Bunkerville.

He believed that he was building Zion. He had faith and commitment, borne out of powerful spiritual experiences that he had as a young man when he knew Brigham Young. When Brigham Young came to the Saints' camp in Iowa asking for volunteers for the Mormon Battalion, Edward, although he was newly married and without any money, was one of the first to stand up and say, "Here am I, send me." Leaving his wife in Iowa with her mother and siblings, he walked to Texas and Arizona and California and finally journeyed to Utah where the first company of Saints had arrived. He then made his way back to his wife in Iowa, where she had stayed in one of the communities the Saints established to help each other as they moved across the plains.

Here is a man of tremendous capacity. I grew up on stories of this type, stories of indomitable courage and faith that grew out of commitment to the Lord and love of the gospel. Over the years, I've come to understand more deeply why Edward did what he did. His legacy is extremely important to me.

I also have an ancestor named David White Rogers, an amazing man of many talents. He was a cabinetmaker and a painter; he created the well-known painting of Joseph Smith and his brother, Hyrum, in profile. He was in Quincy, Illinois, in 1839 just before the Prophet Joseph escaped from jail and the Saints began building Nauvoo. The Church authorities asked for volunteers to go to Missouri to sell land. Mormons had been driven out of Missouri violently, but many members of the Church still held title to land there in Jackson County. This great-great-grandfather, who became

71

a friend of the Prophet, volunteered. A man named Charles Bird went with him. So Brother Bird and my great-great-grandfather went to Jackson County, Missouri, in 1839.

Word spread in Jackson County that two Mormons had come to sell land. A mob confronted them in the town square and formed a circle around them. They had guns, and they intended to kill them. As he later recorded the story, my great-great-grandfather said to the mob, "I claim the right of the condemned man to state my last words." When they told him to speak, he told them he had with him the legal title to land that had been purchased by good people who had come to Jackson County with the hope of building homes and settling there. They had been driven out, but their land was still their land, and "In the name of Israel's God and by His powers, I shall accomplish [its sale]. Only by your committing willful, cold-blooded murder can I be prevented." The men surrounding him faded away, and he sold the land and helped needy Saints move to Illinois with the money. So, one of the reasons I am a Mormon is that I have this legacy of faith of people who were willing to give their lives because they loved the Lord and because they were building Zion.

I also love the doctrines of the Restoration of the gospel of Jesus Christ as well as the embodiment of these doctrines in the organization of the Church. The doctrines help me understand the purpose of my life, and they help me connect my life to the world around me in a way that I find satisfying and powerful. In the doctrines, I find insights and answers that guide me, that reveal new ways of understanding the world. For example, though it may seem like a paradox, the gospel illuminates science. I enjoy science, and so I love the fact that the gospel of Jesus Christ as restored to the Prophet Joseph embraces all truth. It is, in that sense, an integrating force in my life. It integrates my heart and my mind.

That leads me to the Savior. I love how I feel when I read about Jesus Christ, and I love the impact that He has on my life. Sometimes it's hard. I feel pricked in my heart because I'm not as good as I could be. But the gospel lifts me. I feel its pull, the pull to be a better person. When I live my life according to the doctrines that I have been taught, my life is better. I am happier. I feel stronger. I have better relationships. The things that I love, the people whom I love, I love better. My whole life is better when I live the gospel the way I know I should.

Another thing that I love about the Church and the gospel is that we have living prophets. I have had an interesting relationship to prophets in my life, and I have come to understand and respect them. When I was a little boy, about eleven years old, I had a defining experience that has influenced my whole life. It was 1960. I was living in Salt Lake City, and our ward (congregation) had built a new chapel. In June, the prophet and President David O. McKay came to dedicate our chapel.

I remember feeling a compelling desire to be at that dedication that day. Somehow I got permission from my mom and dad to walk to the chapel, about three blocks from my house, two hours before the dedication. One of the reasons I went was to see the prophet in person. When I arrived, hardly any people were there. I was early enough to get a seat right up front in the chapel. I still remember what David O. McKay looked like and what I felt as an eleven-year-old when he walked into that chapel. In my little-boy heart, I knew this was the prophet of God. I knew it, and I felt it. It was a powerful experience that has stayed with me my whole life.

So when our late prophet, President Gordon B. Hinckley, asked me in May 2005 to leave Harvard to serve as president of BYU–Idaho, I had no question in my mind about what I would do. It was not a hard decision because I love God's prophets—and that love is one of the reasons I'm a Mormon. It's been a constant all through my life that we have men on the earth who receive revelation from God. I am grateful that I have the experience of being able to work closely with them in doing the Lord's work.

There are many other reasons I love being a Mormon. The words of the scriptures allow the Lord to speak to us personally, not just through our living prophets but by the mouths of prophets throughout the millennia. I have heard the Lord's voice in the Book of Mormon over and over again—insights that have illuminated problems, challenges, and issues in my life, that have helped me understand the gospel more clearly.

And then there is the power of prayers offered in faith. I have had many experiences in my life in which I have felt and heard the voice of the Lord during my prayers. I have a powerful witness that Heavenly Father hears our prayers and answers them. Of course, He does so in His own time and His own way. The doctrines of The Church of Jesus Christ of Latter-day Saints teach me who God is and what my true relationship is to Him. I feel comfortable going to Him and speaking to Him about anything. I don't have to rely solely on my merits. I can rely on the Savior Himself by going to the Father and praying in the name of the Son.

I love the gospel of Jesus Christ. I love what it means to me. I love how it makes me feel.

AUSTIN COLLIE

AUSTIN KIRK COLLIE is a starting wide receiver for the NFL's Indianapolis Colts who has become known as one of quarterback Peyton Manning's favorite receivers. As a rookie wide receiver with the Colts in 2009, he led all league rookies in receiving touchdowns (seven) and tied for the most re-  ceptions among rookies (sixty). He finished his rookie year on several all-rookie team lists and, in terms of the Colts' history, placed fourth for most catches by a rookie, fifth for most receiving yards by a rookie, and tied for third for most receiving touchdowns by a rookie.

Football is in the Collie family blood; both Austin's father, Scott Collie, and his brother, Zac, played for Brigham Young University. Austin was a Prep Star and Super Prep All-American at Oak Ridge High School in northern California. Among other awards during his high school years, he was voted northern California's Most Valuable Player and earned all-state honors. He also graduated with a 4.0 grade-point average.

He continued this pace in college at Brigham Young University, where he majored in communications, earning all-conference and All-American academic awards while setting multiple BYU football receiving records. In 2005 and 2006, he interrupted his college football career to serve a mission for the LDS Church in Buenos Aires, Argentina.

Austin was named a first team All-American after his junior year at BYU (2008) by CBS Sports.com and a second team All-American by the Associated Press, *Sporting News,* SportsIllustrated.com, and Rivals.com. He also led the nation in receiving yards, with 118.31 per game and 1,538 total yards. He tied the NCAA single-season receiving record with eleven consecutive games of 100 yards or more.

During the off-season, Austin and his wife, Brooke, reside in Austin's hometown in California.

• • •

M Y NAME IS AUSTIN COLLIE, and I currently spend most of the year living in Indianapolis, Indiana, with my beautiful wife, Brooke, and our white Labrador retriever, Bentley. I have the good fortune of being in my second season as a wide receiver on the Indianapolis Colts football team. I'm also a Mormon, which is why I'm writing this essay.

To know me better, you should first understand how much I love the game of football. I was born into a football family. My parents met at Brigham Young University, where my then non-LDS father had accepted a football scholarship from legendary coach LaVell Edwards. My older brother, Zac, also played football at the Y. My father eventually played professionally, and my older brother helped teach me the fundamental skills that a wide receiver needs in order to be successful. So football has been a passion of mine since I was young.

I was part of a great team at Oak Ridge High School in El Dorado Hills, California. During my senior year, I accepted a football scholarship at BYU, and I promised myself I would work hard enough to become a starter as a true freshman in college. It seemed like a long shot to people who didn't know me very well. My family and close friends believed in me, however, and it became a reality. By the end of that first season, I had been named a freshman All-American and the Mountain West Conference's freshman of the year.

That all sounds good, right? Except now I had turned nineteen years old and, like many other young men in our church, had the opportunity to volunteer to serve a mission. It would mean two years of walking great distances, knocking on doors, having doors slammed in my face, and then occasionally finding someone who was looking for a miracle in his or her life.

Even though football is a big deal in our family, it has never surpassed the most important thing we have in our lives—our faith. My father joined the Mormon church while he was a student at BYU. My mother was raised in the Church. Both have strong testimonies of the gospel and encouraged us as we were growing up to gain testimonies for ourselves. Because I took the opportunity to find out for myself about my faith, I was really torn about what I should do.

My success as a freshman at BYU had helped solidify my belief that I could play in the NFL. I faced one of the hardest questions of my young life: *If I left for two years, would I ever be the same football player again?* My mind went back and forth. I found myself leaning more and more toward staying in school, even though I had spent my whole life thinking about and preparing to serve a mission.

That's when my brother Zac pulled me aside. He told me that choosing not to serve a mission was very selfish. He had served in João Pessoa, Brazil, and knew how valuable those two years had been to him and to the many people to whom he had taught the gospel. He cared about my growth as a person and knew that if I didn't go on a mission, I would regret it the rest of my life.

He was right. I was being selfish. I decided to put football aside for two years to serve my Savior. It was one of the best decisions I have ever made. My call was to serve in Buenos Aires, Argentina. I learned to speak Spanish (sort of) in the Missionary Training Center in Provo, Utah, and then spent the next twenty-two months with some of the most wonderful, kind, warm-hearted people I've ever met.

I'm a Mormon because I have seen firsthand the unique happiness that comes from living the gospel. Make no mistake, I've had plenty of challenges in life, and many setbacks. The strength to fight on has come from my beliefs. It has come from relying on the voice of a living prophet who guides our church. Strength has also come from the examples of my parents and others who live worthy lives and are devoted to being good people and to helping others.

Families lie at the center of the Mormon faith. Through the gospel I have learned how I should live so that I can return to the presence of my Heavenly Father and be with my family forever. The gospel has enabled me to marry my wife in a holy temple and to live together with her forever if we follow God's commandments.

When I was a junior in high school, we had a very scary health trial in our family. The moment I heard the news that my mom had been diagnosed with cancer, I was devastated. I remember at first not even being able to speak, and trying to block out the pain in my stomach as my dad began to tell me what the future held for my mom. What saved me? My faith. It gave me peace because I knew that our Heavenly Father was watching and that He cared. I knew that He would help us through this trial if we followed His teachings and maintained our faith.

Photo courtesy of Indianapolis Colts

As a Mormon, I know with certainty that God is our Eternal Father and that Jesus Christ is our Savior. The gospel of Jesus Christ has helped me to understand what my purpose is here on earth and what is expected of me.

You may think of Mormons as being a different type of people. You may be right.

We do believe in certain standards that seem unusual to a lot of people. We don't believe in drinking alcohol or smoking tobacco. This comes from the notion that our bodies are a gift from God and that we should do our best to take care of them. I can promise you that as an athlete I have been tremendously blessed by following these gospel standards.

I have many friends who are not Mormon. I love them. I enjoy talking to them about our faith because I know the happiness and peace it can bring into someone's life. I don't consider myself any better than them, or you, or anyone of any other faith. When I was serving my mission in Argentina I met many great people from all walks of life and many different religious backgrounds. I tried to share the gospel message with as many as I could because I wanted so deeply for them to be blessed the way my family and I have been blessed.

You see, being a Mormon isn't just about the happiness it can bring to your own life. Our faith teaches us the great importance of helping others. Christ came to be our example, and He reminded us, "whosoever will be chief among you, let him be your servant" (Matthew 20:27). When you help others, you feel the warmth of Christ's true love in your heart.

May your heart feel His love, and may your life be blessed.

STEPHEN R. COVEY

STEPHEN R. COVEY has made teaching principle-centered living and principle-centered leadership his life's work. Recognized as one of *Time* magazine's 25 most influential Americans and one of *Sales and Marketing Management* magazine's top 25 power brokers, he is cofounder and vice chairman of FranklinCovey, a leading global professional services firm with offices in 123 countries. FranklinCovey was created in a 1997 merger of Covey Leadership Center with Franklin Quest. It shares Dr. Covey's vision to provide tools for the change and growth of individuals and organizations throughout the world.

In February 2010, Dr. Covey joined the faculty at Utah State University's Jon M. Huntsman School of Business as the first incumbent of the Jon M. Huntsman Presidential Chair in Leadership. His international bestseller, *The 7 Habits of Highly Effective People,* has sold more than 20 million copies in 38 languages throughout the world. Other bestsellers authored by Dr. Covey include: *First Things First, Principle-Centered Leadership, The 7 Habits of Highly Effective Families,* and *The 8th Habit: From Effectiveness to Greatness.* His recent releases include: *Everyday Greatness: Inspiration for a Meaningful Life* (2006), *The Leader in Me: How Schools and Parents Around the World Are Inspiring Greatness, One Child at a Time* (2008), *Predictable Results in Unpredictable*

80

Times (2009), *Great Work, Great Career* (2009), and *The 3rd Alternative* (2011).

Dr. Covey has received the Fatherhood Award from the National Fatherhood Initiative (2003) and the Sikh's International Man of Peace Award (1998). He has also been given the National Entrepreneur of the Year Lifetime Achievement Award for Entrepreneurial Leadership. In 2002, Forbes named *The 7 Habits of Highly Effective People* one of the top 10 most influential management books ever, and a survey by *Chief Executive* magazine recognized it as one of the two most influential books of the twentieth century. *The 8ᵗʰ Habit* was named Best Business Book of 2005 by Soundview Executive Summaries.

Dr. Covey holds a BS in business administration from the University of Utah, an MBA in business administration from Harvard University, and a doctorate from Brigham Young University. He has also received ten honorary doctorates.

Dr. Covey lives in Utah with his wife, Sandra. They are the parents of nine children, grandparents of fifty-two, and great-grandparents of six.

• • •

I AM A MORMON BECAUSE IT'S TRUE: The gospel of Jesus Christ has been restored in its fullness and is found in The Church of Jesus Christ of Latter-day Saints.

I believe this for six reasons:

- First, my parents believed.
- Second, I learned the truth for myself through the true freedom that comes from discipline and wise structure.
- Third, through modern revelation, the Church answers life's toughest questions.

- Fourth, faith helps me serve purposes bigger than myself and my abilities.
- Fifth, seeing is believing.
- Sixth, believing is seeing.

First, *I initially believed because my parents believed.* And they believed because their parents believed. Most of my ancestors were converts from Great Britain and Europe who came across the plains to Utah with Brigham Young. This intergenerational heritage is the foundation of my childhood and faith. In fact, I cannot remember ever doubting either the truth or the supreme importance of the restored gospel of Jesus Christ.

I remember, as a boy, going with my mother into an elevator with the most prominent person in our city. In awe, I asked my mother why she talked to the elevator operator almost the entire time instead of the VIP, whom she knew. She replied that she had never had the privilege of meeting the operator before. "No respecter of persons"—in other words, to respect everyone equally—was a lesson I never forgot.

After hearing me brag to my friends about some of our family adventures, my father taught me another lesson I never forgot: to never brag or drop names, places, or accomplishments—instead to focus on others, to listen to them, and to affirm their worth, potential, and accomplishments. It was this kind of humility, unconditional love, and integrity of life that gave such force to my parents' faith and teachings.

Second, *I learned the truth for myself through the freedom that comes from discipline and wise structure.* I remember how disappointed my parents were, particularly my mother, when I didn't take piano lessons seriously. Instead, I took the course of least resistance and played with my friends instead of practicing the piano. Consequently, I am not now free to play the piano. From that and similar experiences, I learned for myself that true freedom comes from discipline. I learned that freedom wasn't the absence of restraint; rather, it was the fruit of having the kind of structure that promotes the growth and empowerment of people.

This became an invaluable lesson for me when, as a young man, I served a two-year mission for the Church in Great Britain. I accepted structure and rules and the strict discipline of getting up every morning at 6:00 A.M., studying the scriptures for two hours, both alone and with my companion, getting out the door by 9:00 A.M. and proselyting until around 5:30 P.M., with a short break for lunch, and then teaching in the evening from about 6:30 until 9:30, with about an hour's break for dinner and travel. Rather than choosing, I was assigned different companions, and we were to work in unity and harmony through this disciplined process six and a half days a week for two years.

A few years later, I served as a mission president for three years supervising 480 young men and women missionaries. Our motto was "Work, prayer, and love." Again, an amazing thing happened on these missions. From discipline, we literally became "disciples."

With few exceptions, discipline consistently produced more belief and faith and a huge repertoire of freedoms. We learned that love is a verb rather than a feeling, and that love, the feeling, was essentially the fruit of love, the verb. We learned to dedicate ourselves to the service of others with our whole hearts and souls. We learned to not take offense, to love unconditionally, to serve with sincerity and integrity, to repent rapidly when necessary, to forgive as we were forgiven. We learned that to *know* but not to *do* is not to know at all.

The spirit of the discipline we were exercising and the truth of the message we were sharing distilled upon my mind and soul as the dews from heaven. I came to know deeply and independently—for myself—the truth and sacredness of our work, all of which centered on Jesus Christ, the Redeemer of the World and my personal Lord and Savior.

Third, *new and clarifying information contained in revelation given through modern prophets satisfies life's toughest questions for me.*

Some of the questions that are answered include:

• Really, who are we? Where did we come from?

• What is the purpose of life?

• What is our destiny?

• If God is so loving, why is there so much innocent suffering?

• If Christ is the "only way," what about those who live and die and never even learn about Him (most of the human race)?

• If Christ established one church and relatively few join it, where is the justice of God?

• Can family be eternal? If so, how?

• What happens to the spirit when the body dies and before its resurrection?

• How does the resurrection work, anyway?

• What hope is there for one who has been profoundly abused or for one who has made terrible choices in life?

Frankly, I'm both astounded and humbled to see how the restored gospel satisfactorily answers these and many other significant questions.

Fourth, *my faith helps me serve purposes bigger than myself and my abilities.* From many experiences as a parent, grandparent, teacher, writer, and entrepreneur, I've come to learn something priceless that may at first seem perplexing: The more you know, the more you know you don't know, and the greater need you have for faith.

To understand this, think of knowledge as a circle. Where is ignorance? It's on the outside edge of the circle of knowledge. Now, as knowledge increases, what happens to ignorance? It has also grown! Now, what if your purpose as a parent or leader lies outside your circle of knowledge? Will you not require more faith, more belief?

I feel now that my most important work is with my family, not just with my nine children and, at this writing, more than fifty grandchildren and four great-grandchildren, but with the extended and intergenerational family as well. Ultimately, this family encompasses the whole human race, the family of God. Obviously, this purpose transcends my puny powers. Acting on my desire to make a difference, slowly and gradually, I have cultivated a global consciousness and an awareness of the immense suffering that much of the human race experiences every day. This requires more *faith* in the unseen God and also more *work* within His incredible plan and structure to serve both temporally and spiritually His other children.

Fifth, *seeing is believing.* When you see the fruits of belief—that it really works—it strengthens belief. As a professional working extensively with organizations worldwide, I am stunned by the inevitable *upward surge* that happens when leaders are changed at the local or general level of The Church of Jesus Christ of Latter-day

Saints. Also, by sheer contrast, I am overwhelmed by the trust and empowerment given to every Church member—by an open pulpit; by extensive, lifelong, lay participation; by an unpaid ministry; by a welfare plan wisely balancing "help out" with "help up"; and by carefully programmed attention to the needs of children and youth and families and single adults. It's truly exceptional and amazing to see an organization institutionalize its values. "Ye shall know them by their fruits" (Matthew 7:16).

Sixth, *believing is seeing. Believe* is another great verb. I choose to believe. Then, when I act on my belief, I am truly happy. My family is happy and unified. Belief gives purpose and meaning and order to life. It explains things. Because I believe, I "see." I understand.

Connecting with divine roots produces good things, including a deep change in our nature. The gospel gives us the key to true identity. It is Christ-centered rather than self-centered. Christ said, "I am come that [we] might have life, and that [we] might have it more abundantly" (John 10:10). Developing an abundance mentality is the opposite of what is known today as "identity theft." It is also the opposite of the cultural DNA that causes people to compare themselves to other people and to see ever-greater conflict over a decreasing pie. Such people have a hard time being genuinely happy with the successes of other people.

Christ's gospel, if truly embraced to its ultimate end, creates in us an abundance mentality where people do not compare themselves with others. There is no identity theft. When man found the mirror he began to lose his soul. He became more concerned with his image than with his true self. By believing, the Christ-centered person gains the vision to see not only who God and Christ are but who he or she is. This ability to see affects everything else in life.

The Christ-centered person begins to feel a mission to bring the spirit of Christ to every person who comes into the world. This mission inspires us toward timeless and universal principles such as fairness, justice, mercy, and service. It is no longer our accumulation but our contribution that matters as we concentrate on what we can do for the benefit and blessing of other people. The Savior's entire life and His infinite atoning sacrifice exemplify this way of life.

The more we attach ourselves to Christ's infinite Atonement, the more we receive continuously the benefits and fruits of it. One of its fruits is the abundance mentality, a life where one genuinely promotes the welfare and happiness of other people. This other-centeredness is where our own happiness comes from.

In summary, I am a Mormon because of my heritage. I am a Mormon because my disciplined obedience and repentance lead to greater freedoms, including knowledge of truth. I am a Mormon because my church satisfies my need for explanation and because my faith leads me to do more than I am capable of for the benefit of others. I am a Mormon because the Church as an institution works and is life-changing. And I am a Mormon because I choose to partake of Christ's abundance.

MARGARET MEADE COWHERD (PEGGY)

MARGARET MEADE COWHERD (Peggy) is chief financial officer of Global Business Travel for American Express in New York. The Global Business Travel organization is one of the world's largest travel agency networks, with locations in more than 140 countries worldwide and clients ranging from small businesses to multinational corporations. It provides a combination of industry-leading technology, travel management consulting, strategic sourcing, and supplier negotiation support, alongside global customer service available online and offline.

Ms. Cowherd's career began at International Business Machines Corporation. In her last role with IBM, she spent two years as a regional controller in the Global Services organization, which provided technology services to both internal and external customers. Ms. Cowherd was the first female controller in the Global Services organization. She and her team provided financial support for a 5,000-person operational organization. During her tenure, the region met or exceeded all financial targets.

Prior to joining American Express, Ms. Cowherd worked for Goldman Sachs for three years as vice president in the technologies division in New York. She was responsible for all aspects of financial management of the $2B budget. Ms. Cowherd and her team developed and implemented an automated invoice-processing system designed to reduce processing and authorization time and pay invoices on a more timely basis. Additionally, she and her team developed and implemented the first formalized forecast process in the company, designed to improve knowledge and accuracy of expense projections.

Ms. Cowherd holds a BS in business administration from the University of Connecticut. In her spare time, she teaches Sunday School and also enjoys spending time with her family and keeping up with her active niece and nephew, Rachael and Ryan.

• • •

ABOUT ELEVEN YEARS AGO, I was faced with a decision to move to Scottsdale, Arizona. I had been offered a job to help run a new, smaller company in Scottsdale. I would be leaving behind a long career with IBM and moving away from my family and friends. Initially, I thought the risks were far too great, both personally and professionally, to accept the offer. I had not previously been to Scottsdale, nor did I know anyone there. I prayed for guidance and then knew that I should go.

While I was living in Arizona, I had learned about the Mormon church from someone who had worked for me. I admired and respected him and continued to seek more information about the Church. He told me about his family's home evenings together, and shared some of the practices and offerings for children, which I thought were terrific. I had gone to the Mesa Temple one night after work. I remember how beautiful the grounds were around the temple, and the sweet peace I felt in the air. If you have seen one of the temples at night, fully lighted, you know what an impressive sight that can be. I also went into the visitors' center that night and spoke to some of the attendants. I distinctly remember the softness in their eyes, and their sweet spirits. Even though the surroundings were foreign to me, when I was on the temple grounds, I felt as though I was coming home after having been gone for a while. There was something so familiar in what I felt, yet there was so much I needed to learn.

I decided to take the lessons from the missionaries, and I attended Church services while I was learning. I was baptized soon after finishing the lessons, becoming a member of The Church of Jesus Christ of Latter-day Saints. I joined this Church because I felt the confirmation of the Spirit that it was the right choice for me. It is clear to me that God had a hand in my life and knew very well why I was moving to Arizona. He knows and cares about each of us personally. I believe that everything in life happens for a reason, and I truly believe that trusting in the Lord is the answer to every problem.

We all experience challenges in our journey through life, and we have our ups and downs. I think of it as a kind of Ferris wheel: You can't always be at the top, but you're not always at the bottom, either. When things aren't going so well, there is strength in knowing that God is watching over you and that He is in control. He has you in the palm of His hand, no matter how bleak things may look at some point in time.

At times, when I am going through trials, I think about how nice it would be if God would just remove me from the situation and let me move forward. I've learned through my adversity that this is not what the purpose is. God will help bring you *through* the adversity, not *out* of the adversity; that way you learn and He strengthens you. These are growing times and learning times. As you quiet your heart, you will feel His peace. As you sense your weakness, you will receive His strength. As you let go of your will, you hear His guidance. When you pick yourself up, you will be lifted by the wind of His Spirit.

One of the most difficult periods of my life was when my father was diagnosed with cancer. Ours is a very close, loving family, and this was a devastating experience for us. During such trials, we realize how fragile our mortal lives are, but having an eternal perspective was very comforting to me. My greatest source of strength and peace during my father's illness was to be able to go to the temple, where I could feel very close to Heavenly Father. Sometimes I needed to go every week.

In this case, as with other trials, I had to learn to let go of my own will. That's a difficult thing to do for a strong-willed person like myself. You feel as though you are going to lose control if you let go. It's hard to let God take over and to trust that He knows best and will help you through whatever you have to face. My father passed away, and that was certainly not my will. I prayed for miracles. I prayed for God to heal his body and to give him a few more years of quality life, but that was not Heavenly Father's will. He had other plans for my father. But I can tell you, based on my personal experience, that the Lord has shown His continuing love and compassion through my exercise of faith. There have been little rays of sunshine along the way. Despite the grieving and the pain and the loss, I have felt my father's spirit very close to me, and I know that is Heavenly Father's doing. There have been occasions when I've been commuting to work, at random times during my day, or working outside in my garden, when I have felt his warm presence near me. My eyes well up with tears and I just know: He's there, and he is watching over me. Although I miss him, and I can't give him a hug, and I can't see his twinkling eyes or his smile, I know he is all right. I know I'll see him again, and that knowledge comforts me and gives me peace. That's one of the principles of the Mormon church I love the most—the focus on the reality of eternal life.

The point is, there is a way to greater peace, to greater happiness and understanding. Going to church on Sundays helps me to continue to grow in my knowledge of the gospel, develops my

91

understanding and my compassion, and replenishes my strength for the following week. I find that if I take the time to be in the right frame of mind and focus on what's being said in church, instead of letting my thoughts wander to everything else that is going on in the world, invariably there is a message conveyed to me that I needed to hear. There is so much noise and interference in our day-to-day lives that we don't always hear what God is trying to tell us. These experiences have strengthened my determination to accept and be obedient to Heavenly Father's will.

I have also learned to rely on the power of prayer. I still vividly remember my father kneeling by his bedside to pray every evening before he went to sleep. He continued to do so until he was physically not able to kneel down by his bed. My mother told him, "God will know what's in your heart. Just say your prayers while you're lying in bed." I am so grateful for the loving parents I have been blessed with, and for the wonderful example they have been for me. They have shown their great love and concern for my brother, my sister, and myself. They have prepared us well, and have taught us good values. They have helped me to grow and become the person I am today. When I kneel by my bedside, it helps me to have a more centered focus. I am comforted when I take the time to kneel and focus my attention and my thoughts in prayer. I know I will receive Heavenly Father's guidance if I am willing to accept it.

I can tell you that in a time that calls for strength, you will summon it if you believe in Heavenly Father. As you listen to Him, follow His will, and live His commandments, He will draw you close and give you peace. In times when you need hope, you will receive hope. He has always placed a special person in my life when I needed one the most. Someone always happens to be there to help me through my times of need, whether it is a family member, a friend, or someone who just calls me out of the blue. We do have a Heavenly Father who loves each of us, who knows us personally and understands our every need. His only desire is for us to be happy and to accept His will. He will bless and sustain us if we do so.

This I know: If you walk with Heavenly Father, He will never fail you. He will always be by your side.

LEW CRAMER

Before moving to Utah in September 2006 to establish the World Trade Center Utah, Lew Cramer served as a managing director of Summit Ventures International, a Washington, D.C.–based strategic business consulting firm focusing on international business development, major project financing, and advocacy issues for both domestic and global companies.

Previously, Mr. Cramer served as the Director General of the U.S. and Foreign Commercial Service, leading the U.S. government's commercial staff of 1,400 employees at more than 120 embassies overseas and in 65 offices throughout the United States. His government service in the Reagan and Bush I administrations also included Assistant Secretary of Commerce for International Trade; Deputy Assistant Secretary of Commerce for Science and Electronics; Executive Director of President Reagan's EXPORT NOW business initiative, and White House Fellow with the U.S. Trade Representative.

He has worked extensively in the global telecommunications and broadband sectors, including as vice president for MediaOne International and US WEST, responsible for their international government and multilateral financial institution relations and public policy for numerous wireless and broadband investments in more than thirty countries. From an initial capital investment of approximately $2 billion, these international investments were valued at over $15 billion when merged into AT&T in 2000.

Mr. Cramer is currently serving as chair of CDC Development Solutions (formerly known as Citizens Development Corporation), an international organization established by the first President Bush to foster business development in the former Soviet Union. He also serves on the board of the Financial Services Corporation and the American Management Association. He has served as chair of the Global Affairs Council of the American Management Association, as a member of the U.S. Department of State's International Communications and Information Policy Advisory Board, as an international advisor to the chair of the International Chamber of Commerce in Paris, and as a board member of the U.S. Telecommunications Training Institute.

For over a decade, Mr. Cramer taught international business at Georgetown University and the University of Southern California. He has lectured and written extensively on international business and government topics around the world. Previously, he practiced corporate law in the San Francisco Bay area and in Los Angeles, California. Mr. Cramer holds BA and JD degrees with honors from Brigham Young University. He and his wife, Barbara, live in Salt Lake City, Utah, and are the parents of six children.

. . .

I T HAPPENED DURING MY FIRST WEEKS at college in 1967. I was an eager freshman participating in a longtime autumn football tradition at Stanford University. Every fall, before the annual Big Game against archrival University of California, Berkeley, energetic Stanford students constructed a huge bonfire in a dry lake bed on campus, fueled by thousands of wooden fruit crates collected by the freshman class from farmers in the Palo Alto area. My assignment that afternoon was to ride on top of an ancient open-bed truck to ensure that its collection of precariously balanced wooden crates stayed reasonably intact while we sped toward our bonfire destination.

Obviously more full of enthusiasm than of common sense, I undertook this duty with an equally foolish classmate as the driver. We careened through the dusty back roads of the Santa Clara Valley, me sitting grandly on top of dozens of crates piled high in the back of the speeding truck. About fifteen minutes from our destination, I distinctly heard a voice: "Get off those crates." Startled that I could hear anything in the wind rushing by me, I looked around to confirm that I was indeed still alone atop the crates. I was, and everything appeared to be as much "clear sailing" as when our wild ride had begun.

Again I heard the voice, warning me much more emphatically: "Get off those crates NOW." Although I still felt quite safe, I dared not disobey the insistent voice. I scrambled down the crates into the protected rear end of the truck bed. At that very moment, the driver entered a crossroads and suddenly took an inexplicable right turn onto a narrow dirt side road framed by several large oak trees. As the truck passed beneath them at about 45 miles per hour, a broad horizontal branch looming across the road collided with the topmost crates, powerfully sweeping off much of my presumed safe perch.

Hearing that insistent warning at the crossroads, then heeding it to escape certain death, was an intensely sobering experience for an eighteen-year-old college freshman. I had been raised in a Mormon home in the small (in those days) and heavily Mormon-influenced community of Mesa, Arizona. I left the sanctuary of my nurturing family to attend a top-level university in the midst of the turbulent 1960s, when every value, especially religious, was under serious attack. Smart and sophisticated professors, questioning classmates, and even good friends constantly challenged the very core of my religious beliefs.

Shaken by my near-death experience at the Palo Alto crossroads—and bolstered by the obvious inference that someone, somehow, was solicitous of my future path in life—I undertook a rigorous and systematic investigation of what I truly believed about the Mormon faith in which I had been lovingly raised. As a direct benefit, during the intervening four decades my daily life has been blessed continually and immensely by my strong personal faith in my Savior Jesus Christ and by my solid commitment to and daily involvement with The Church of Jesus Christ of Latter-day Saints.

Let me share with you a few reasons, coupled with personal examples, reflecting on why I am honored to be a Mormon.

I have felt the Spirit of God confirming the important decisions in my life. After the spiritual challenges and religious discoveries of my college freshman year, I was strongly impressed that I should interrupt my schooling to serve as a Mormon missionary in northern Germany. This mid-college decision was uniformly baffling to my fellow students and my professors, but proved to be one of the decisive blessings of my life. My two years of full-time commitment to serving Christ and His children, which included daily scripture study and constant reliance on the guidance of the Lord's Spirit, forged a lifelong foundation for understanding the blessings of a Mormon way of life.

Those sacred experiences also taught me how to recognize when and how the Spirit of God communicates truths to me. This understanding of the intervention of the Spirit has since guided me repeatedly in significant personal decisions. For instance, when my future wife and I were praying about our potential marriage plans, the reassuring confirmation of the Spirit of God was a welcome comfort, and we knew that our intended course of action was correct. A similar comfort has guided us numerous times as we have made family, career, and other key decisions.

Being a Mormon provides me with excellent guidance on the best ways to live my life. After several years of practicing law in California, I felt impressed that I should accept an offer to work as a White House Fellow in the Reagan Administration. This opportunity to move my adventurous wife and our family of five young children to Washington, D.C., dramatically changed my life. I left life as a West Coast corporate lawyer to become an East Coast international trade negotiator and business executive.

In 1987, in my position as a Reagan trade official, I was privileged to lead one of the first U.S. government high technology trade missions to the People's Republic of China. China was a much different, much simpler place in those days, and considerable controversy surrounded proper diplomatic protocol in the newly emerging Chinese business environment. Particularly delicate for the head of a U.S. government delegation was the issue of appropriate diplomatic etiquette. I was tutored carefully in preparation for our many meetings.

I faced one key obstacle: As delegation head, I was expected to initiate and participate in numerous alcoholic toasts with our senior-level Chinese hosts. To do otherwise would be deemed a serious breach of protocol. As a practicing Mormon, I was candid with my U.S. government colleagues: I was not going to drink alcohol at these meals, no matter how critical. So we agreed on an alternative approach. I was hopeful that our Chinese hosts would somehow be understanding of my dilemma, but my colleagues were doubtful that any other option would be acceptable.

As the first meal of our historic trip began, and before the drinks were brought out, I initiated a memorable discussion with my Chinese counterpart, explaining that for personal religious reasons I was uncomfortable drinking the traditional Chinese *gan bei* toast. To my surprise and relief, he immediately ordered me several orange sodas for the toasts. He then used our personal discussion to initiate a helpful and far-ranging conversation on the differences between our two nations in a positive and friendly manner. His graciousness defused a potentially uncomfortable situation and built an important friendship. During the following weeks of our trade mission, the other members of our U.S. delegation became so overwhelmed by the number of toasts that by our final meetings in Shanghai, all eighteen delegates were gratefully drinking orange soda with me.

Being Mormon makes me and my family happier. As a young missionary waking up in the pitch-dark mornings of the coldest months in Berlin—hungry, tired, and cold—I consistently felt the happiest I had ever been in my life. This joy came from serving Christ and His children and from sharing His message of eternal life and love with a world much in need of this strength. As a Mormon, I continue to be blessed daily with this joy because Christ's message provides me with the ultimate "long view." I know that this life is only a part—an essential part, but nonetheless only a part—of the eternal perspective promised by Christ. Remembering this long-term landscape is powerful because it allows me to minimize the challenges and slights of everyday living and to concentrate on the more important aspects of life. Once a friend asked me what I would do if I won the lottery. My reply was simple: I have *already* won the lottery. I have an incredible wife and family, a wonderful job and friends, and the knowledge that I can be with my family eternally through my faith in Jesus Christ.

Being a Mormon means being part of an amazing international social network. Maybe it comes from our common values, common experiences, and common commitments. Whatever binds Mormons together also provides a helpful and robust social connection anywhere in the world. In August 1984, when our family flew from Los Angeles to Washington, D.C., to join the Reagan administration, we arrived at our unfurnished rental home late on a Saturday night with children who needed to start school on Monday morning. We showed up for our Mormon church services on Sunday morning, and by the end of the day, we had sufficient furniture, friendship, and information about shopping and schools to begin our new life. In my many years of international work and travels, I have generally found that the most helpful local information invariably comes from attending Mormon church meetings in foreign locales.

I have the opportunity to honor the many sacrifices of my Mormon ancestors. My ancestry on my mother's side includes faithful members of the Mormon church stretching back six generations to its founding. Sacrifices for our shared faith are chronicled by grave sites in Sweden, England, and Scotland as well as in other cemeteries in Europe and along the Mormon Trail. Several of my Hatch ancestors served faithfully in the Mormon Battalion's historic infantry march from Iowa to California and back to Utah, all on foot.

By contrast, my father was a career U.S. Army officer who was originally a Protestant farm boy from Nebraska. Impressed by what the Mormons did during the Great Depression to help their own people, he joined the Church during World War II after meeting a committed Mormon girl. If I were not to be a faithful member, joyfully building the Mormon church in today's challenging world, I am certain these ancestors would disown me in the world hereafter!

Finally and ultimately, I am a dedicated and believing Mormon because I have been blessed by the Spirit of God with the firm conviction—strengthened daily over six decades of life—that God loves each of us. God wants us to experience joy on this earth, and therefore He has provided incredibly helpful ways for this joy to be shared with our families. He has done this by reestablishing His original church on earth through the Prophet Joseph Smith. Today a living prophet receives ongoing revelations from God to bless the daily lives of people throughout the whole world as he guides God's own church—The Church of Jesus Christ of Latter-day Saints.

JASON DEERE

JASON DEERE has made a career out of writing hit songs and developing hit artists. His music is known as life-affirming, with an ability to trigger deep emotions about love, heartache, simple joys, and getting through life's challenges.

His song *Love's Lookin' Good on You,* written for Lady Antebellum, went double-platinum. He has also penned memorable tunes for Little Big Town, LeAnn Rimes, Jessica Simpson, Jim Brickman, SHeDAISY, BeBe Winans, Natalie Grant, Point of Grace, Wanessa Camargo, Leonardo, Luiza Possi, The Wreckers, James Wesley, Stealing Angels, and Due West. His already lengthy list of film and television credits is growing.

When Jason isn't cranking out hits, he is devoted to helping other artists become major label recording acts, such as SHeDaisy, Due West, Ryan Shupe & the RubberBand, and Little Big Town. Songs he produced and remixed for Trace Adkins and Joe Nichols have also climbed to the top of the charts. He has a special passion for working with the best artists in the business while inspiring others to reach for success.

Jason wrote, recorded, and produced two award-winning albums about the history of The Church of Jesus Christ of Latter-day Saints. Many of the songs on *Joseph: A Nashville Tribute to the Prophet* were born in special moments of sacred reflection, and he wrote *The Trek: A Nashville Tribute to the Pioneers* after combing through volumes of pioneer journals and spending long hours in quiet contemplation.

Jason is the guiding force behind the Nashville Tribute Band, which has performed hundreds of concerts from the U.S. to Canada to Australia and China. His latest CD in the LDS trilogy, *The Work: A Nashville Tribute to the Missionaries,* was released in 2011.

• • •

MY FATHER, MONTE DEERE, grew up amid difficult circumstances in Amarillo, Texas, in the 1940s and '50s. Football was his only way out of a less than desirable future. After years of hard work, and with a little luck, he received a scholarship in 1959 to play at the University of Oklahoma. He was the quarterback, coached by the great Bud Wilkinson. After college, he became a fighter pilot in the United States Air Force. For whatever reason, this youthful and likely overconfident man humbled himself enough to listen to the words of Gary Cox, a friend and fellow pilot from Idaho, as a testimony was shared. In 1968, my father joined The Church of Jesus Christ of Latter-day Saints. He has never looked back.

At the time, my mother was pregnant with me. She had been raised Baptist, and one could say she was a little stubborn. She did not join the Church until I was almost six years old. Her wavering testimony, particularly of the Prophet Joseph Smith, took years to solidify, like slow-drying cement. So I am a Mormon because my parents became Mormons. But anyone who knows me knows I am much too stubborn and independent to do something because my parents did it.

One Sunday when I was about fifteen, I was sitting next to my mother in one of our Oklahoma sacrament meetings when I noticed she wasn't singing the congregational hymn. Being a smart-aleck kid,

I ribbed her and said, "Sing." She looked at me with daggers. On the way home I rather delicately asked her, "Why were you not singing that hymn?" She carefully said, "I was raised Baptist, and I was taught to never praise a man, so I will not sing 'Praise to the Man.'" I realized for the first time that my mom, who I saw as quite perfect in every way, possibly had a limited testimony of the Prophet Joseph. It caused me to question the Prophet's relevance and my own testimony.

Around this same time, my friends at school were asking me why I was a Mormon and why my church put so much emphasis on this "Joe Smith" guy. My cherished spring breaks and summer vacations, spent with my maternal grandparents in Oklahoma, were turning into "save Jason from the Mormons" sessions. Two of my favorite people in the world were strategically presenting every argument from anti-Mormon literature they could find for hours at a time. By age fifteen I knew more about the man Joseph Smith than I did about almost anyone. I felt a need to sift through the good, the bad, and the ugly of what I had been told to find out if this man was someone my Father in Heaven wanted me to know about.

After studying for a year at Brigham Young University, I chose to serve a two-year mission. My two older brothers had served missions in Guatemala and Honduras, and I watched their experiences closely through their letters. I knew my brothers wanted me to serve a mission. I knew my parents wanted me to serve a mission. I knew my Young Men's leaders at church wanted me to serve a mission, and I definitely knew my bishop wanted me to serve a mission. But I wanted to know that the God in heaven who made me wanted me to serve a mission. At two o'clock one morning in the late spring of 1988, I walked onto the second green at the Trails Golf Club on the banks of the Canadian River in Norman, Oklahoma, and got down on my knees and prayed a sincere prayer. I prayed specifically to

know if my Heavenly Father wanted me to serve a mission for The Church of Jesus Christ of Latter-day Saints.

Then came the answer without words, the sure knowledge without experience—the feeling that I have only ever felt when the Spirit of the living God has filled my heart and soul to the point where my eyes flood with joyful tears. Done. I would wear the black missionary badge for twenty-four months.

I was called to serve in the Nevada Las Vegas Mission. Four months into my mission, my companion, Elder Orr, and I rode our bikes home to our pink trailer house on Boulder Highway. (That's right, a pink trailer—we were unusually humble while living there.) We had just taught a discussion, and the restoration of the gospel was weighing heavily on my mind.

I walked outside onto the dilapidated redwood deck covered by worn green artificial turf and sat down to my thoughts in the cool desert air. In what seemed like seconds, the words and melody to a song, "Lamb to the Slaughter," literally floated onto the pages of my journal. As I wrote the song down, my heart again filled with the

Spirit of God, and my testimony of Joseph Smith, the prophet of this final dispensation in which I live, was forever confirmed within me.

At twenty-one years of age, I had a firm testimony of the restored gospel that I could not and would not deny. But did I feel like a Mormon? Yes and no.

I have often called myself a "satellite Mormon" because I was raised in Oklahoma around so few members of my own religion. No comfort zone existed in being a Mormon in my hometown. I never had a Mormon friend that we didn't have to drive great distances to visit. I never had a Mormon girlfriend. I certainly didn't have any Mormon pioneer blood in my veins. My relatives more likely played a part in blessing the pioneers with their trials.

Almost everyone in the congregation of my youth was a convert to the Church, many of whom wore their imperfections right on their sleeves. Some put cigarettes out at the door on Sunday, quite literally. General Authorities of the Church visited us only on rare occasions. I knew they existed, for I saw them twice a year as images were pulled in from the giant satellite dish outside our chapel onto a TV screen inside. But they were from the "mother ship" in Salt Lake City, where the mass of "Utah Mormons" seemed to have a monopoly on my own religion. To me we seemed like outsiders trying to make the most of the principles of Mormonism as they fermented in the lives of faithful Oklahomans. Those were beautiful years among wonderful people. I will forever cherish them.

I married my wife, Sonja, in 1991 and moved to Nashville in 1994 to pursue making a living by writing songs and producing records. In 2003, my bishop asked me to teach early-morning seminary, a daily scripture study class for Mormon high school students. I had no idea how accepting this calling would change the course of my life. I spent countless early mornings with twenty-four of the most wonderful young people I have ever known. As I taught that fall, my heart and soul were fixed on the restoration of the gospel. I was teaching an Old Testament class in the mornings, and at night I was reading everything I could get my hands on about Joseph Smith and his early converts.

I had not written any songs of a religious nature since "Lamb to the Slaughter." I had no desire to be a Mormon music artist when talent like Michael McLean and Kenneth Cope existed. However, that fall songs began to come, blessings to me, to my understanding of the early years of our modem church. Sonja started to play the crude work tapes of the new songs in her car and my kids started asking questions, leading to valuable gospel discussions in our family. I played a few of the songs for my friend Dan Truman in his home. We were both moved to tears and realized that we had to do something with this concept.

Dan is a member of the successful country band Diamond Rio. At that moment he was too busy to be involved in another album project. But he made time, and he and his wife, Wendy, put their hard-earned money on the line to make *Joseph: A Nashville Tribute to the Prophet*. The album covers LDS history from Joseph's First Vision in 1820 to his martyrdom in Carthage, Illinois, in 1844. Let's face it: it was a redneck Mormon record. We didn't expect anyone to care.

Sheri Dew, the CEO of Deseret Book Company, heard it and loved it. (She was raised on a farm in Kansas; maybe that had something to do with it.) She called me up and said, "Well, this isn't what we usually do around here, but it's got the Spirit in it, and we want to put it out." They released the album in the summer of 2005, and to our amazement people did care. During the past several years, Dan and I, along with a group of talented musicians and singers that we call the Nashville Tribute Band, have toured the world, doing more than 450 shows in front of hundreds of thousands of people, testifying of the restoration of all things as Christ established them in His earthly ministry. In 2007, we put out another album, *Trek: A Nashville Tribute to the Pioneers,* which covers Latter-day Saint history from the trials of the Saints in Nauvoo to the entrance of the first Mormons into the Salt Lake Valley in 1846.

These years have forever changed me. The experience of writing, producing, and touring the *Joseph* album helped me clearly understand the dispensation in which I live—that my Father in Heaven has a specific plan for these latter days and that I can labor for my own joy within that plan. The experiences associated with *Trek* have healed a lifelong "disconnect" for me. While doing research, I read journal after journal from the pioneering members of the Church. One day I realized that not a single journal entry was written by anyone from the state of Utah! The Mormon pioneers were *all* my people to begin with, each from towns and villages around the world. They followed their hearts, just like I have tried so hard to do, and they found truth and light in the restored gospel. These people became *my* people. I feel I have been adopted into the body of the Saints as I have come to respect and honor their faith. My conversion feels complete and oh, the joy this brings to me!

Why am I a Mormon? Not due to any one significant event, but rather to a road map of events. If the individual experiences ever lose their luster over time, as a collective body they will lift me into the eternities as I praise God in gratitude for the rock-solid foundation upon which the gospel of Jesus Christ has allowed me to stand. For as long as I am able, anywhere people will listen, I will be found joyfully singing and talking about my passion for the gospel of Jesus Christ.

LARRY ECHO HAWK

LARRY ECHO HAWK, an enrolled member of the Pawnee Nation of Oklahoma, is the eleventh Assistant Secretary-Indian Affairs to be confirmed since Congress established the position in the 1970s. He oversees the Department of the Interior's responsibilities for managing tribal and individual Indian trust lands and assets and for promoting the self-determination and economic self-sufficiency of the nation's 565 federally recognized American Indian and Alaska Native tribes.

Prior to his appointment, Mr. Echo Hawk was a professor at Brigham Young University's J. Reuben Clark Law School for fourteen years where he taught federal Indian law, criminal law, criminal procedure, evidence, and criminal trial practice. A former U.S. Marine, he began his law career as a legal services attorney for impoverished Indian people in California, then practiced law in Salt Lake City. Starting in 1977, he served as Chief General Legal Counsel to the Shoshone-Bannock Tribes of the Fort Hall Indian Reservation for over eight years.

Mr. Echo Hawk was elected Attorney General of Idaho in 1990. With this election, he became the first American Indian in U.S. history to serve as a state Attorney General. In the 1980s, he served two terms in the Idaho House of Representatives and as the Prosecuting Attorney for Bannock County, Idaho.

Mr. Echo Hawk has also served on the American Indian Services National Advisory Board and Board of Trustees. He was appointed by President Clinton to the Coordinating Council on Juvenile Justice and Delinquency Prevention, responsible for coordinating federal efforts to combat juvenile delinquency in the United States. Other boards he has served on include the Indian Alcoholism Counseling and Recovery Housing Program and the American Indian Community Resource Center.

Mr. Echo Hawk was born in Cody, Wyoming. His family later moved to Farmington, New Mexico, where his achievements as a public school athlete led to an NCAA football scholarship at Brigham Young University. At BYU he played every game of his career on the varsity football team (1967–1969). He received his BS from BYU in 1970 and his JD from the University of Utah in 1973. He also attended Stanford's MBA program (1974–1975). He has received numerous awards and honors, including Distinguished Alumnus Awards from both BYU (1992) and Utah (2003) and George Washington University's prestigious Martin Luther King medal for his contributions to human rights (1991). He was the first BYU athlete honored to receive the NCAA's Silver Anniversary Award (1995).

Mr. Echo Hawk and his wife, Terry, have six children and twenty-four grandchildren.

• • •

ECHO HAWK: THAT IS THE ENGLISH translation of the name given to my great-grandfather, a Pawnee Indian born in the mid-1800s in what is now called Nebraska. Among the Pawnee, the hawk is a symbol of a warrior. My great-grandfather was known for his bravery, but he was also known as a quiet man who did not speak of his own deeds. As members of his tribe spoke of his good deeds, it was like an "echo" from one side of the village to the other. Thus he was named Echo Hawk.

According to accounts of the first white men who encountered the Pawnee people, the Pawnee were estimated to number about 20,000. Under the laws of the United States they had the right to occupy 23 million acres of land on the plains of Nebraska. When my great-grandfather was nineteen years of age, the Pawnee people were forced to march several hundred miles to a small reservation located in the Oklahoma Indian Territory. Like so many other tribes before them, they had their own Trail of Tears. Fewer than 700 Pawnee survived many years of hardship.

That is a painful history. But the pain was not limited to one generation. The federal government took my father from his parents and sent him to a boarding school where he was physically beaten if he spoke the Pawnee language or practiced his native culture. My sister was sent home from a public school because her skin was the wrong color. I heard a public schoolteacher describe Indians as "savage, bloodthirsty, heathen renegades." Perhaps most painful, during my early childhood my family had no expectation of achieving a higher education and becoming doctors, lawyers, or engineers. A college education seemed beyond our reach.

But out of that pain was born promise. All six children in my family went to college. Three of us became lawyers. The most vivid realization of that promise for me came in 1999, when I ran for the office of attorney general of Idaho, a daunting task. No member of my political party had been elected as attorney general in twenty years, nor a person from my county elected to any statewide office in thirty-eight years. In all the history of the United States, an American Indian had never been elected to any state constitutional office (such as governor, lieutenant governor, secretary of state, or attorney general). A political writer for the largest newspaper in Idaho wrote: "Larry Echo Hawk starts with three strikes against him: he is a Mormon, Indian, Democrat." I went out and worked as hard as I could. On election night, when I received a call from my opponent conceding the election, I felt the full promise of America.

For me, life began to change at the age of fourteen when two missionaries from The Church of Jesus Christ of Latter-day Saints came into my home and presented the missionary lessons. Up until then I knew very little about Christian religion and had seldom attended any church. I was baptized, but I did not have a testimony of the restoration of the gospel of Jesus Christ through the Prophet Joseph Smith.

I was, however, glad that my family had been baptized. Prior to joining the Church I had doubts about whether my family would stay together because my father had a drinking problem. After we were baptized, my father quit drinking and family life was much better. However, I continued to live much the same as I had before I was baptized. Fortunately my parents made me go to church every Sunday. Though it had little influence at that time, I had the benefit of listening to Sunday School teachers, priesthood leaders, and sacrament meeting speakers.

In Farmington, New Mexico, between my junior and senior

years of high school, my priests quorum advisor, Brother Richard Boren, took a special interest in me. He was a successful lawyer, and I admired him very much. He told me repeatedly that I could go to college and get a good education. He also said if I wanted to do well in sports, I had to work at it by setting goals and developing myself.

Although I wasn't a bad athlete, I wasn't anything special. With his encouragement and guidance, I set my goal to become a good football player. We set up a program of weight lifting, running, and skills development. I was small, so I began mixing up a special weight-gaining formula to drink. It tasted awful, but in one year I gained twenty pounds. My football coaches could hardly believe their eyes. I thought I was going to be a defensive back, but the coaches listed me as a quarterback—a disappointment because the captain of the football team was the starting quarterback. I feared that I would again be on the bench. But I gave it everything I had on the practice field. After a few days of practice, I came into the locker room and saw my name listed as the first-team quarterback. I had beaten out the captain of the football team!

A life-changing moment occurred during two-a-day practices before the first game of the season. While I was playing with my brother and two friends, a ball hit me squarely in the eye. It was a serious and painful injury. The doctor told my parents that I might lose the sight in that eye. He bandaged both eyes and sent me home to lie in bed for a week. You can imagine how devastating this injury was because I had worked so hard, and the first game of the season was just a week away.

For the first time, I started to think seriously about the other things Brother Boren had talked about: the gospel of Jesus Christ, the teachings of the Book of Mormon, and the power of prayer. I remember slipping out of bed to my knees. It was the first time in my life that I had ever prayed intently. I remember saying, "Heavenly Father, please, if you are there, listen to my prayer and help me not lose the sight in my eye. I promise, if I can just keep the vision in my eye, I will read the Book of Mormon." When the bandages came off, my sight came back to near perfect vision within a week. I kept my promise and immediately started reading the Book of Mormon.

I was able to travel with the team to the next game in Colorado, but I didn't think I was going to play. We fell behind by two touchdowns in the first half. During halftime, the coach told me to be ready because I might get a chance to play. I remember being on one knee, like football players sometimes do to rest and watch the game. I just dropped my head and said a prayer "with real intent" (Moroni 10:4) because I was about to face my biggest challenge on the athletic field. This would be my chance.

The coach sent me into the game to run a bootleg, pass-run option. After the fake, I could tell after a few strides that I wouldn't be able to run the ball for a gain. I saw one of my teammates downfield, planted my foot, and threw the football as far as I could. As soon as I released the ball, I was clobbered. Lying on my back, I heard a loud roar in the stadium and wondered whether they were cheering for my side or the other side. I jumped up and saw my teammate with the ball sixty-eight yards down the field in the end zone. A touchdown! That was the greatest moment of my teenage life. To me, it was an answer to my prayer. That night my team came from behind to win the game. The next day my name was in the headlines of our local newspaper.

I had not been a good student through junior high and high school. I struggled because my mind was not focused on school. I loved sports but not academics. The Book of Mormon was the first large book that I ever read from cover to cover. I read ten pages every night, never missing a nightly reading. When I finished the entire book, I knelt down and prayed. At that moment I had my first strong spiritual experience. I knew then the Book of Mormon was true. Until that moment I had not realized that Heavenly Father had been watching over me and giving me answers to all my prayers for healing and for a witness of truth.

It seemed to me that the Book of Mormon was about my Pawnee Indian ancestors. The Book of Mormon talks about the Lamanites, a people who would be scattered, smitten, and nearly destroyed. But in the end they would be blessed if they followed the Savior. That is exactly what I saw in my own family's history. When I read the Book of Mormon, it gave me very positive feelings about who I am, knowledge that Heavenly Father had something for me to accomplish in life, and instruction in how I could be an instrument in His hands in serving the needs of other people.

Before the end of my senior year in high school, I had scholarship offers to play football for the University of New Mexico and Brigham Young University. My hard work, encouraged by Brother Boren, had paid off, opening the door to a college education. But, more important, a seemingly freak accident had opened a spiritual door through which celestial blessings have continued to pour on me and my family.

While I was a student at BYU, I heard President Spencer W. Kimball speak several times. He was well known as the Apostle who had a great love for Indian people. He gave a speech entitled "This Is My Vision" in which he related a dream about the Indian people. He said, "I saw you as lawyers. I saw you looking after your people. I saw you as heads of cities and of states and in elected office" (see Dell Van Orden, "Emotional Farewell in Mexico," *Church News,* 19 February 1977, 3). To me it was like a challenge from a prophet of God. I carried an excerpt from that talk in my scriptures. At a certain point in my life, I reread the passage where he said we could become leaders of cities and states, and even though I had never envisioned running for elective office, I knew that I could and should do it.

When I graduated from BYU, I decided to become a lawyer for one reason: to help Indian people. After graduating from law school,

I spent nine years working as the attorney for Idaho's largest Indian tribe and saw a marvelous awakening under laws that now help Native Americans to become self-sufficient and economically strong.

During the Vietnam War, I volunteered for service in the U.S. Marine Corps. Soon after I arrived in Quantico, Virginia, for boot camp, I found myself standing at attention in front of my bunk in our barracks along with fifty-four other Marine Corps recruits. I met my drill instructor when he kicked open the door to the barracks and entered while yelling words laced with profanity. He was a tough, battle-hardened veteran, previously wounded in Vietnam. He confronted each recruit one by one. Without exception, he found something about each recruit to ridicule with vulgar language. I dreaded my turn. He grabbed my duffel bag and dumped my personal belongings onto my bunk. Looking through my things, he grabbed my Book of Mormon. I braced myself for his attack. Instead, he stood close to me and whispered, "Are you a Mormon?"

As instructed, I yelled, "Yes, Sergeant Instructor!" I expected he would then rip into me and my religion, but he paused, raised his hand holding my Book of Mormon, and then, in a very quiet voice, said, "Do you believe in this book?"

Again I yelled out, "Yes, Sergeant Instructor!"

At this point I was sure he would yell out disparaging words about Mormons. But he just stood there in silence. Finally he walked back to where he had dumped my personal things and gently laid my Book of Mormon down. He then walked to the next recruit, whom he ridiculed and disparaged with vile language.

I have often wondered why that Marine Corps drill instructor spared me that day. But I am glad I was able to say without hesitation that I am a Mormon and that I know the Book of Mormon is true. That testimony is a precious gift given to me by the Holy Spirit with the help of two missionaries, a priests quorum leader, and a prophet of God. For this I am very grateful.

RICHARD AND LINDA EYRE

RICHARD AND LINDA EYRE are popular speakers and authors on the topic of parenting and families. They find it remarkable and gratifying that in every one of the forty-five countries where they have made presentations, parents have similar hopes, dreams, and worries about their children regardless of economic, religious, geographic, or cultural differences.

Together they have authored numerous work/family balance and parenting books, one of which, *Teaching Your Children Values,* became the first parenting book in fifty years (since Dr. Spock's *Baby and Child Care*) to reach No. 1 on the *New York Times* bestseller list. They had two books released in 2011: *5 Spiritual Solutions for Everyday Parenting Challenges* and *The Entitlement Trap.*

Richard and Linda have also appeared together on many national network TV shows, including *Oprah, The Today Show, Prime Time Live, 60 Minutes,* and *Good Morning America,* and they once did regular segments on the *CBS Early Show.* Their parenting website, www.valuesparenting.com, provides ideas, guidance, and creative programs for families throughout the world.

The Eyres' most important production is their nine children

("one of every kind"), who through the years have helped them formulate the ideas they have passed along to other parents. The second-generation Eyres have earned university degrees from Wellesley, Harvard, Columbia, and BYU. Each of them has interrupted a university education to spend two years abroad studying, doing missionary work, and/or providing humanitarian service. They also do their part to spread awareness of the importance of family through their own speaking, books, blogs, and websites. To date, twenty-three grandchildren have been added to the Eyres' treasury. The family's favorite projects so far have been humanitarian expeditions to Ethiopia, Kenya, Bolivia, India, and Mexico. Their Eyrealm Foundation focuses on strengthening families in the developing world.

Richard has an MBA from Harvard, is president of his own management consulting company, and is a ranked senior tennis player. He has served as a mission president for The Church of Jesus Christ of Latter-day Saints in London and as a director of the White House Conference on Parents and Children. He also ran as a candidate for governor of Utah. (Linda is so glad he didn't win!)

Linda is a teacher and musician, and she is the cofounder of International JoySchools.com, an in-home program for teaching preschoolers the joys of life. She and her husband have both served on numerous arts, university, and nonprofit boards.

• • •

MANY YEARS AGO, while I (Richard) was a student at the Harvard Business School, I had a French classmate who told me point-blank that he would one day be the president of France. I had some political ambitions of my own at the time, and Dominique and I became friends. We found agreement on the fact that we viewed Harvard not so much a path to wealth as a path to power. Power was the ultimate goal, we decided, and could lead to wealth if we wanted it to, while the reverse was not necessarily true. We successfully petitioned the dean to start an elective class at the school called "Power."

Looking back, we are both amazed how shameless we were in our ambitions—and how wrong! As a member of the Mormon church, to think that power was the end, rather than the means to other more worthy ends, was a misconception of the first order.

With passing years, as we have raised our children and watched life unfold, it has become increasingly clear to us that the real goal, the real end toward which all of our means should direct themselves, is family. God's family!

Family is where we will find our greatest fulfillment, our greatest peace, our greatest joy. And family is, in two very distinct and wonderful ways, eternal. (More on that in a moment.)

The interesting thing is that most of us, and most people on the planet, know that family is what matters. Public opinion polls show that most people give family life a high priority in their lives.

Why, then, is it so difficult to make our expenditure of time and mental energy match up with our priorities? And why is it so very hard, perhaps harder than any other challenge we face, to develop committed, nourishing marriages and to raise responsible, happy kids in cohesive, lasting, values-driven families? Part of the difficulty is that most people are not able to keep their focus on their family day after day, and they do not have an adequate backup or support system for what they are trying to teach and to do in their homes.

To a large extent, that is why we are Mormons.

The Church of Jesus Christ of Latter-day Saints helps us, in a rather wonderful and dramatic fashion, to keep our attention and our focus on our family! The Mormon church has possibly the most family-centric theology and culture on earth. Its organization of lay leadership and its programs for children and youth seem designed and conceived to strengthen families and to help parents raise their children.

Indeed, that really *is* how and why the Church was designed and conceived. Harold B. Lee, a Mormon prophet and former President, referred to the Church as "the scaffolding with which we build eternal families."

We are Mormons first and foremost because we love the teachings of the Church and believe that it contains Jesus Christ's restored and complete gospel.

But, on the basis of practicality as well as faith, we are also Mormons because of all that the Church does to strengthen, build, and support our marriage and the raising of our children.

To explain what we mean by that, let us review five basic parenting advantages or "spiritual solutions" that come to us through our Church membership:

1. *We believe that our children are literally our spirit brothers and sisters.* They lived, as we did, in a premortal life with God, our Heavenly Father. Here and now, on this physical earth where we come to learn and progress by experience, children are born to us as our greatest stewardship. They teach us even as we teach them, and we believe we can return together to God as intact families in the life after death. These beliefs give us a respect for our children and a larger perspective that makes an amazing difference in our parenting.

2. *We can pattern our parenting after God's.* Viewing God as the literal father of our spirits allows us to strive to parent our children as He parents us. We can try to emulate His unconditional love, His treatment of each of us as an individual, and His example of teaching and nurturing us. Knowing that He lets us go into a mortality of choices, options, and agency influences our outlook. As we consciously try to follow this same pattern in our own home, it improves everything.

3. *We have a direct channel to God, the real Father, on behalf of our stewardship of others of His children.* This gives our prayers a personal and specific tone as we ask for insight and for help in understanding and caring for those we believe have been sent directly to us from God. We believe we are entitled to personal inspiration and revelation from our mutual Father as we strive and struggle to raise responsible and righteous children in difficult times. We rely on this "direct-channel" prayer often, feeling a little of the sentiment once reportedly expressed by Abraham Lincoln: "Sometimes I am driven to my knees by the overwhelming conviction that I have nowhere else to go."

4. *The Church's organization and programs give us enormous help and backup in teaching faith and values to our children.* It is hard to conceive of a support mechanism more complete than our children and youth classes, the Boy Scout and Young Women programs, and the parenting instruction for adults. Plus the Church provides a culture of clean living. Dating, dress, and behavior guidelines encourage, support, and reward our children's good choices. Frankly, we don't know how we could have raised our children in this pernicious world without the support of the Church.

5. *We believe that the Savior's Atonement, His Holy Spirit, and His priesthood can reside in our homes and affect our children and our families directly.* Fathers can give their children priesthood blessings, and children receive the gift of the Holy Ghost when they are eight years old. We see the family as the basic unit of God's government and ultimately of His heavenly kingdom where our families will be part of His family. It is this larger framework and God's own spirit and power that give us a chance to succeed.

Families, as mentioned earlier, make us eternal in two ways. First, we are immortalized by our children, who will be here when we are gone. Second, families themselves are eternal—our family and marriage bonds survive death to become not only the crowning achievement of our mortality but the greatest blessing and vehicle of our eternal life and eternal progress.

So . . . we still watch the French newspapers occasionally, looking for Dominique and wondering about his progress in achieving his power goal of becoming the president of France. But we also know that the power that Dominique and I were seeking back in graduate school was not the real power. Real power is the insight, perspective, programs, and priesthood of God that allow us to succeed in the greatest of our relationships and our stewardships—our families.

LARRY GELWIX

FOR THE PAST THIRTY-SIX YEARS, Larry Gelwix has served as the volunteer head coach of the Highland Rugby team in Salt Lake City, Utah, currently ranked as the number-one high school age team in the United States. Coach Gelwix and his teams have won twenty national high school and youth rugby championships and have produced a varsity record of 418 wins and just 10 losses in those thirty-six years.

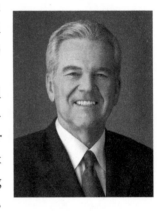

This unparalleled win-loss record caught the attention of Hollywood, resulting in the motion picture *Forever Strong*, the true story of Coach Gelwix and the Highland Rugby team. Following a successful national release in theaters, *Forever Strong* played as the in-flight movie worldwide for US and international airlines and received numerous favorable reviews in the national media.

Coach Gelwix has received the prestigious Pioneers of Progress Award from the Days of '47 Committee, recognizing and honoring modern pioneers. He has also received the Best of State award as Best High School Coach in the state of Utah and the Educational Service Award from the Utah Department of Corrections. He was recently named as the recipient of the Brigham Young University Outstanding Service Award. The national media has labeled Coach Gelwix the "Winningest Coach in America."

Professionally, Larry Gelwix serves as CEO of Columbus Travel in Bountiful, Utah, and is a nationally recognized travel expert and former CEO of an airline. He is the on-air host of the syndicated radio broadcast *The Travel Show*. He is also featured on the *Getaway Guru* television series.

Larry Gelwix received his bachelor's and master's degrees in organizational communications from BYU. He has served in many Church callings, including bishop, high councilor, Young Men's president, and full-time missionary. He and his wife, Cathy, are the parents of five children and have three grandchildren. The Gelwixes are currently serving as mission president and "mission mom" in the California Fresno Mission while their youngest son serves as a full-time missionary in the Canada Calgary Mission.

• • •

I AM A MORMON BECAUSE the principles and values taught by The Church of Jesus Christ of Latter-day Saints are true. They work in our personal lives, in our business lives, and in our families. The gospel of Jesus Christ is the perfect game plan. I see this every day in my coaching.

For example, one of the lessons I've learned as a coach is that if you want to be a champion, focus on the final score. There is a coaching term, "end game," meaning, where do I want to be at the end of the game and how am I going to get there? What is my "end game"? I have to coach a full game—and I expect my players to play the full game. You can never give up *or* let up.

Consider this: Suppose you were a football player, and somehow you knew with absolute certainty, not 99.9 percent, but 100 percent, that your team would win. You even knew the final score, and you knew all this *before* the game even started. You might not know how you were going to get there, but you knew you would win—and it all depended on just one thing: YOU. You will win if, and only if, YOU personally give it YOUR absolute best—your best attitude, your best effort. You probably will not be the best player on the field. You will see more talented people all around you. But the outcome has nothing to do with them. It's all about you. If you hustle and do your best, you win . . . guaranteed.

You're not going to play a perfect game. You may fumble the ball sometimes. You might miss a tackle, throw an interception, or step out of bounds. In other words, you're probably going to make some mistakes along the way, but never intentional mistakes. Winning is all about your attitude and your effort.

If that really were the deal, suppose your team was down twenty-one points in the first, would you give up? Of course not! Why? Because you already know how the game ends based upon your attitude and effort. Or what if you're up by fifty or sixty points at halftime? Would you put it all on cruise control and say, "Hey, I can let up now. This game's in the bag!" No, because you know everything can change based upon your attitude and effort. What if you're down by eighteen points with two minutes to go? Winning seems impossible. Would you quit? Never! Because you already know the final score.

Well, it doesn't work that way in sports, but this is exactly what happens in life, and it's what the gospel of Jesus Christ teaches us.

The most frequent question my players are asked is, "What do you want to be when you grow up?" I hear all the answers, "I want to be a lawyer, a doctor, a schoolteacher, a carpenter, owner of my own business," and so on. I tell them, "That's great, but it really doesn't matter *what* you want to be as long as it's honest, you have a passion for it, and you will be able one day to support yourself and a family." As important as the question is, "What do you want to be?" it is not *the* most important question. *The* most important question is not "What do you want to be?" but "WHO do you want to be?" You see, "who" we are, not "what" we are, is our final score.

When we truly understand that who we are is our final score, then even when things go bad for us—people betray us, we have problems with our family, health, or business—we keep our focus on our "end game," the final score of "who" we are, not "what" we are. That's what the Lord asks and expects of us—our best attitude and best effort. And when we lead with our best attitude and effort, "after all we can do" (2 Nephi 25:23), we always win—and we understand it's never about us, it's always about Him.

It's tough to play the game on your toes all four quarters, it really is, but that's what a champion does. The biggest obstacle to greatness is goodness. When we're good at something, we don't always feel the pressure to push ourselves to greatness, which means living up to our full potential. We sometimes find we can "get by" by giving less than our best. I have learned that the difference between a good team and a great team is that a great team plays with a laser-like focus on attitude and effort, while always keeping an eye on the end game or final score.

I tell my players, "Never surrender, never quit, no regrets!" The gospel of Jesus Christ guarantees us the victory. There are promises made at baptism, at confirmation, promises made at priesthood ordination and in the temple blessings. That's the final score.

In the midst of a Winter Quarters, or a Haun's Mill, or when facing trials like the Martin and Willie handcart companies did, or if our children make choices that are not right, even as we may experience health problems or divorce or any other calamity in life, we can hold on to the final score. We already have the Lord's promise of how the game ends. This is why, when we can't see what's beyond the horizon, we can with faith in God's promises still pick up our handcart and head West. Before the game even started—that is, in our premortal world before we came to earth—our Heavenly Father had already told us what the final score would be if we would consecrate all that we have and all that we are to Him. That's how common, ordinary people like you and me can just keep going. No visions, no angels, just simple faith. It comes down to faith and trust in our coach, in our team, in our playbook. "Look unto me in every thought; doubt not, fear not" (Doctrine and Covenants 6:36).

I've learned that the Holy Ghost is the only agent of change. It's the Holy Ghost that changes hearts and changes lives. We have three responsibilities in the change process: we love, we serve, and we invite, invite, invite, and invite others to change and come unto Christ. I've said to a lot of young men: Go on a mission. To some it may seem like the most ridiculous, silly, nonsensical thing to do. Think about it. You're nineteen years old. You're going to give up school, home and family, a social life, your car, sports, friends, maybe a scholarship. You're going to give up the good life. For what? To go out and lead a highly regimented, spartan life of rejection? It makes no sense! And it won't make any sense until you add one element into the equation—that at the end of the day, the gospel of Jesus Christ really is true. The Church of Jesus Christ of Latter-day Saints is what it claims to be. Joseph Smith saw and heard what he said he saw and heard. We are led by a modern prophet. Once you add this into the mix, going on a mission is the most logical, "of course" thing you could ever do. It becomes a desire rather than an obligation.

As a young man, I had a testimony and wanted to serve a mission. My father was not a member of the Church. My grandparents on my father's side of the family couldn't understand it. They said, "You're going to do what? You're going to leave school and be a missionary? How much are they going to pay you?"

"Well, nothing."

"You're going for nothing?"

"Yes. In fact, I have to pay for it. That's why I've been saving money at my summer jobs all through high school."

"You're going to take your college money and pay for it? You're going to go on a mission?"

To them it was like, "Are you crazy?" It made absolutely no sense to them because they didn't have that testimony borne of the Holy Ghost. But once you add testimony in, then everything we do, everything we're asked to do, every commandment, makes perfect sense. Sacrifice has been a part of the gospel from the beginning. The first thing Adam and Eve did when they left the Garden of Eden was to offer a sacrifice. I've taught my players, "Being a champion is hot, sweaty, dirty work." Champion athletes know and understand that sacrifice, dedication, hard work, and selflessness are all part of their final score.

In sports you've heard the expression of a "go-to guy." When the game is on the line, you want the ball to go to Michael Jordan. You want Steve Young to throw the pass. That's a go-to guy. The world sometimes has a problem accepting Joseph Smith and the First Vision. Think about it: God and Jesus Christ appear to a fourteen-year-old, unschooled boy and tell him he's going to restore the true gospel of Jesus Christ to the earth? But look at it from the Lord's point of view. How long had Heavenly Father and Jesus Christ known Joseph Smith? Did they see him as a fourteen-year-old boy? No, he was a "go-to guy." For eons of time they had given him assignments, callings, things to do, and handed the ball to him. They passed it to him and he caught it. For eons he had shown up for practice. For eons he did the drills and learned the plays; he knew the game plan. To Heavenly Father and Jesus Christ, it wasn't a fourteen-year-old boy who showed up in the grove in 1820. God called on His go-to guy, someone He knew and trusted. I believe that every person who is willing to put it all on the altar of service and sacrifice was and is a go-to guy.

There is a passage in the Pearl of Great Price, in the book of Moses, describing how the Lord called Enoch. Enoch asks the Lord, "Why is it that I have found favor in thy sight, and am but a lad, and all the people hate me; for I am slow of speech; wherefore am I thy servant?" (Moses 6:31). Here's a kid who gets his mission call, so to speak, and he says, "I can't do this. I don't talk very well. I'm not popular. I can't. Why me?" Now look at verse 32. The Lord says to *"go forth" and just do it. Be faithful, be obedient, follow the game plan, and I'll put the words in your mouth.* So here's the unpopular young man with low self-esteem, can't speak very well, and doubts his own abilities, but takes the Lord at His word. In Moses 7:13, we see what happens when we partner with the Lord, when we accept Him as our coach and follow His game plan. We read that Enoch's faith was so great that mountains and rivers moved, and the armies of the enemy fled, "so powerful was the word of Enoch, and so great was the power of the language which God had given him." Why? Because he partnered with the Lord.

One of the most critical decisions you make in most things is who your partner will be. Partners can make you or break you. We spend a lot of time and energy picking our partners, and for good reason.

Now think about the gospel. How often does the Lord say, "Prove me herewith"? "Just try me." In other words, He is inviting us to make Him our partner. Read Mosiah 2:22 in the Book of Mormon, where King Benjamin says, "And he [the Lord] never doth vary from that which he hath said." What does that mean? God doesn't lie. God doesn't change the deal. God doesn't do secret stock options. He doesn't undercut you or engage in back-room dealing. Whatever the Lord or His appointed priesthood leaders say, from the local level to the top, when speaking under the guidance and direction of the Holy Ghost, you can take it to the bank. You can cash it. It will always be good. That is what you want in a partner.

What pulls our identity together—in fact, what pulls everything together—is when we choose what team we're going to play for. We would never switch jerseys and play for two teams in the same game, so why do we sometimes fall for the biggest lie of the century in our personal lives? "I can lead a secret double life." "I can live with one foot in Babylon and one foot in the promised land." It was a lie in our premortal life, and he who is the father of all lies is selling the same big lie today (see 2 Nephi 2:18).

Choose what team you're going to play for, put the Lord's jersey on, be grateful for what and who that jersey represents, focus on the final score by always giving your best attitude and best effort, and you will win. I have learned that there are only two pains in life. There's the pain of hard work and the pain of regret. The pain of hard work is tough, it stretches us, but at the end of the day we are grateful for the pain of hard work because we are a better and stronger person. But if we don't do our best, the pain of regret will never go away.

I am a Mormon because the principles and values of The Church of Jesus Christ of Latter-day Saints are true. They work in our personal lives and in our families. I want to wear the Lord's jersey 24/7 because I have a testimony of Him.

TERRYL GIVENS

TERRYL GIVENS was born in rural upstate New York, but he spent his childhood in Arizona and Virginia. He received his bachelor's degree in comparative literature from Brigham Young University in 1980 and did his graduate work in intellectual history (Cornell) and comparative literature (UNC Chapel Hill), working with Greek, German, Spanish, Portuguese, and English languages and literatures. After receiving his PhD from UNC in 1988, he accepted an appointment at the University of Richmond, where he now serves as Professor of Literature and Religion, and the James A. Bostwick Professor of English.

Professor Givens teaches courses in Romanticism, nineteenth-century cultural studies, and the Bible and Literature. He has published in literary theory, British and European Romanticism, Mormon studies, and intellectual history. Professor Givens's early work focused on literary studies, specifically romanticism. His dissertation and early publications were on the classical theory of mimesis and its dissolution in the nineteenth century. He also published *Dragon Scales and Willow Leaves,* a well-regarded children's book.

Shifting his research emphasis to the intersection of literary and religious studies, Professor Givens published *The Viper on the Hearth* in 1997. He used his background in literary criticism to survey anti-Mormon literature from the nineteenth century to the present, exploring the challenge anti-Mormons were presented with in seeking to justify persecutions of a religious sect in a supposedly religiously tolerant nation.

His book *By the Hand of Mormon* is considered an important contribution to Mormon studies as the first academic survey of the significance of the Book of Mormon to believer and skeptic alike that has been published by a major academic press (Oxford University Press). In it, Professor Givens argues that the Book of Mormon has been important primarily for its extratextual historical claims (based simply in its existence) rather than for its contents. In addition, he makes a case for "dialogic revelation" as a novel contribution of the Book of Mormon.

Terryl Givens served as a missionary for The Church of Jesus Christ of Latter-day Saints in São Paulo, Brazil, and has served as bishop in his local ward (congregation) for several years. He now lives with his family near Richmond, Virginia.

• • •

FAITH, IN MY EXPERIENCE, is a choice. The call to believe is a summons to engage the heart—to attune it to resonate in sympathy with principles and values and ideals that we devoutly hope are true and that we believe to be true but not on certain grounds. There must be grounds for doubt as well as belief, for only in these conditions of equilibrium and balance, equally "enticed by the one or the other" (2 Nephi 2:16), is my heart truly free to choose belief or cynicism, faith or faithlessness. Under these conditions, what I choose to embrace, to be responsive to, is the purest reflection of who I am and what I love.

Immanuel Kant believed the two sources of the most supernal awe and reverence were "the starry heavens above and the moral law within." More broadly, I recognize in his words the two sources of my own decision to believe. What story provides the most credible scenario for the universe's luminous beauty (as well as unspeakable anguish) and my place within it? And what story gives the most likely account for the deepest yearnings and intimations of the human heart? Whichever cosmic plot we construct to make sense of it all, we are acting in faith. As Fitz James Stephen said, "In all important transactions of life we have to take a leap in the dark. . . . If we decide to leave the riddles unanswered, that is a choice; if we waver in our answer, that, too, is a choice: but whatever choice we make, we make it at our peril." So this is why I choose to believe, taking each riddle in turn.

Astrophysics provides a credible account of the origin of the stars, and Darwin might explain the development of the human eye. But neither can tell me why the night sky strikes me with soul-piercing quietude or why my mind aches to understand what is so remote from bodily need. Regarding the first, the mystery of how we experience the world in all its beauty, David Belinksi asks, "How do the twitching nerves, chemical exchanges, electrical flashes, and computational routines of the human eye and brain provide a human being with experience? The gap opened between casual sequences that with a moving finger we can trace from one point to the next and the light enraptured awareness to which they give rise is unfathomably large because it spans an incommensurable distance."

And regarding the second, the insatiability of human curiosity, John Polkinghorne writes, "our surplus intellectual capacity, enabling us to comprehend the microworld of quarks and gluons and the macroworld of big bang cosmology, is on such a scale that it beggars belief that this is simply a byproduct of the struggle for life." George Bernard Shaw said it a little differently: "My dog's brain serves only my dog's purposes. But my brain labors at a knowledge which does nothing for me personally but make my body bitter to me and my decay and death a calamity."

The best sense I can make out of this riddle is that there is some independently existing principle of intelligence and agency within me, which is impelled by its eternal identity and potential to move toward greater understanding of and love for this universe. As Joseph Addison wrote, "There is not . . . a more pleasing and triumphant consideration in religion than that of the perpetual progress which the Soul makes toward the perfection of its nature."

And what of what Kant called "the moral law within"? My response to human acts of barbarism and violence is more than a studied rejection of behavior that is counterproductive or socially detrimental. The tears I shed at stories of abuse, or heartbreak, or my neighbor's or children's pain involve more, I have to believe, than a biologically inherited tribal solidarity. And similarly, the rejoicing I feel in witnessing a quiet gesture of selflessness, a noble sacrifice, or a tender exchange is a mystery that transcends my genetic makeup. "The believer finds," wrote Henry James, "that the tenderer parts of his personal life are continuous with a *more* of the same quality which is operative in the world outside of him, and which he can keep in working touch with, and in a fashion get on board of and save himself, when all his lower being has gone to pieces in the wreck."

The simplest explanation for these powerful inner currents of emotion and moral sense is that they are of long standing and are anchored in a source that exists prior to and independent of present circumstance. As Clement of Alexandria argued with plaintive eloquence, our turning in dismay from our base inclinations, in order to embrace goodness and virtue, can only be a decision born of experience. Repentance, in his story line, is prompted by a shadowy recollection, and thus is an act of reversion rather than conversion. It comes when premortal memories filter through to us, creating a vague "reminiscence of better things. . . . There follows of necessity, in him who has come to the recollection of what is better, repentance for what is worse. Accordingly, . . . the spirit in repentance retraces its steps. In the same way, therefore, we also, repenting of our sins, renouncing our iniquities, . . . speed back to the eternal light, children to the Father."

Augustine agreed that the conclusion was inescapable. "Happiness is known to all," he reasons, "for if they could be asked with one voice whether they wish for happiness, there is no doubt whatever that they would all answer yes. And this could not be unless the thing itself . . . lay somehow in their memory." Then, making the observation personal, he asks rhetorically, "But where and when had I any experience of happiness, that I should remember it and love it and long for it?" Like the woman looking for the lost coin, "She would not have found it if she had not remembered it."

These considerations persuade me that a certain account of my soul's origin, nature, and destiny makes the most sense of how I experience this world of mortality. But there is more about Mormonism in particular that gives added definition to such a vague outline of faith. Many kinds of God are conceivable, and have been conceived, as being the source of those eternal truths and realities that inform our spiritual natures. But only one can I personally believe to be worthy of my adoration and love. First, He would have to be a God of infinite empathy. A God without body or parts is conceivable. But a God without passions could not engender in this heart either love or interest.

Early Christianity knew such a God. The Church's first theologian, Origen, asked, "Does not the Father and God of the universe somehow experience emotion, since he is long-suffering and of great mercy? Or do you not know that when he distributes human gifts he experiences human emotion? . . . The Father himself is not impassible. If he is asked, he takes pity and experiences grief, he suffers something of love and . . . for our sake he experiences human emotion." He would be, in other words, the God reintroduced to the world through Joseph Smith. A God who prevents all the pain He can, assumes all the suffering He can, and weeps over the misery He can neither prevent nor take upon Himself.

Second, He would have to be a God devoid of jealousy. Genuine love always desires the highest good for the objects of its affection. As Addison wrote, "It must be a project pleasing to God himself, to see his creation forever beautifying in his eyes, and drawing nearer to him, by greater degrees of semblance." Plato had written much earlier that the Creator "was good, and one who is good can never become jealous of anything. And so, being free of jealousy, he wanted everything to become as much like himself as was possible." This God, long lost to the world, we also hear again in modern scripture, bestowing as much grace and as many gifts as we are "willing to receive," even to our participation in "the divine nature." This is a God I am powerfully drawn to and gladly worship.

It is not a coincidence that the principal guideposts in my spiritual pilgrimage thus far come outside my faith tradition. But that's my final point. They don't. The restored gospel is a gospel of liberality and generosity. My faith encompasses and embraces them.

It took the most important influence of all, my wife, Fiona, who is a lapsed Catholic, lover of the temple and all things beautiful, and fervent disciple of the weeping God of Enoch (Moses 7:28–37) to teach me that the church John the Revelator saw in vision was not taken from the earth; it retreated into the wilderness. There, it did not wither and die. Rather, it was "nourished for a time." Joseph Smith saw the Restoration as a bringing of that church back out of the wilderness, a restoration of the "ancient palace" now reduced to ruins, a reassembling of all the good and beautiful in the world and in the Christian tradition that had been lost or corrupted from Eden forward.

Joseph's vision reminds me of the philosopher Spinoza, who "rejected the orthodoxy of his day not because he believed less, but because he believed more." From the time of that insight, I stopped asking in despair, not just "where are our Dantes and Miltons," but "where are our Thomas Trahernes and George MacDonalds and John Cassians and Gregory Nazianzens?" They are right where they have always been. They are in the "prepared place." Even today, the church I love has invisible borders. In a modern revelation, the Lord referred to "those which I have reserved unto myself, holy men that [even you, Joseph] know not of" (Doctrine and Covenants 49:8). There is a greater congregation, consisting of holy persons living and dead, who love the Lord and are sanctified by that love. The kinship I strive to attain, the dialogues I struggle to engage, with the living Saints and with the Henry Mores and Edward Beechers of that church, create my truest sense of belonging. As for The Church of Jesus Christ of Latter-day Saints, I find the central and enduring facts of the Restoration to be its teaching of the true God and the restoration of the authority that channels His love to us in particularly powerful ways, through sealing ordinances that bind us eternally in covenant relationships to God and to loved ones.

I find endless byways to explore and celebrate in Joseph's expansive vision of past and future worlds, human origins and human destinies, and a God whose heart beats in sympathy with ours. When I grow exasperated with the deadening lesson manuals and the foibles of Mormon culture and the excruciating inefficiencies of bureaucracy, I remember that God foresaw it all. "Patience and faith" would be necessary to remain faithful, as we were told on the very day of the Church's organization (Doctrine and Covenants 21:5). I have made my peace—as did Parley Pratt and a devastated generation of Saints—with the failure to realize at this time the Zion of hope and promise we expected to find. Never mind, I tell myself. There are sufficient materials at hand to fashion a life of faith and patience. The project is ongoing. That it takes at times a concerted act of will makes the choice a doubly meaningful act.

THOMAS B. GRIFFITH

THOMAS B. GRIFFITH was appointed to the United States Court of Appeals for the D.C. Circuit in June 2005. Raised in McLean, Virginia, he graduated from Brigham Young University *summa cum laude* and from the University of Virginia School of Law, where he was an editor of the law review.

Prior to his appointment to be a federal appeals court judge, Griffith had been the chief legal officer of the U.S. Senate, a partner in a major law firm in Washington, D.C., and the general counsel of Brigham Young University.

• • •

I AM A CONVERT TO The Church of Jesus Christ of Latter-day Saints. I count my decision to join the Church the single best and most important choice of my life.

I was sixteen years old at the time, a junior in high school living in McLean, Virginia, a suburb of Washington, D. C. Although no one would have mistaken me for devout, I was interested in religion and had regularly attended the Episcopal church with my family since I was a child. I enjoyed church. At twelve, I completed catechism and took my first communion. At fourteen, I became an acolyte. Being involved in the liturgy of the church, especially Holy Communion, I had the sense not only that I was part of a venerable tradition, but that I was also involved in something sacred. I could easily imagine myself going into the ministry. Even so, I had little sense that Jesus Christ was a living, dynamic presence, and I was agnostic as to the truthfulness of the New Testament claim that He was the Son of God whose bodily resurrection was a sign of His divinity.

Because of my interest in religion, I was open to the invitation of a Mormon friend to attend a scripture study class at her church that met each weekday at 6:30 A.M. before school began. There I discovered about twenty high school students taught by a young married couple. The friendliness and informality of the class appealed to me. I was especially touched by the students' open expressions of faith in Christ and love of family, things I had not said before publicly nor heard expressed by my peers. The discussion that day was about the Book of Mormon and how it fit into the Mormon canon alongside the Old and New Testaments. At the end of the class, the teacher gave me a copy of the Book of Mormon and encouraged me to read it.

I took the book to school that day. During my first class, I slipped the Book of Mormon inside the textbook I was supposed to be reading and began to leaf through its pages. Initially, my attention was drawn to the illustrations depicting scenes that were new to me, but then I started reading the text. When I did, something unexpected and marvelous happened, something I can't put fully into words. All at once, I was overcome with a sense of wonder. Joy filled my heart, and my mind came alive with excitement. I experienced a powerful sense that what I was reading was true, that it was ancient, that it confirmed the trustworthiness of the Bible (especially the New Testament account of the life of Christ), and that the rest of my life would be inextricably intertwined with this book and its message. I had never before experienced anything like this. I wanted to know more, much more.

I soon found myself attending meetings at the local Mormon

chapel each Sunday afternoon following my service as an acolyte in the morning. As I learned more about the Mormon experience over the next few months, I was deeply impressed that the Mormons I met were reasonable people who truly believed the audacious claim that The Church of Jesus Christ of Latter-day Saints is the successor to the New Testament church. These people were pragmatists, firmly grounded in the world of the rational, the world of critical inquiry. The congregation I attended included members of Congress, business men and women, lawyers, doctors, scientists, university professors, PhDs, and even the Administrator of NASA. Two years later, I was a student at Brigham Young University, learning from professors with doctorates from the finest universities in the world. And they, too, believed this claim.[1]

The bold claim of Mormonism is not based on a new reading of scripture or a different approach to worship. Instead, it is based on a series of miracles that took place in modern times. For some critics, the recency of these events makes the assertion that they actually happened less plausible. Surely rational moderns can't believe in miracles! But for Latter-day Saints, their significance lies primarily in their recency. They witness to God's present involvement in human affairs. Three events in particular make up the heart of the Mormon witness.

Joseph Smith's Vision. In the early nineteenth century, Joseph Smith was a teen living with his family on the frontier of western New York. Caught up in the excitement of the Second Great Awakening, two questions dominated young Joseph's thinking: How could he be forgiven of his sins? Was there a church on the earth authorized to carry on Christ's work? After wrestling with these questions for some time, Joseph followed the injunction in the Epistle of James in the New Testament that "If any of you lack wisdom, let him ask of God, . . . and it shall be given him" (James 1:5). He retired to the seclusion of a grove near his home to seek answers through prayer. A vision ensued in which Joseph saw and spoke with God the Father and the Lord Jesus Christ. He was told that his sins were forgiven, but that the church founded by Christ and His apostles was no longer on the earth.

Priesthood Authority. Latter-day Saints believe that Christ's church was reestablished through Joseph Smith. Central to that belief is the claim that ancient prophets and apostles, now resurrected, came in bodily form—not in apparition—to Joseph Smith and others and gave them priesthood authority to organize anew Christ's church. John the Baptist, Peter, James, John, Moses, Elijah, and other ancient worthies visited Joseph Smith and conferred on him this authority. The Church is led today by the same apostolic authority that directed the New Testament church.

The Book of Mormon. In preparation for the reestablishment of Christ's church, an angel gave Joseph Smith an ancient record on golden plates that he translated through miraculous means. The record tells of Hebrew pilgrims who left Jerusalem in about 600 B.C. on a journey that took them to ancient America. Named for its primary compiler and editor, the Book of Mormon covers roughly a thousand-year period and recounts the religious history of this group and their descendants. The book is not a theological treatise, but rather an account of the struggles, triumphs, and tragedies of real people. Perhaps the most remarkable feature of the Book of Mormon is its account of how this group looked toward the birth of Christ with an anticipation that was rewarded by His ministry among them as Risen Lord after His resurrection.

Like the larger Christian tradition of which it is a part, it is vital to the Mormon claim of unique and distinctive authority that these events actually happened. As Ross Douthat has observed, "The Christian story is not . . . a theological or philosophical treatise. It's not a set of commands or insights about our moral duties. Nor is it a road map to the good life. It has implications for all of those questions, obviously. . . . But fundamentally, the Christian story is evidence for a particular idea about the universe: *It recounts a series of events that, if real, tell us something profound about the nature of God, and His relationship to His creatures.*"[2] As with the testimony of first-century Christians that the resurrected Jesus was seen, touched, and heard by eyewitnesses—a witness that is the foundation of Christianity's claim to unique authority that commands our attention and deserves our devotion—Latter-day Saints proclaim that God has acted in our time in a miraculous fashion that has also been seen and experienced by eyewitnesses.

Although Joseph Smith's vision in the grove was a private encounter between a boy and God, the conferral of priesthood authority and the recovery of the Book of Mormon involved eyewitnesses who made the same claims about what took place as did Joseph Smith. There is, for lack of a better word, a "physicality" about these events. For example, Joseph Smith and his companion Oliver Cowdery report that John the Baptist and Peter, James, and John placed hands on their heads while ordaining them to the priesthood. Smith and Cowdery *felt* those angelic hands on their heads. This is not the stuff of mystical vision. It is a straightforward claim that angels appeared in the clear light of day in bodily form and acted at God's direction.

Likewise, Joseph Smith wasn't the only person to see and handle the golden plates. At least eleven other people felt the plates, hefted them, and examined the writing on them. Each stood by his claim that the plates were real, which is all the more noteworthy in the case of those who later parted ways with Smith over his direction of the Church. Joseph Smith dictated the bulk of the translation of the Book of Mormon in the presence of others over a period of about eighty days. Its authenticity has been the subject of a robust debate. Although believing Latter-day Saints do not rely primarily on scholarly works to justify their faith in the book's truthfulness, they point to sophisticated literary, linguistic, anthropological, and archeological studies that lend support to the claim that the Book of Mormon could not be the product of the nineteenth century, but was written in ancient times by authors with deep cultural ties to the Near East.[3]

I have found the careful and prayerful study of the Book of Mormon to be, like that of the Bible, a source of inspiration, guidance, and challenge. And as in the Bible, the witnesses of Christ set forth by the Book of Mormon authors—each with a voice as distinct from one another as Paul is from John—testify of His saving power and grace.

Because these claims do not arise from the subjective realm of the visionary, they are susceptible to some measure of rational analysis and scrutiny. We can make informed judgments about whether they were more likely to have happened than not. If these events did not take place, if they are nothing more than fanciful tales concocted by imaginative, devious, or even pious frauds, Latter-day Saints have little of worth to offer the world. But if these events were real—if Joseph Smith saw and talked with God the Father and the Lord Jesus Christ, if he received priesthood authority under the hands of ancient prophets and apostles, and if he is the transmitter of ancient scripture specially prepared to bear witness of a living Christ to a world in which faith is under assault from the forces of secularism— then Mormonism has something marvelous to offer all.

I am a Mormon because I am convinced these events actually took place. That conviction comes from the testimony of the Holy Spirit to my heart and mind and as a result of my best efforts to test, probe, question, and challenge.

In particular, Latter-day Saints affirm the reality of the literal bodily resurrection of Christ and His ongoing involvement in the affairs and lives of all humankind. As Joseph Smith and a colleague wrote, "And now, after the many testimonies which have been given of [Christ], this is the testimony, last of all, which we give of him:

That he lives! For we saw him, even on the right hand of God; and we heard the voice bearing record that he is the Only Begotten of the Father—that by him, and through him, and of him, the worlds are and were created" (Doctrine and Covenants 76:22–24). With this witness of Christ's living reality comes the declaration that His atoning sacrifice is not only the central act in the history of the universe but also the most important event in each of our lives. It is through Christ's Atonement that God the Father draws us to Him in love and moves us toward others in love. Mormon scripture, belief, ritual, and practice all center on the Atonement of Christ.

Mormonism's focus on participating fully in the Atonement of Christ creates a lifestyle that has been rightly called "religion on steroids."[4] Mormon life centers on the family, and there is much encouragement of devotional activity in the home. The backbone of Mormon family life is made of daily family prayer and scripture reading, Monday evenings set aside for religious education and recreation, and Sundays filled with worship services and meetings.

For a committed Latter-day Saint, the activities of the local congregation, called the "ward," are second in importance only to family life. Two features of the way a ward is organized work in tandem to create a close-knit community of faith. First, a Mormon doesn't choose which ward to attend. Membership is based on where one lives. Second, there is no paid clergy at the local level, which means that almost everyone in the ward has some responsibility. There is much sweat equity.

One careful observer remarked, "Church involvement teaches us compassion and patience as well as courage and discipline. It makes us responsible for the personal and marital, the physical and spiritual welfare of people we may not already love (may even heartily dislike), and thus we learn to love them. It stretches and challenges us, even when we are disappointed and exasperated, in ways we would not otherwise choose to be stretched and challenged. Thus it gives us a chance to be better than we may have chosen to be—but need and ultimately want to be."[5]

But Mormon life is not intended to be confined to the family and the ward. Those are but training grounds for Christian living in the larger world. The work of the Church is to see that "the whole human family be linked together in indissoluble bonds."[6] This impulse drives the Mormon passion for researching family history and building temples in which ordinances are performed that link humankind to God and to one another by covenant. This imperative calls for a generosity of spirit captured in this description of the type of Christian discipleship Mormonism seeks to create: "A man filled with the love of God, is not content with blessing his family alone but ranges through the whole world, anxious to bless the whole human race. . . . [His duty] is to feed the hungry, to clothe the naked, to provide for the widow, to dry up the tear of the orphan, to comfort the afflicted, whether in this church, or in any other, or in no church at all, wherever he finds them."[7]

The life of the Church is a laboratory for Christian living that I find to be inspiring, challenging, and deeply gratifying. The commitment called for takes much time and significant resources, but it hardly seems a sacrifice if one believes, as I do, that this is Christ's church reestablished on the earth in our day.

NOTES

1. Studies have shown that, unique among the major religions, commitment among Jews and Mormons increases with their level of educational training. Stan L. Albrecht, *The Consequential Dimension of Mormon Religiosity,* 29 B.Y.U. STUD. 57, 103 (1989). And Brigham Young University, the Church's flagship school, has graduated more students who go on to complete doctorates than all but nine other universities in the world. See *Brigham Young University: 2009 Academic Rankings,* http://yfacts.byu.edu/viewarticle.aspx?id=273 (last visited July 29, 2009).

2. Ross Douthat, "The Implications of Christmas," *The Atlantic,* http://rossdouthat.theatlantic.com/archives/2008/12/the_implications_of_christmas.php (December 25, 2008), emphasis added.

3. Oxford University Press has published a reliable account of the debate over the provenance of the Book of Mormon. See Terryl L. Givens, *By the Hand of Mormon: The American Scripture That Launched a New World Religion* (New York: Oxford University Press, 2002), 89–184. Two recent titles by Oxford discuss the complexity of the literary structure of the Book of Mormon. See Terryl L. Givens, *The Book of Mormon: A Very Short Introduction* (New York: Oxford University Press, 2009), and Grant Hardy, *Understanding the Book of Mormon* (New York: Oxford University Press, 2010). That Oxford has published sympathetic accounts of the book's origins may invite the curious to actually read and study it. As Thomas O'Dea observed: "The *Book of Mormon* has not been universally considered by its critics as one of those books that must be read in order to have an opinion of it." Thomas O'Dea, *The Mormons* (Chicago: University of Chicago, 1957), 26.

4. Jason Szep, "In U.S., Mormons Are in the Spotlight," *Reuters,* June 10, 2007, available online at http//www.reuters.com/article/lifestyleNolt/id USN 527023320070610.

5. Eugene England, *Why the Church Is as True as the Gospel* (Salt Lake City: Bookcraft, 1986), 5.

6. George Q. Cannon, *The Life of Joseph Smith the Prophet* (Salt Lake City: Deseret Book, 1986), 516.

7. Joseph Smith Jr., *History of The Church of Jesus Christ of Latter-day Saints,* ed. B. H. Roberts, 2d ed., rev., 7 vols. (Salt Lake City: Deseret Book, 1971), 4:227; *Times and Seasons* 3, no. 10 (March 15, 1842):732.

DAVID HALVERSEN

DAVID HALVERSEN was born in Salinas, California, and grew up in Spanish Fork and Ogden, Utah. He graduated from Weber State College in Economics and Business and did his graduate studies in Economics at the University of Utah. In his business career, he began as a consultant with Boeing and Wharton Econometric Associates. He served in management positions in Xerox, General Electric, and Avon Products, Inc., and recently retired as Group President for Tupperware Brands Corporation, where he had responsibility for countries across Asia, Latin America, and North America. He has held several positions in the Church, including bishop and stake president, and he is currently president of the Orlando Florida Temple for the Church. He and his wife, Lana, have three sons and seven grandchildren.

• • •

GROWING UP IN THE CHURCH of Jesus Christ of Latter-day Saints was a time of laying a foundation—gaining the ability to believe, to have faith, and then to act. That foundation and inspiration I owe to my parents. My father was called to serve as mission president in New Zealand in the midst of World War II. My parents sacrificed much and accepted the call without hesitation. I was born en route to New Zealand while they were waiting to board a ship leaving the U.S. mainland as the war continued to rage. My parents' sacrifice for the Lord during this difficult time will always remain an inspiration to me.

All my friends when I was growing up were members of the Church, and I don't recall any major challenges. The Church provided many opportunities to serve, even in my teenage years. I was called as the Sunday School president in our ward (congregation) when I was seventeen by a bishop who desired the youth to develop leadership skills in preparation for serving missions. Later, I was called to serve as a missionary for two years to New Zealand—a country where I had spent my first three years as a child. To this day I still have a great love for the Polynesian people.

There come times in our lives when our foundation is put to the test. When I graduated from Weber State, I was awarded a National Science Foundation Fellowship to the University of Utah in Economics. At this time, my first real experiences with being testing arrived. In our graduate school program, most were not Mormons. It was in the sixties, and many student activities were different from what I had previously faced. Although I was invited to join professors and students in parties where drinking was commonplace and other activities were clearly not appropriate, I declined the offers. Some professors singled me out for not joining them, and one in particular confronted me and stated: "You're never going to make it in the business world if you aren't willing to drink and socialize in certain ways." I can still remember the conviction with which he made his statement, which eventually turned out to be so wrong.

In due time, doors were opened in the business world that provided me opportunities to follow the principles I had been taught throughout my life. Living the standards of the Church gave me a way to live my life and feel good about what I was doing, while also serving as a way to help others who felt similarly but did not know how to deal with some compromising situations.

Soon came the opportunity to work with a Nobel Prize winner and his team in a consulting position at the University of Pennsylvania. I learned another principle very quickly—my "university of life" was just beginning. Suddenly, during a very difficult time in the economy, I received an unexpected job offer that took me into the consulting world a long way from home. This job offer set the pathway leading to several additional career opportunities in Xerox, General Electric, Avon Products, and finally Tupperware Brands. Each in itself was a university degree, but most of all each provided a chance to work with and associate with outstanding individuals. I found that during my entire career, the gospel principles upon which my life was centered became the foundation for all my leadership responsibilities—wherever in the world those responsibilities took me.

There is tremendous power in living by example and setting a course early. As a junior corporate officer, I was representing headquarters at an awards celebration in Paris, France. An individual proposed a toast for several award winners, and when it came time to raise the wine glass, I picked up my water glass. In an instant, a voice thundered from the other end of the hall, "Stop! Dave Halversen, you are new to France. We always toast with wine!" I responded, "I'm fine, thank you." But the person insisted. He walked up to the front table where I was sitting and began to dramatically explain in front of all what I should do. The whole event stopped and went so silent you could hear a pin drop as everyone awaited my reaction. When he finally saw that I was not wavering, and that I would not drink the wine despite his pleas for French tradition, he returned to his seat, and the toast continued with my water. While a little uncomfortable for everyone, to say the least, this experience set a tone for the way people in the corporation viewed me from then on. They saw me differently and knew that there was something different about my lifestyle and beliefs. The story must have traveled quickly because, after that, people would order water for me at functions before I even said a word.

Being a Mormon means that certain standards and values are established that simplify making good choices, even when one is confronted with embarrassing or pressure situations. Although challenges have come in many different ways during my lifetime and career, having the Church's standards as a foundation has certainly made my decisions easier.

The more difficult decisions in my life have been those that required relying on the guidance of the Spirit, and then having the faith to know that things would be okay. As my career path emerged, I found that listening to the promptings of the Spirit created circumstances for me to serve the Lord while progressing in the business world. After I had served as a bishop in our ward for only about a year and a half, the situation at work was changing and an offer came to leave Connecticut and go to Florida for an attractive position. My concern was my calling in the Church—leaving the flock, so to speak, when I had only served for such a brief time. I went to the stake president (my Church leader) for counsel and told him of the job offer. He informed me that he had had a feeling that I would be leaving. He then said, "I've prayed about it. The Lord wants you to go." I learned much that day from a leader who lived his life to receive constant inspiration and guidance to help those for whom he had responsibility. Looking back at my life since I took on a new job responsibility in Florida some seventeen years ago has solidified in my mind that the guidance by a kind stake president was truly inspired.

While prayers are answered in different ways—most times through subtle means—there have been times when the direction has been unmistakably clear. In those times, the course of my career has been impacted. A few years after moving to Orlando to work for Tupperware Brands Corporation, I began to sense that something else was about to change. One night I awakened at 3:00 A.M., and into my mind came words as clearly as if someone were talking straight to me: "David, this morning you are going to walk into the chairman's office and you're going to say the following. . . ." I listened and remembered the exact words. Of course, I did not sleep for the rest of the night.

In the morning, I made an appointment with the chairman. When I walked in, I communicated the exact words that I had been given. After a brief conversation, I returned to my office. About ten minutes later, he called me in and said that he had spoken to other senior officers and would be moving me from being a senior staff officer to make me a Group President over one-third of the corporation's world businesses. The Lord answers prayers in distinct ways and also inspires others to open ways for us. I'm grateful for a corporate leader who was inspired that day by the Holy Spirit.

In my new position I was guided many times on a day-to-day basis on what to do and how to use the teachings of the Savior in treating people for whom I had responsibility. I realized that my having served in the Church as a bishop and a stake president proved to have a positive influence on those with whom I associated at work. To transact international business reviews, the executive committee of the corporation would be on international video conferences every month. While going back and forth on needed strategies and actions, the chairman would often stop and turn to me and say, "Bishop, tell them why you go to church every Sunday," or, "Bishop, why do you use the same books of scripture all the time?" or, "Bishop, why do your missionaries go out two by two?"

The chairman, while not a religious person, had a respect for the Church because of its organization and ability to teach its members all over the world the same things at the same time. He would often use my responses to teach business applications from true gospel principles as part of training or making decisions. One interesting event happened during a large luncheon to promote corporate charitable giving. Out of the blue, the chairman stated, "David, come and tell everyone why you pay tithing or ten percent to your church." Although that was a shock at first, I quickly realized what a great opportunity it was to teach how giving back to something in which I strongly believe is not a sacrifice, and that in life we will always owe more than we receive. I've found throughout my business career that gospel principles could be applied anywhere in the world, whether I was in Asia, Latin America, Europe, or home in North America.

Knowing that you can be an example of these principles helps keep them in the forefront of your mind. I remember being interviewed for a thirty-minute show on CNBC Asia. Afterward, the news anchor said, "I can tell that you enjoy your work. You have about 800,000 people reporting to you in your organization. What is it like?" I responded that it was a great privilege to be in a position to inspire so many people with things I know will change their lives.

Over and over, it has been very special to receive promptings from the Spirit to guide me in so many ways. Looking back at my career, I realize that the Church has provided me with many opportunities to learn and grow that have greatly blessed me in business. I am far from being an extrovert and or desiring to be out front in public, but the many opportunities to serve in leadership positions have afforded me great training to speak to small groups or to thousands of people in various settings. I have learned every day how much the contributions of many who serve with you help bring the true results of success. It truly is the sacrifices of the often unseen that touch lives and bring so many blessings. Most of all, I realize and am most grateful for the sacrifices of my wife and children over the years as I traveled throughout the world.

A great principle I have learned is that we all sometimes walk on borrowed light. We know of great parents, great leaders, and other special people who have had inspirational experiences. But eventually we need to receive our own light, to humbly listen and have our own spiritual experiences. Certainly my testimony of the Savior is most precious to me. That testimony comes with a willingness to make the effort and then listen to His voice through the Spirit.

Let me share a final personal experience. There had been a period of time when I had been getting up in the morning before the family and spending time reading and studying about the Savior's life and His teachings. I did this for several months. Then one morning there came a very special and overwhelming feeling, so powerful that I knew without a doubt who the Savior was and what He meant in my life. The next Sunday, I arose and prayed for that same feeling again. This time a different feeling came, accompanied by this clear thought: "I gave the answer to you already; now go out and do something with what you have been given." I believe that is what we are about—getting the right answers and doing something with that direction. That's what being a Mormon does: it changes your life, and possibly the lives you touch, each day.

MULIUFI (MUFI) FRANCIS HANNEMANN

MUFI HANNEMANN served as the twelfth mayor of the city and county of Honolulu, the thirteenth-largest municipality in the United States. He took office in January 2005 and was reelected with an 80 percent public approval rating.

As mayor, Mr. Hannemann had a remarkable record of achievement, including an emphasis on public safety that led to the FBI's naming Honolulu one of America's safest large cities, and that enabled his administration to commit the city to hosting the November 2011 Asia Pacific Economic Cooperation Summit of world leaders. He led the development of Oahu's first rail transit system, established the Department of Emergency Management, expanded ambulance facilities, and led a major overhaul of the first-responder telecommunication network. His administration's focus on infrastructure yielded improvement of sewer networks, refuse treatment facilities, recycling, and road resurfacing as well as national recognition for expansion of public online services. His strong city fiscal policies led to high bond ratings and national awards for financial integrity.

Mr. Hannemann played a pivotal role in averting the closure of the Pearl Harbor Naval Shipyard and revitalizing Chinatown as an arts and culture district (yielding Honolulu a national outstanding achievement award). He involved Honolulu City in supporting the agricultural industry by reducing property tax rates on farmland and opening a farmers market in downtown Honolulu. He also drove successful efforts to reduce demands on Hanauma Bay Nature Preserve and to save Waimea Valley from development. He helped found the Hawaii Council of Mayors, enabling the state's four mayors to collaborate on intercounty issues, state legislation, and other matters affecting local government.

Honolulu-born, Mr. Hannemann graduated from Harvard *cum laude* with a bachelor's degree in government (1976) and was a Fulbright Scholar at Victoria University in New Zealand. He has the distinction of having served in four presidential administrations: Carter, Reagan, Clinton, and Bush II.

His many honors include the American Public Transportation Association's 2010 Local Distinguished Service Award, Easter Seals Outstanding Advocate Award, and recognition by the American Diabetes Association–Hawaii Chapter for his unparalleled fundraising efforts. He created the Pacific Century Fellows, modeled after the White House Fellows, that is mentoring promising young leaders. In 2008 and 2009, he was named "Best Public Official" by *Honolulu Magazine,* and in 2009, the readers of *Honolulu Weekly* judged him "Best Local Politician."

In January 2011, Mr. Hannemann became President and CEO of the Hawaii Lodging and Tourism Association, an organization devoted to representing the interests of Hawaii's hospitality industry through education, political action, and member benefits.

Mr. Hannemann is married to Gail Mukaihata Hannemann, the chief executive officer of the Girl Scout Council of Hawaii. They reside in 'Aiea, where he formerly served on the stake high council and currently serves as his high priests group instructor.

Y MOTHER, FAIASO, was a full-blooded Samoan member of
The Church of Jesus Christ of Latter-day Saints. Her father,
Paramount Chief Pinemua Muliufi Soliai of Nuuuli, introduced the
Church into his village in the face of great opposition from his fellow villagers and other village chiefs of a different Christian faith.
Mother was influential in my father's conversion and baptism before they married in 1936, and by the time I was born, my parents
were active members of the Church. So I was raised Mormon because of my parents. I've remained a
Mormon because of the values that
my parents imbued in me during
my upbringing in the Church.

One of my mother's favorite
scriptures was: "Train up a child in
the way he should go: and when
he is old, he will not depart from
it" (Proverbs 22:6). Early on, my
parents taught us the Church's values through family home evening,
scripture study, and attending our Church meetings. My father,
Gustav, of Samoan-German-English ancestry, was a bishop when
I was growing up, and the Junior Sunday School Coordinator was
my mother. Every step along the way, either a relative or close friend
was my Scoutmaster or my quorum adviser or my Sunday School
teacher.

Of course, I also developed a testimony based on personal experiences and other things that have stood the test of time. Part of
gaining a stronger testimony for myself came from observing what
the gospel has done in the lives of other people, including examples
from the scriptures and from people who clung tenaciously to their

faith. The scriptures enabled me to hear and learn from Jesus Christ Himself. I also had the everyday examples of our Church's General Authorities and our prophet, President Thomas S. Monson.

In addition, I have seen the power of the priesthood work its way in people's lives, whether performing an ordinance myself or watching others. My uncle, David Hannemann, the only surviving sibling on my father's side of the family and the eighty-year-old patriarch of our family, is a former president of the Hawaii LDS Temple and the most spiritual man I know personally. I watch him and learn from him as he continues to administer the affairs of our extended family.

My first real test away from the influence of my family was as a freshman enrolling at Harvard. My first five siblings were born in Samoa, but my youngest sister and I were born and raised in Hawaii. When my parents moved to Hawaii in 1953, they felt strongly that one of their sons or daughters should go to Harvard. I was the one. My mother was a stay-at-home mom and would walk me to the library to borrow books. She told me over and over that three things were important: the Church, family, and education.

In Samoa, my mother was the daughter of a paramount chief, and inherent in that were all the trappings and benefits of being of a chiefly family. My parents left a good life in Samoa in pursuit of a better life. They wanted their children to get a premium education and to be able to pursue the American dream. My mother was a very wise woman who was the disciplinarian in our family, yet was always quick to demonstrate compassion.

In Samoa, my father was a well-educated man who graduated from high school at the age of thirteen and became a teacher and a principal. He too was of royal lineage, as his maternal aunt was Queen Makelita, one of the few women who rose to the title of Tui Manua. He was a leader in both the Church and the community. When he became a naturalized American citizen, he took his civic responsibilities very seriously. He always voted and always encouraged others to obey the law. In the U.S., to allow my mother to stay home with the family, my father worked—not one, not two, but three jobs.

It was not unusual for my dad, after working these multiple jobs, to come home and drill me on my homework. He was a math whiz, and when I needed any kind of help, I would go to him. One time I had to write a book report on *Moby Dick*. The movie was going to be shown on TV, but our TV was on the blink. I remember my father, as tired as he was, making several phone calls until he found someone who said to bring me over. My dad walked me to this distant relative's home and sat with me on the couch watching *Moby Dick* to help me, along with the book, to do my book report. My father was the educator in the family, but my mom set the goal of my going to Harvard.

I knew at an early age that my parents had made sacrifices for their children. When I left for Harvard at age eighteen, I was on my own, but my mother and father never wavered in their confidence that I would stay close to the Church. Some people would ask my mother if she worried about sending her son away from Hawaii to the East Coast. She always answered "No, no. I've taught him well."

Then came my most earth-shattering experience. I lost my mom. She passed away after my freshman year, and I thought the whole world was going to collapse. Her example and my membership in the Church guided me to stay and finish at Harvard as opposed to taking an easier path of coming home to care for my father, now a widower. I started at Harvard as a government major in 1972, and I graduated cum laude in 1976.

My parents were the best example I have ever seen of a loving couple. They were devoted to each other. They supported each other. My upbringing in the gospel and their examples made me believe that I must finish what I had started. I had to do it. My parents did train me well, and I've remained steadfast in believing in the gospel of Jesus Christ. My LDS roots started with my parents and have continued with me as I've grown.

People sometimes ask me if I majored in public speaking or if I took debate classes. Any such ability I have comes from my parents' training. My father, a great master of the scriptures, could give a talk and quote a couple dozen scriptures off the top of his head without opening the standard works. That approach was part of my upbringing. I have a fond childhood memory of being assigned to give short talks at Church and not being allowed to read the talks from a paper. Our parents would discipline us by taking away an opportunity to play if we didn't memorize our talks and do them well. That's how strict they were. These early childhood experiences are extremely valuable to me.

For a couple with limited means, my parents did well. My father attributed his ability to make ends meet to his faith in the gospel. We worked hard and we prayed hard. We were taught early the power of prayer, not just to ask the Lord for help, but to thank God first. In high school, other students thought I had migraine headaches because before an exam, before a game, or before eating food, I would always bow my head and cover my eyes with the palm of my hand. I was actually praying. Then after the game or exam, as I was taught by my parents, I prayed again to express gratitude—not so much for victory, but that no one got hurt or that I was able to get through the exam okay. This was a testimony-building experience for me, and it has stayed with me all my life.

I owe a lot to the teachings I received as a youth in the Church. Now, as an adult, I am privileged to pass on to the next generation these values and principles that I learned at an early age. I believe in mentoring. I believe in providing leadership and guidance to younger siblings and family members and others by passing on what I have learned.

When I was mayor of Honolulu, I never made a decision on behalf of the people of the city that I did not take to the Lord in prayer. I explained to my cabinet that a burning in my bosom meant it was the right decision; a stupor of thought meant I had to go back to the drawing board. I've learned that the Lord rarely answers our prayers when we want it, where we want it, and how we want it. We have to become sensitive to the subtle promptings of the Spirit to know when our prayers are being answered positively or when the Lord is saying, "This is not right" or "You need to try harder."

Another important part of prayer is preparation. We shouldn't just ask the Lord, "Should I do A, B, or C?" We should go to Him and say, "I have options A, B, and C. I'd like to do B, and this is the reason why." When we have done our part, it works. It's like taking an exam. We can't just expect the Lord to help us get an A. We have to study. Then we can ask for extra help from the Spirit to push us through.

I have always been blessed with wonderful gospel instructors. Every step along the way, even at Harvard, wonderful people taught from our Church's standard works by weaving in what they were reading or studying at law school or business school. At the end of the day, though, life comes down to the basic tenets of the gospel, which are simple. What makes the difference is actually living the commandments—something that will be a challenge for each of us our entire lives.

Mormons see the role of our Church as aiding us as we strive toward being more Christlike in all that we do. To be Christlike, I believe, is to be on the lookout to help others—and not just those who are the easiest to help, like immediate family members. Sometimes we need to embrace people who have a different point of view. In the world of politics, to "turn the other cheek" is a difficult thing to do. While some individuals and organizations may not like me or believe what I say, I can still strive to act in their best interest.

Christ gave us many examples of how He loved His enemies, how He reached out to those who wronged Him. His way was not "an eye for an eye" or "a tooth for a tooth." He required discipline, but He also had compassion and sensitivity. His ultimate example, the pinnacle of His teachings, was what He did on the cross when He said, "Father, forgive them; for they know not what they do" (Luke 23:34). He asked for forgiveness for His tormentors, just as He offers it to all of us on condition of repentance.

Members of The Church of Jesus Christ of Latter-day Saints have a code of conduct that includes everything from not drinking to giving a ten percent tithe to honoring the relationships within our families. In politics, that bar is raised even higher. Yes, it is a challenge, but it's not one that I'm uncomfortable with. I try to be as knowledgeable as I can be about the gospel and as prayerful as I can be about the issues so that I can make the right choices. Our Prophet, Joseph Smith, said it best: Teach them correct principles and let them govern themselves.

It's not only important to be comfortable with the challenges of being held to a higher standard. I also hope to let people know the benefits of living an LDS life. For example, our Word of Wisdom is a healthy lifestyle that everyone would benefit from emulating, whether LDS or not: not just abstinence from alcohol and tobacco, but getting enough rest and observing moderation in all things. The Mormon work ethic and our awareness of the larger community as we provide humanitarian aid and assistance can guide others. It's in the nature of LDS Church membership to reach out to others.

The way we pray can also make a difference to people. Once a year in Honolulu, the governor and the mayors come together to do a breakfast prayer service. As mayor of Honolulu, I often offered the prayer. Afterward people would sometimes request a copy. My staff replied that I did not write my prayers down. When people expressed surprise, my staff said, "When he prays for us or with us in cabinet functions, he doesn't come with a scripted prayer, and when he calls on us to pray, he encourages us to pray the same way. He believes you should pray from your heart." When LDS members pray publicly, we help others learn who we are.

God's plan for happiness in this earthly life is the gospel of Jesus Christ. More important, His church, The Church of Jesus Christ of Latter-day Saints, has a plan of happiness for the eternities. This time on earth is about preparing for a life in the eternities where we can be with those we love most—our families—forever. To me, the single biggest difference in being a Mormon is living a life in harmony with that ultimate, long-range view.

MATTHEW S. HOLLAND

MATTHEW S. HOLLAND is the president of Utah Valley University, where he has been serving since June 2009. Before assuming this position, President Holland was an associate professor of political science at Brigham Young University, where he taught courses in political philosophy and American political thought.

A popular teacher, President Holland has a commitment to applied learning concepts that led to his selection as BYU's "Civically Engaged Scholar of the Year" in 2008 by Utah Campus Compact. His scholarly research on how ideals of Christian charity influenced the development of American political life garnered national attention. In 2007, his book, *Bonds of Affection: Civic Charity and the Making of America,* was published by Georgetown University Press. In 2005, he won Princeton University's James Madison Fellowship.

President Holland graduated from Brigham Young University with honors in 1991 and was valedictorian for the political science department. That same year he was awarded the Raoul Wallenberg Scholarship for a year of graduate study at the Hebrew University of Jerusalem. Before going on to earn his master's degree and PhD in political science at Duke University, President Holland served as chief of staff for the top executive of the international consulting firm Monitor Group and, later, as special assistant to then-Governor Michael O. Leavitt of Utah.

Currently, President Holland serves on numerous community boards, including the editorial advisory board of the *Deseret News* and the boards of the Utah Valley and Salt Lake City Chambers of Commerce. He and his wife, Paige, have four children.

• • •

M OST SIMPLY PUT, I am a Mormon because Mormonism is true.

To be clear, by Mormonism I mean the gospel of Jesus Christ as fully restored through His latter-day prophets.

To be candid, by making such a declaration, I stand unfashionably out of step with much of the academic world I have inhabited for most of my professional life.

When Plato began teaching students in the very first "academy," he was following in the footsteps of his teacher Socrates, who declared that "a lover of learning must from youth on strive as intensely as possible for every kind of truth" (Plato's *Republic*, 485d). Central to Socrates' view was the notion that not only did certain unchanging truths exist, but such truths were the most real and desirable things the soul might pursue. The job of the academy, then, was to assist the student in the search for those eternal verities.

The irony of contemporary academic life—relative to what Plato and Socrates started—is that the whole notion of eternal truth is generally called into question or just dismissed. And the only thing more suspect than philosophical certainty about the nature of human existence and morality is religious certainty about such matters. To walk in this kind of setting with sureness about the divine origins, ways, and purposes of human life is to be seen often as a real

curiosity and, in some cases, a downright threat to the intellectual community.

I wish not to overstate things. In the contemporary academy, I have terrific colleagues who either share my views or share some kind of sympathetic religious world view or are, at least, highly respectful of what I hold sacred and true. I would also note that at public schools and universities, it is not just prudent but completely consistent with principles of liberty (principles deeply affirmed by my religious understanding) that teachers and administrators not use their positions to proselyte or privilege their particular faith in the curriculum and classroom.

Yet, the fact remains that certain philosophies and attitudes that often emanate from and prevail within the world of higher education create a temptation like that faced by Jeremiah of old to "not make mention . . . nor speak any more" of one's core religious convictions in any way or in any place other than one's own home or private place of worship. Just like Jeremiah, this is untenable to me, for God's word is "in mine heart as a burning fire shut up in my bones" (Jeremiah 20:9). I cannot deny that word nor can I be kept from all public affirmations of it.

A word, then, about how I came to my convictions. For some, a testimony of the truthfulness of the restored gospel of Jesus Christ can come very quickly—in a single, intense moment of inspiration or in a rapid series of powerful spiritual witnesses and intellectual illuminations. I have watched this happen in other people's lives a number of times. My own convictions have come in a different way, however. I am unable to point to a single moment, or even a quick series of moments, of conversion. Rather, my convictions have come "precept upon precept; line upon line" (Isaiah 28:10). Through a steady, lifetime diet of gospel-related teachings, experiences, questionings, meditations, and reasonings, I have simply come to know—undeniably so—that the messages and doctrines of The Church of Jesus Christ of Latter-day Saints are true.

While the process has been more gradual for me than for some, the product of gospel knowledge has ultimately come with all of the truth-confirming power so picturesquely promised by Alma, a prophet in the Book of Mormon. Speaking to those who want to "know of a surety" that the teachings of God's prophets are true, Alma urges an "experiment" (Alma 32:17, 26–27). The experiment begins by planting the word of God in the heart and nourishing it through study, prayer, and meditation. This experiment is an act of faith because, at least at first, there is an unavoidable sense of uncertainty about such teachings (see v. 27). If this act of faith is not prematurely aborted, Alma assures that the word planted in the heart "will begin to swell within your breasts." The fact that you can "feel these swelling motions" is simply the first palpable signal that what you have been considering is "real" (vv. 28, 35).

Beyond the feelings of the heart, the properly and faithfully nourished word of God also unmistakably informs and affects one's mental and spiritual faculties: "your mind doth expand . . . your understanding doth begin to be enlightened . . . it beginneth to enlarge [your] soul" (vv. 28, 34). But even this is not all. In one of the most unique images developed in all of scripture, Alma also indicates that the word starts to blossom into intellectual-spiritual "light" that can not only be "discerned" but "tasted." More to the point, these gospel truths "beginneth to be delicious to [you]," causing you to want to "feast" upon the word of God and the most delicious and satisfying fruit it produces (v. 42). Here, it is worth turning to Joseph Smith, who neatly captures and even further develops the same image in his King Follett discourse, where he says that "this is good doctrine. It tastes good. I can taste the principles of eternal life, and so can you. They are given to me by the revelations of Jesus Christ; and I know that when I tell you these words of eternal life as they are given to me, you taste them, and I know that you believe them. You say honey is sweet, and so do I. I can also taste the spirit of eternal life. I know it is good; and when I tell you of these things which were given me by inspiration of the Holy Spirit, you are bound to receive them as sweet, and rejoice more and more" (*Teachings of the Prophet Joseph Smith* [1976], 355).

The fact of the matter is that the restored gospel of Jesus Christ is real and sweet, and the more I study and try to live it, the more real and sweet it becomes.

Among the sweetest messages and realities I have discovered in Latter-day Saint theology is the notion that God can do infinitely more with my life than I could ever hope to do on my own. It starts with the most loving, redemptive, and powerful act of all time: Christ's Atonement, which holds out the hope of rescue from every iota of discouragement, dissipation, and divine distance fostered by sin—the inevitable mistakes we all make as mere mortals in this fallen world. And, as if this matchless offer were not enough, Heaven also stands ready to help us succeed far beyond our natural abilities, turning weaknesses into strengths, consecrating the performance of all our duties unto the welfare of our souls, and providing unseen and miraculous forces of support in the battles of life.

I have turned to and received these graces too many times to doubt that they are real. In fact, I consciously rely on them daily. And, like Frost's road less traveled, they have "made all the difference" in my personal and professional life. They are manifestations of just one of a most delicious set of doctrines that fasten me to Christ and an active commitment to His living Church led by His living oracles.

Ultimately, then, I am a Mormon because, being an earnest seeker of truth from my youth, and having tasted what I have tasted, I could be no other.

VALERIE M. HUDSON

VALERIE M. HUDSON is a professor of political science at Brigham Young University. In January 2012, she will become Professor and George H. W. Bush Chair in the Bush School of Government and Public Service at Texas A&M University, teaching in the masters of international affairs program. Her research foci include foreign policy analysis, security studies, gender and international relations, and methodology.

Professor Hudson's articles have appeared in such journals as *International Security, Journal of Peace Research, Political Psychology,* and *Foreign Policy Analysis.* She is also the author or editor of several books, including (with Andrea Den Boer) *Bare Branches: The Security Implications of Asia's Surplus Male Population* (MIT Press, 2004), which won the American Association of Publishers Award for the Best Book in Political Science and the Otis Dudley Duncan Award for Best Book in Social Demography and was featured on *60 Minutes* and in the *New York Times, The Economist,* and other news publications.

Born in Washington, D.C., Dr. Hudson joined The Church of Jesus Christ of Latter-day Saints in 1971. She attended Brigham Young University, where she received her BA in political science, with minors in international relations and Russian. She obtained her

PhD in political science from Ohio State University. She taught at Northwestern University and at Rutgers University before joining the political science faculty at BYU in 1987.

Dr. Hudson was named to the list of *Foreign Policy* magazine's Top 100 Global Thinkers for 2009. Winner of numerous teaching awards and recipient of a National Science Foundation research grant, she served as the director of graduate studies for the David M. Kennedy Center for International and Area Studies for eight years and is vice president of the International Studies Association for 2011–2012. Dr. Hudson is one of the Principal Investigators of the WomanStats Project, which includes the largest compilation of data on the status of women in the world today. She is also a founding editor of *SquareTwo,* a founding editorial board member of *Foreign Policy Analysis,* and an editorial board member of *Politics and Gender* and the *International Studies Review.* She is married to artist David Cassler, and they are parents of eight children.

• • •

I AM A CONVERT to the Mormon church from Roman Catholicism, and I gained my testimony as the result of spiritual experiences that I cannot deny. In this essay, however, I will discuss why, as a feminist, I remain a steadfast member of The Church of Jesus Christ of Latter-day Saints (LDS).

It is difficult to be raised in one of the Abrahamic faiths (Judaism, Islam, Christianity) and not absorb some fairly unpleasant conclusions about women. Depending on the religion and sect involved, one may be taught that the first woman was feebleminded or a murderess, a fact that mars all her daughters; that a woman's body is unclean; that God meant women to submit to their husbands and in general be subservient to men; and that divinity is male and male alone. (Of course, echoes of such teachings can also be found in other faith traditions.)

After decades of studying LDS doctrine concerning women and carefully distinguishing it from LDS cultural understandings and practices that sometimes contradict that doctrine, I have been liberated from the erroneous and harmful beliefs about women that haunt those raised in Abrahamic traditions. How remarkable and in some senses ironic to have experienced "women's lib" by conversion to Mormonism!

The following main points of doctrine make Mormonism the most feminist of all the Christianities in my view:

First, the restored gospel teaches that the term *God* means an exalted woman and an exalted man married in "the new and everlasting covenant" (Doctrine and Covenants 132:19–20). In other words, no God exists without men and women loving each other as equals. Heavenly Father is not an eternal bachelor; he is married to our Heavenly Mother. The one who is an eternal bachelor is Satan.

Second, the restored gospel teaches that all will have their male or female bodies forever. A body is not a curse, but a great gift that each soul had to prove worthy to receive. Women readers, your breasts, your womb, your ovaries are not unclean cursings, they are blessings. Also, marriage is forever; we will have children forever; and the life of being a woman married to my sweetheart and having children forever is the life that will bring me the fullest joy in the eternities—as it has here on earth.

Third, LDS doctrine teaches that men and women are equals before the Lord and before each other. *Equal* does not mean "identical," just as no two men are identical and yet they stand as equals before each other and before the Lord.

Elder L. Tom Perry, an Apostle of the Church, said in 2004: "There is not a president or a vice president in a family. The couple works together eternally for the good of the family. . . . They are on equal footing. They plan and organize the affairs of the family jointly and unanimously as they move forward."[1] What an incredible vision, especially for a Christian denomination, many of which believe in some type of submission of wives to husbands. The LDS Church does not preach submission of wives.

In my opinion, we cannot fully understand how revolutionary this doctrine is unless we go back to the story of the Garden of Eden. Three points distinguish the restored gospel telling of that story:

1. Latter-day Saints do not believe that the Fall was a great tragedy. Rather, we believe that it was foreordained for our progression and thus was a blessing.

2. Latter-day Saints do not believe that Eve sinned in partaking of the fruit of the First Tree, the tree of the knowledge of good and evil.

3. Because we do not believe Eve sinned, we also do not believe she was punished by God for her role in partaking of the fruit, but rather rewarded.

God's plan of happiness for His children mandated that they leave their heavenly home and receive a mortal body, enter into full agency to choose between good and evil by being separated from God, and then return once more to their heavenly home to be judged for how they used that agency. That is, the plan was to be a "round," if you will: it would take us from our heavenly home and, if we walked that path well, it would bring us back now more like our heavenly parents, with much more knowledge and a desire to choose the right—so much more than we could have acquired if we had stayed in heaven with a diluted version of agency.

However, the *children* had to *choose* to leave and bring to pass a separation from their divine parents. And so in the Garden were placed a son and a daughter of God, and two trees. Two persons, two trees.

Both trees represented doorways along the journey of the great plan. The First Tree, the tree of the knowledge of good and evil, symbolized the doorway leading from heaven to earth and the ordinances of entering mortality with a mortal body, with full agency, and having the light of Christ awakened within. The Second Tree, the tree of eternal life, symbolized the ordinances of salvation and exaltation—the doorway back to our heavenly home.

Through women, souls journey into mortality and gain their agency. In general, through women nurturing their children with love, the light of Christ is awakened within each soul. And we should include in that list of souls Jesus the Christ. Even Christ our Lord was escorted to mortality and veiled in flesh through the gift of a woman, fed at His mother's breast, and awakened to all that is good and sweet in the world while in her care. Women escort every soul through the veil to mortal life. I find it interesting to think that even Adam, who was created before Eve, entered into full mortality and full agency only by accepting the gift of the First Tree from the hand of a woman. In a sense, then, Adam himself was born of Eve. Eve was created second not because she was derivative of Adam: she was created second to highlight that the giving of the gift of the First Tree was the gift to be given by women in the great plan.[2]

If Eve was foreordained to give this good gift as her stewardship in the great plan, then she did not sin. As Elder Dallin H. Oaks, an Apostle of the LDS Church, has said, "Some Christians condemn Eve for her act, concluding that she and her daughters are somehow flawed by it. Not the Latter-day Saints! Informed by revelation, we celebrate Eve's act and honor her wisdom and courage in the great episode called the Fall."[3] We believe that our heavenly parents were happy and grateful that Eve offered her gift, as were the rest of God's children.

Eve, then, was not the worst among women; Eve was the best among women! She was perhaps the most courageous, the most faithful. It was also right, then, that the first mortal being that the resurrected Jesus showed Himself to was a woman. Jesus' performance of the Atonement repaid Mother Eve's faith in the plan, her courageous opening of the door represented by the First Tree.

Did God curse Eve? According to Genesis 3:17, the *ground* was cursed for the sake of Adam and Eve. Is this a cursing of Adam and Eve? In the teachings of the Mormon church, we do not believe it was a curse meant to punish them—it was a curse meant to start the law of opposites that undergirds agency: virtue vs. vice, pleasure vs. pain, light vs. darkness, truth vs. lies (see 2 Nephi 2:11–13). Eve was told she would labor in childbirth. Was this a cursing of Eve? Again, from the LDS perspective, absolutely not. To have children and be able to fully give the gift of Eve is one of the most soul-satisfying parts of a woman's life that she will experience here or in the hereafter (if circumstances have prevented it here).

In the King James Version of the Bible, we are told that Eve, as part of her punishment, was told that Adam would rule over her. Is that what Mormons believe? Actually not. Elder Bruce C. Hafen, a General Authority in the LDS Church, says: "Genesis 3:16 states that Adam is to 'rule over' Eve, but . . . *over* in 'rule over' uses the Hebrew bet, which means *ruling with,* not ruling over. . . . The concept of interdependent equal partners is well-grounded in the doctrine of the restored gospel."[4]

So Latter-day Saints, alone among all Christian religions, assert that not only did Eve not sin, but she was rewarded for her courage and wisdom, and God was assuring her that just as she fulfilled her role in the great plan of happiness, Adam would step up to the plate and perform, entitling him to rule with her. This is revolutionary and astounding doctrine among all the Christianities!

What gift will Adam give to further the great plan? Latter-day Saints believe that Adam and his sons will give the gift of the fruit of the Second Tree to those children of God worthy to receive it, just as Eve and her daughters give the fruit of the First Tree to all who are worthy to partake of it. The fruits of the Second Tree are the ordinances of salvation and exaltation. These ordinances are administered through the priesthood by the sons of God. Just as the doorway through the veil into this life is administered and guarded over by the daughters of God, so the doorway through the veil that brings us home is administered and guarded over by the sons of God. Those who have accepted the gift of the Second Tree from the hands of the sons of God will pass through that veil back to that celestial place where they can be with their heavenly parents once more.

Just as Adam was asked to hearken to Eve and receive the fruit of the First Tree, Eve is asked by God to hearken to Adam in accepting the fruit of the Second Tree. Two people, two trees—two hearkenings, two gifts given, two gifts received, two stewardships.

This means that priesthood, in the LDS understanding, is not some "extra" given to men and denied women. Priesthood is a man's apprenticeship to become just like his Heavenly Father, and women have their own apprenticeship to become like their Heavenly

Mother. The ordinances of body and of agency—pregnancy, childbirth, lactation (the spiritual ordinances of the First Tree)—are not less powerful or spiritual than the ordinances of the Second Tree.[5] Women have their own godly power.

Some have erroneously felt that the Mormon church and its male leaders preside over all members' families, somehow indicating that men are to rule over women.

Nothing could be further from the truth. The restored gospel helps us see that the Church is intended to be the gift that the sons of God give to the family, just as the daughters of God give the gift of birth and nurturance to the family. The Church, then, is but an auxiliary to the family. The family stands above it in the eternal plan. Elder Jeffrey R. Holland, an Apostle of the LDS Church, has said, "There might be wards and stakes [congregations] in heaven— I don't know anything about them—or there may well be some other organization that we don't know much about. What we do know will exist in heaven is families. And most of what has been revealed about our afterlife, our eternal life, our celestial life, focuses on family organization."[6] The family is the divine organization, one in which women and men rule as equals. President James E. Faust, of the First Presidency of the LDS Church, said: "Every father is to his family a patriarch and every mother a matriarch as coequals in their distinctive parental roles."[7]

I remain a steadfast member of the Mormon church because for the first time in my life, I understand why it is not a curse to be born a woman and how it can be claimed that men and women stand before God and before each other as true equals. In fact, one of the most profoundly feminist acts one can commit is to share the restored gospel of Jesus Christ with others. It restores not only right relations between man and God but right relations between men and women, making it the strongest, most progressive force for women in the world today.

Notes

1. L. Tom Perry, "Fatherhood—An Eternal Calling," *Ensign,* May 2004, 71.

2. Alma Don Sorensen, "The Story of Eve," in Alma Don Sorensen and Valerie Hudson Cassler, *Women in Eternity, Women of Zion* (Springville, Utah: Cedar Fort, 2004), 68–101.

3. Dallin H. Oaks, "The Great Plan of Happiness," *Ensign,* November 1993, 72–75.

4. Bruce C. Hafen and Marie K. Hafen, "Crossing Thresholds and Becoming Equal Partners," *Ensign,* August 2007, 24–29.

5. Analiesa Leonhardt, "The Sacrament of Birth," *Square Two,* Vol. 3, no. 1, Spring 2010, http://squaretwo.org./sq2ArticleLeonhardtBirth.html

6. Worldwide Leadership Training Meeting, February 9, 2008 (Salt Lake City: The Church of Jesus Christ of Latter-day Saints), 12.

7. James E. Faust, "The Prophetic Voice," *Ensign,* May 1996, 4.

JON M. HUNTSMAN SR.

JON M. HUNTSMAN SR. is founder and executive chairman of Huntsman Corporation, a global manufacturer and marketer of specialty chemicals.

Forty years ago, he began a small entrepreneurial plastics packaging business. Originally known for pioneering innovations in packaging and later for rapid and integrated growth in petrochemicals, its operating companies today manufacture chemical products used in a wide range of industries. Huntsman Corporation, as of 2010,  employs more than 12,000 individuals in multiple locations worldwide with annual revenues exceeding $9 billion.

Mr. Huntsman earned his undergraduate degree at the Wharton School of Business at the University of Pennsylvania and subsequently earned an MBA from the University of Southern California. He has been awarded thirteen honorary doctorate degrees.

Mr. Huntsman was a U.S. Naval Gunnery Officer. He served under President Richard M. Nixon as Special Assistant to the President and as White House staff secretary.

Jon Huntsman authored a book on corporate ethics, entitled, *Winners Never Cheat: Everyday Values We Learned as Children (But May Have Forgotten)*. The second edition, *Winners Never Cheat:*

Even in Difficult Times, was listed on the *Wall Street Journal*'s Best Sellers List.

Mr. Huntsman is widely recognized as one of America's foremost concerned citizens and philanthropists. His lifetime humanitarian giving, including contributions to the homeless, the ill, and the underprivileged, exceeds $1.2 billion, and he has assisted thousands of people, both domestically and internationally. The *Chronicle of Philanthropy* placed Mr. Huntsman second on its 2007 list of largest donors.

With his wife, Karen, Mr. Huntsman founded the Huntsman Cancer Institute in 1995 to accelerate the work of curing cancer through human genetics. The Institute is now one of America's major cancer research centers dedicated to finding a cure for cancer as well as a state-of-the-art hospital treating cancer patients.

Among other recognition, he has received a Medal of Honor from the American Cancer Society (2008), the American Red Cross Excellence in Governance Award (2006), and the Freedom Foundation Great Humanitarian Award (1996).

Jon and Karen Huntsman are the parents of nine children. They have fifty-six grandchildren and four great-grandchildren.

• • •

THE CHURCH OF JESUS CHRIST of Latter-day Saints is a remarkable anchor in the lives of individuals. Not only does it anchor a husband and wife, it anchors children to the family through both Church programs and the priesthood.

Karen and I raised nine children. Our youngest is severely mentally handicapped, and our oldest was the governor of Utah and is currently a candidate for President of the United States. As they were growing up, we took the programs of the Church for granted to some extent—that is, family home evenings, scripture study,

family prayer, family dinners, going to Church together. That was forty years ago.

Recently our beautiful daughter Kathleen passed away, leaving seven children between the ages of nine and nineteen. We now have seven additional children to raise. Here we are in our early seventies, asking what will best help these children in a world that has changed so dramatically and in which technology has such an impact on the lives of young people. The only solution we could find was to go back to those simple programs suggested by the Church.

In this busy world of Internet and texting and every type of new toy, Mormon young people know that nothing can replace dinner together; nothing supersedes family home evening or reading scriptures together. No one misses family prayer. Once a family prays together, they have a greater capacity for communicating. Oftentimes in prayer, children communicate what's really on their minds and in their hearts. Their challenges are expressed in their prayers. From both a macro point of view and a family point of view, these prosaic moments are critical in our lives. These basics of the Church help us overcome or rise above whatever is happening in the world around us.

Most people would say that the Huntsmans have everything. To the outside world, it looks like we live a life of leisure with the Midas touch. But as you peel the onion back a little and look under the layers, you can see heartache. You can see tragedy. My mother died of cancer in her fifties. I was holding her in my arms when she passed. It had a huge impact on me as a young man in my twenties. And I said to myself, *if ever the good Lord allows me to make any money, to become prosperous, it will be my life's challenge to do everything possible to help eradicate cancer.*

At that time, I was an egg salesman in Los Angeles. My father had been a rural schoolteacher, and we were born without anything but hopes and dreams. Since then, we've taken a lot of chances. Entrepreneurs take chances. When you don't have any money, you have to buy something for nothing. You have to convince people that you merit being a keeper of the keys to the gate, that you can manage people and return some type of financial or humanistic or charitable return on their investment.

I bought some businesses that large companies in the chemical industry wanted to unload. I was able to buy them on the basis that I would pay the sellers several years downstream. They had faith in me. They placed trust in me. Part of why they wanted to deal with me was because I was Mormon. They said, "We know you're honest. We know you're hardworking. We know you'll pay your bills." And I paid every one of them one hundred percent, plus interest.

The year 2011 was our fortieth year in business, and we are more profitable today than we've ever been. During those forty years, I found myself hanging from the cliff by my fingernails on more than one occasion. We have been through recessions and energy crisis problems, and our attorneys have advised us to declare bankruptcy on three occasions. But we decided that one way or another we were going to fight through it and succeed at all costs.

You see, we always had a goal in mind—and no one was going

to stop our intent to conquer cancer. My mother died of cancer, my father died of cancer, and my stepmother died of cancer. I have had cancer personally four times. Most people don't realize that 40 percent of the people who get cancer have a genetic predisposition. For them, it's just a matter of when. Today we have the largest genetic cancer research center in the world, with access to more than eleven million names of people we can help by diagnosing their future through their past. We feel the Lord has blessed us to be able to live through these terribly difficult business times to do our part in eliminating this dreaded disease among those cases that come from one's genetic makeup.

My mother and father were not active in the Mormon church. I grew up in a tough part of Idaho where not many members were active. But, as a boy of five, I sold the *Idaho State Journal* door-to-door for five cents a copy, and I would pay tithing. We left Idaho when I was seven years old and moved to a Navy base during World War II, and I continued to tithe. My mother and father would question, not in a negative way, "Why do you pay tithing? Why do you keep such an accurate record of all the money that you make so you can give the bishop 10 percent?"

I never understood it myself until one cold morning in February 1971, when I received a phone call from the chief of staff at the White House, calling on behalf of the President of the United States. I had been appointed by President Nixon to oversee the U.S. welfare program, which at that time had the second largest federal budget behind the Department of Defense. The White House chief of staff, H.R. (Bob) Haldeman, asked me to interview for the position of White House staff secretary, a very senior position for such a young man. I would also become the first Mormon to become a Special Assistant to the President of the United States.

I remember fumbling through my pockets and handing the White House guards my American Express card when they asked for my driver's license. Over the course of two days, I was grilled by the president, the vice president, the chief of staff, and members of the White House staff. This position was very close to the president— responsible for the ingress and egress of all papers and documents to him and also responsible for White House personnel and finances. They had narrowed it down to fourteen applicants, and I was again in Mr. Haldeman's office. He looked me right in the eye and said, "I want to know one thing. Are you a full tithe payer in your church?"

I stopped dead in my tracks and answered, "Yes, sir, I have paid tithing since I was five years of age."

He said, "I need ask no further questions. You have the job. If you've paid tithing all your life, then you are a man of integrity and honor, and you deserve to be next to the President of the United States." Had I said no, or "Someday I intend to pay tithing," it would have changed my life dramatically. I think about that day every time I pay my tithing. You can never be overdue with the Lord.

It's difficult to express, but I've always felt the Church was an enormous blessing. I've never questioned its leaders. I've never tried to find excuses for my membership, even though I attended Ivy League universities and operated businesses around the world. I mention these things because maybe the Lord does touch certain people so that they don't question. I have always been humbled and grateful to be a member of The Church of Jesus Christ of Latter-day Saints and to bear the priesthood of God.

This doesn't mean I haven't stumbled or fallen or made mistakes or said and done things I shouldn't have said or done. The greatest blessing in our lives is the gift of the Atonement of Jesus Christ. The Atonement gives us four important things: First, the great opportunity to be with God the Father and His Son Jesus Christ through the eternities. Second, the joy of being with our families forever—including, for me, my daughter Kathleen, my parents, and other loved ones who have gone on before. Third, the gift and power to repent of our mistakes, a means by which we can move on in life if we have fallen in a chuckhole or stumbled along the way. All mortals make mistakes. All people are put on earth to see not whether they falter but whether they will get back up and get moving. The Lord gave us this wonderful law of repentance.

Finally, fourth—the one I feel is the most important gift that's ever been placed on the earth for mankind—is the gift of healing. We can heal from our imperfections. We can heal from our addictions. We can heal from the sins we may have committed. Some people don't understand that the Atonement is the simple blessing of being forgiven of our sins in order to heal the wounds we have inflicted upon ourselves. Through the Atonement, we can move forward in life, positive and happy, with a sense of honor and integrity.

I learned this important lesson during a time I had the privilege of serving as the stake president (the ecclesiastical leader) for Howard W. Hunter, then the prophet and President of the Church. He was a dear and trusted friend. On one occasion, I felt the Spirit move me to go by his home to see how he was doing. When I knocked on the door, his wife said, "President Huntsman, come on in. We knew you would come by. President Hunter told me a few minutes ago, 'President Huntsman will come by our home this evening to see how I'm feeling.'"

When I went in, he was leaning back in his recliner, looking pale and quite ill. When I asked him what I could do to help, he said, "I would like a priesthood blessing. Would you be kind enough to give me one?" I said I would be honored and humbled to do so and asked if he wouldn't mind explaining the nature of his illness.

He responded, "Today I had an ill thought toward another man, and it's made me physically and emotionally sick all day. Every bone in my body aches. My heart burns because I had a negative thought in my heart toward another person. Would you bless me that any harsh thoughts toward any man or woman would dissipate immediately and be eradicated from body and heart, mind and soul?"

So I placed my hands on his head and, as soon as I did so, I thought of Matthew 5:8: "Blessed are the pure in heart: for they shall see God." I had just put my hands on the head of a man who was so pure in heart that it made him physically ill if he had negative feelings toward anyone. That was one of my greatest experiences, to learn from such a pure man the impact of carrying ill thoughts toward another.

Having the gospel of Jesus Christ with His gift of repentance has given me enormous confidence because Jesus Christ made it possible for me to repent. I can get failure behind me and be positive and move on in life because, as a Mormon, I have been taught to accept the Atonement, the great gift the gospel of Jesus Christ offers to all.

FIROZ KING HUSEIN

FIROZ KING HUSEIN grew up as a Muslim in Bombay, India. After obtaining his bachelor's degree in civil engineering from the University of Bombay in 1969, he came to the United States to continue his education in civil engineering. He had never heard of Mormons or The Church of Jesus Christ of Latter-day Saints, but was introduced to Brigham Young University through a friend and graduated there with a master's degree in civil engineering in 1971.

King is president and owner of Span Construction & Engineering, Inc.; Freedom Management, Inc.; and Eagle Building Systems, Inc. Span C&E has been the number one pre-engineered steel builder in the United States for the past nineteen years, including building more than 62 million square feet for Costco in the U.S. and other countries. Span, in partnership with Okland Construction, also built the Indoor Practice Facility and Student Athlete Buildings as well as the Gordon B. Hinckley Alumni Building at BYU.

In 1993, King was named the Honored Alumni of the Year by the Brigham Young University College of Engineering and Technology. He has also received BYU's Distinguished Service Award (2005) and President's Award (2009). He serves on the Executive Committee of the President's Leadership Council at BYU–Provo, on the President's Leadership Council at BYU–Hawaii, and on the

Deseret News Editorial Advisory Board. He currently serves in the Church as a bishop in Monterey, California. King is married to the former Diane Clark of Afton, Wyoming, and they have four children.

. . .

M Y FATHER PASSED AWAY when I was eleven, leaving my mother, my two brothers, one sister, and me to make our own way in Bombay, India. I remember feeling scared, overwhelmed, uncertain about the life in front of me, and wondering where my father went when he died and what would happen to him—and to me.

Although we were Muslim, my mother sent us to a private Catholic school where English was the primary language. She paid for this and our other needs by teaching embroidery to high school girls in our small home, using old treadle sewing machines. I was mostly a C student until a high school English teacher gave me an A on a term paper and expressed confidence in me—a real turning point in my life. She helped me believe in myself. I decided to work hard, and from that point forward I got straight As.

Being an A student enabled me to study civil engineering at the University of Bombay, and I started dreaming about going to America for my graduate degree. Then came July 20, 1969. We did not have a TV, so I was glued to the radio, listening to everything that was happening as America landed men on the moon. Neil Armstrong's words, "That's one small step for man, one giant leap for mankind," were chiseled into my mind. "In America," I thought, "anything is possible."

Two months later I flew from Bombay to New York, then to Houston, hoping to attend graduate school in engineering at Rice University. But I was not happy in Houston, partly because I was homesick. When I complained to a friend back home, she wrote me about her cousin who was attending Brigham Young University, a school I had not heard of. I called him, looking for moral support. He raved about BYU and sent me an application.

Filling it out, I came to an "ecclesiastical endorsement" page that mentioned being interviewed by a bishop. When I called my friend's cousin back and asked, "What's a bishop?" he had me open the phone book and look up Church of Jesus Christ of Latter-day Saints. I found a list of "wards" in the Houston area and eventually reached a bishop's wife who informed me that the bishop would be home that evening, but that I could also meet him on Sunday at church.

The next Sunday, the bishop explained to me that although it was not necessary to be a member of the Mormon church to attend BYU, I would have to agree to live by BYU's honor code while there. This meant, among other things, abstaining from alcohol, tobacco, coffee, and tea. None of these was a problem for me, despite tea being the common drink in India. I grew up drinking it with my breakfast, but around age nine began throwing up on the way to school. I figured it was a reaction to the tea, so I stopped drinking it.

In January 1970, I boarded a Greyhound bus in Houston in a short-sleeved shirt and without a coat (having only seen pictures of snow) and headed for Provo, Utah, and BYU. I was assigned to a "family home evening group," a group of students who met for activities every Monday evening. I started dating the only other non-Mormon in the group and through her eventually met Diane Clark from Star Valley, Wyoming.

Diane and I soon began dating. By December, our relationship had become serious. Things boiled down to a single issue: She would not marry a non-Mormon, and I would not join the Church just to marry her. Wanting to get through school quickly, I took heavy course loads and graduated with my master's in civil engineering in only three semesters, so we parted in January 1971. As I left for

Boston to seek employment, I remember telling her that she would certainly marry a returned Mormon missionary.

Some of the girls I dated in Boston were sophisticated and fashionable, but after each date I usually came home feeling something was missing. I kept in touch with Diane until Christmas 1971, when she told me she was engaged. I just said, "Oh. Well, I guess I don't feel like talking anymore," and we hung up.

Then sometime in January I came to my apartment to eat lunch and pack my bags for a business trip. Just as I was walking out the door to leave for the airport, I looked around the room, saw the telephone, and was prompted to call Diane. She informed me that she had broken off her engagement a few days before and that her phone was scheduled to be disconnected in a few minutes as she was headed home to get ready for a semester abroad in France. Had I not called her at that moment, we likely would have lost contact altogether. We agreed to communicate through letters while she was in France. While she was overseas, she twice received clear manifestations through the Spirit that she would marry me, although she did not tell me until later. We were married in November 1972 in Massachusetts.

I attended Church with Diane regularly, but did not take the missionary discussions. While I was at BYU, missionaries had taught me the "first discussion." They had given me a Book of Mormon and asked me to read it and get baptized the next Saturday. That was the last time I saw them.

Diane felt uncomfortable in the East, so periodically I would check for employment opportunities out west. In 1977, I was offered a job in Fresno and headed to California, leaving Diane and our boys, ages four and eleven months, in New Hampshire until we could sell our house. Before I left, the baby had to be admitted to the hospital with pneumonia and had barely been released when I had to leave. That weighed heavily on my mind. Also, finances were tight because we had a house payment in New Hampshire and I was renting a small apartment in Fresno. I was in a new job in a new place, away from my wife and children. I was needed in California. I was needed at home with my family. I worried constantly.

One day I left the office to get some lunch. I was in the habit of listening to music on my car radio, but this time what I heard on the radio were hymns. I then realized that I had tears in my eyes. I stopped at a traffic light, and in the middle of this internal turmoil I looked up to see two Mormon missionaries crossing the street right in front of my car. Everything else went blank; all I could see were these two "angels." I immediately knew what this meant and what I needed to do. I went to my apartment and called Diane. I said, "Lock the house, give the key to the realtor, and move here with the boys. I am getting baptized."

She then told me that she had been on her knees most of the night before, praying to the Lord: "I can't go on anymore. I need my husband to receive a testimony of the gospel." I was baptized in Star Valley on Christmas Eve, 1977. Before being baptized, I didn't think doing so would make much difference; looking back now, the differences are almost beyond my ability to express. It was the best decision I ever made.

In the years since BYU, I had tried to read the Book of Mormon several times, but had taken an intellectual approach. After I was baptized and received the gift of the Holy Ghost, the Book of Mormon just opened up to me. It is still a precious book to me, and I read from it almost every day. But all along my main obstacle was accepting Jesus Christ as the Son of God. As a Muslim, I believed that Jesus Christ was only a prophet, sent to the Christians.

Shortly after I joined the Church I was called to teach seminary, an early-morning scripture class for high school students. I taught for four years, going through all of the LDS "standard works": Old Testament, New Testament, Book of Mormon, and Doctrine and

Covenants. This was a wonderful way for a new convert to learn the gospel. At the end of each lesson, the teacher was encouraged to bear testimony of what was taught. I grew spiritually as I did so.

One of my most sacred experiences happened when I taught the New Testament. I received a very clear manifestation of the resurrected Christ. God knew what I needed, and I was blessed with the confirmation that Jesus Christ is indeed the Son of God and our Savior. I know it is unusual, but in my case I received a testimony of the Book of Mormon and of Jesus Christ as my Savior *after* I joined the Church.

Since I joined The Church of Jesus Christ of Latter-day Saints, my entire life has changed because my priorities have changed. I used to sleep eight hours each night; now I manage with four or five. I used to sleep until noon on Sundays; now it is my busiest day of the week, starting early in the morning and often continuing late into the night. I cannot remember the last time I was sick, even with a cold. I am blessed with more energy and can do more with my time than I could before I became LDS. When people ask me why I serve in the Church, I always say, "It is my way of giving thanks to the Lord for everything He has blessed me with." I try to live by the success formula the Lord gave us in Matthew 6:33: "Seek ye first the kingdom of God, and his righteousness; and all these things shall be added unto you." I wish I had the words to describe the "all" that has been added to me.

I have a firm testimony of the law of tithing. I pay my tithing, and I receive back everything I need and then some. I used to wonder about and fear what happened to my father when he died. Now I have a testimony of the life hereafter and of temple work. Fear and anxiety have been replaced with peace—the inner peace that only the gospel can give me. I go to bed every night without any remorse or inner concerns. The blessing of peace is one of the most precious gifts of the gospel that I enjoy.

As a bishop myself now, I have been blessed to witness lives being changed through the miracle of forgiveness and the power of the Atonement. I am grateful for the Spirit and cannot imagine living without its influence. I have the Savior as my friend. I have felt His hand guiding and protecting me, not only in my personal life but in my family affairs, in my Church responsibilities, and even in my business.

I am living the American dream, but not in the way I originally envisioned it. When I came to America I had envisioned being successful in the "ways of the world." Coming to the United States from India, where my mother earned money for my education by teaching machine embroidery—having started with only a $500 loan from a Muslim Education Trust—has not turned out as I thought. It has turned out far, far better. I am living a blessed life with the gospel of Jesus Christ as my anchor. Now I know that "anything is possible" with the help of the Lord. I am deeply grateful to be a Mormon. I would not trade my membership in this Church for anything in the world.

JANE CLAYSON JOHNSON

JANE CLAYSON JOHNSON is the former network anchor of *The Early Show* on CBS. As a CBS News correspondent, she reported for *The CBS Evening News* and *48 Hours*. Prior to joining CBS, Jane was a network correspondent for ABC News, where she reported for *World News Tonight with Peter Jennings* and *Good Morning America*. Jane began in television at KSL in Salt Lake City.

Jane has covered three U.S. presidential campaigns, the Columbine High School massacre, the Oklahoma City bombing of the federal building, and the events of September 11 and their aftermath. Her news assignments have also taken her around the world from muddy refugee camps in Macedonia and streets crammed with protestors in Indonesia to China and Australia and beyond.

Of such experiences, Jane once wrote: "It is in moments of incredible suffering and despair that I have repeatedly witnessed the inextinguishable human spirit flare up to push back the darkness. I believe that those sparks of compassion and courage have a divine origin."

Honored with many journalism awards, including an Emmy and the Edward R. Murrow Award, Jane is the recipient of an honorary doctorate degree from Utah State University. She graduated from Brigham Young University with a degree in journalism in 1990.

In 2007, Jane published the best-selling book *I Am a Mother*, which detailed her decision to leave her career in New York City to become a mother full time. Jane can now be heard occasionally on National Public Radio.

Jane is a native of California. She and her husband, Mark W. Johnson, now make their home in Massachusetts. Jane has two young children and three teenage stepchildren.

• • •

MORE THAN TWENTY YEARS AGO, I traveled with a group of students from Brigham Young University to the Holy Land for a semester abroad. During the months spent in and around Jerusalem, I immersed myself in the scriptures, yearning to know more of my Savior as I literally walked where He had walked. I spent hours at the Garden Tomb. Studying. Pondering. Praying.

I came to know that Jesus Christ lived, that He died and was resurrected.

Of course, I had been taught these things all my life, but my experiences in the Holy Land cemented my personal faith. I felt the Spirit whisper to my heart that the gospel of Jesus Christ is true and timeless; that the truths He taught on the hills of Galilee two thousand years ago are the same truths we teach today in homes and chapels around the world; that we are able to testify of these truths because a loving Father in Heaven appeared with His Son, Jesus Christ, to a fourteen-year-old boy who had faith—and a question. In answering that question, they commenced the restoration of the gospel of Jesus Christ on the earth.

I am a Mormon because my parents are Mormons, as were their parents and grandparents. I am a Mormon because the values and standards espoused by our leaders resonate with me and lead to things that are good. But, above all, I am a Mormon because I cannot deny that affirmation of faith that came as I sought to know more about my Savior those many years ago.

But the gospel of Jesus Christ is not just what I believe; it is who I am.

My church lifts me, strengthens me, and motivates me to be good . . . and to do good. The first principles and ordinances of the gospel are simple: faith, repentance, baptism, receiving the gift of the Holy Spirit. As I obey the commandments, seek the Lord's will in my life, nourish my faith, and repent, I grow stronger as a person. And as I share my personal blessings, my family is strengthened and those around me are uplifted. The gospel is a tremendous gift in my life, and I treasure it.

Has it always been easy? Absolutely not! There have been seasons of heartache and questioning, struggling and reevaluation, in both my personal and professional life. There were most certainly moments during my career in the network news when I thought, "Gosh, it would be so much easier to *not* believe."

But I couldn't do it. I could never *not* believe. Over time, I gained respect because of my beliefs—and, at times, in spite of them. I learned how to grow both professionally and spiritually at the same time. I allowed my faith to guide me through that wonderful season of life.

Now I am immersed in a new season of life, one full of carpools and homework and piano practicing and play dates. This season is far removed from the last. But the gospel and my relationships with family and friends remain a constant. I would not have it any other way.

As a wife and a mother, I cannot imagine any life other than one that is centered on the gospel of Jesus Christ. It motivates me to be a better person. My husband and I try to teach our children

to be kind, empathetic, generous, and loving. We say family prayers together and learn about Jesus Christ by reading scriptures and telling stories from the Bible. Every Monday night, we have dedicated family time, where we talk about faith and service, developing good character, and doing hard things.

One of my greatest desires is that my children share in my faith and love of the gospel. This is not something I can simply give to them. It is something each of them—like each of us—must learn for themselves. The best I can do is to emulate the principles of the gospel that mean so much to me, to teach my children the path that Jesus walked and to have faith that they too will want to follow it.

During those months more than twenty years ago when I actually walked in the Savior's footsteps, I came to know the Lord. I remember one Sabbath afternoon in particular when I opened my heart to the Spirit as I took out my violin and began to play "I Walked Today Where Jesus Walked." It was a moment of tremendous peace and a confirmation of my Savior's love for me. After I had finished playing, a beautiful woman in the congregation came forward, put her arms around me, and said, "I can tell that you love the Savior."

I have never received a greater compliment.

It is what I hope to pass on to my children and to theirs: I am Mormon because I love the Lord Jesus Christ.

MARK W. JOHNSON

MARK W. JOHNSON is cofounder and chairman of Innosight, a strategic innovation consulting and investing company, which he cofounded with Harvard Business School professor Clayton M. Christensen. He has consulted to *Global 1000* and start-up companies in a wide-range of industries and has advised the U.S. government and Singapore's government on innovation and entrepreneurship.

Mark has published articles in *Harvard Business Review, Sloan Management Review, Business Week, Forbes*, the *Washington Post, Advertising Age,* and *National Defense.* His award-winning book, *Seizing the White Space: Business Model Innovation for Growth and Renewal,* was published in 2010 by Harvard Business Press.

Prior to cofounding Innosight, Mark was a consultant at Booz Allen Hamilton. Before that, he served as a nuclear-power-trained surface warfare officer in the U.S. Navy. Mark received an MBA from Harvard Business School, a master's degree in civil engineering mechanics from Columbia University, and a bachelor's degree with distinction in aerospace engineering from the United States Naval Academy. He currently serves on the board of the U.S. Naval Institute.

Mark and his wife, Jane Clayson Johnson, and their children live in Massachusetts.

• • •

As I met with the missionaries over a course of weeks and months in the year 2000, I experienced a sort of revelation. It didn't involve angels or visions or even an overpowering feeling of the Spirit. My revelation was more of an unveiling, perhaps even a rediscovery. As we discussed the principles of the gospel, the plan of salvation, and the Restoration, I felt as if everything I already knew about God and religion and its influence in our lives was enhanced. This made sense! There was no paradigm shift, no moment when I suddenly had to throw out old beliefs and accept something new.

For me, embracing the gospel of Jesus Christ as presented by the missionaries simply felt right. And so I entered the waters of baptism, based on my faith that this was what the Lord would have me do with my life. Becoming a member of His Church motivated me. I felt as if the gospel could make me a better person, and I was excited at the prospect of making covenants with God—covenants that would not only bless and enhance my life but would also challenge me to live a higher law.

Of course, I was still a novice in the gospel at the time. So when my business partner and friend Clayton Christensen helped me secure a ticket to attend the dedication of the Boston Temple a few weeks after my baptism, I didn't completely understand what would happen. I thought it might be something like a sacrament meeting, with prayers and worship and singing. I certainly didn't fully grasp the significance of being able to sit in the celestial room as then-Church President Gordon B. Hinckley offered the dedicatory prayer.

But the moment I bowed my head and closed my eyes in obedience to President Hinckley's request to do so, an extraordinary

feeling—like a rushing of wind—passed through my entire body, culminating in my head. I didn't hear anything or see anything, but I felt a power I had never experienced before and have yet to experience again. The Spirit washed through the room. No one was left untouched. I turned to my right to see a woman in her seventies beaming with the glow of the Spirit. And then I turned to my left to see a young boy, maybe seventeen, basking in that same light. It was magnificent! I found myself helplessly crying with joy, and I knew for myself (not just by the faith of others) that the Church I had joined was true. I continued to cry, even past the service, not wanting to stop.

As the Spirit of the Lord dug deep into my soul that day, a realization began to formulate in my mind. Ten years later, this realization has crystallized and become my mantra, if you will. It is that the first principles and ordinances of the gospel, though simple and sometimes tritely rehearsed, are truly the overriding principles of happiness in our lives.

Weeks before the temple dedication, I had taken a leap of faith and told the missionaries I would accept their challenge to enter the waters of baptism. I had met with the bishop and stake president, where we discussed the principle of repentance and where I felt a significant measure of peace and love because I knew the Lord was willing to forgive my sins if I would humbly submit. And then came the ordinance, the actual baptism by immersion, followed by the laying on of hands to receive the gift of the Holy Ghost.

In the coming weeks, I continued to have faith that my decision to join the Church was correct; I knelt in prayer daily seeking repentance and to better myself; I took the sacrament each Sunday as a symbol and reminder of my baptismal covenant. And then, just weeks later, in the temple of the Lord, I received a gift of the Spirit, a wave of wind and fire rushing through my soul, confirming to me that this is the Lord's Church, that I am God's son, and that I can attain eternal happiness through following His commandments.

This pattern has been repeated over and over in my life. It is true that I have never again experienced the overpowering rush of the Spirit I did that day in the temple. But I have repeatedly received confirmation of His love and gifts of His Spirit when I have had faith, repented of my sins and shortcomings, and continued to renew and keep my covenants with God.

As I approached a long-distance courtship with Jane, I saw this pattern in play. So many small miracles happened along the way that allowed me to be again in the temple, this time with my sweetheart across the altar, where we made covenants with each other and God.

As I served in the bishopric of a young single adult ward in Boston, I saw the joy that comes as ward members and leaders work together to live the principles of the gospel and continue the pattern of faith, repentance, baptism, and receipt of the Holy Ghost. I marveled at the way in which prayers are answered and lives improved through following this pattern.

Indeed, it is a pattern from which I never want to stray. The gospel inspires me to do and be better. Through prayer, scripture study, worshipful church attendance, family home evenings, and everything that is part of gospel living, I find greater joy than I imagined possible. I feel as if the gospel encourages me to become something in life, not just know something or feel something. Following the gospel plan is liberating. And that is why I am a Mormon.

JEFFREY MAX JONES

JEFF JONES is a Mexican statesman and businessman. He joined Mexico's minority National Action Party (PAN) in 1995. He was elected to one term in Mexico's lower house, the Chamber of Deputies, from 1997 to 2000, representing Chihuahua's First District, and then to a term in the national senate, the *Senado de la Republica,* in the year 2000. Senator Jones served as president of the Border Affairs committee and on the Agriculture and Agrarian Reform committees, soon becoming known as an innovative, solution-oriented thinker. His senate service ended in 2006, with Mexico's one-term limit for legislators.  During his term as senator, he was the highest-ranking Mormon ever to serve in the Mexican government.

When Jeff was first invited to run for office, he told party members, "You're crazy. I'm white and I'm Mormon." However, they were not deterred, and he eventually won over the people of Chihuahua with his grassroots campaign efforts and affable mannerisms. After his election he gained a reputation for complete honesty and for being a person who could not be corrupted.

From 2006 to 2009, the former senator served as undersecretary of agribusiness development with SAGARPA *(Secretaría de Agricultura, Ganadería, Desarollo Rural, Pesca y Alimentación),* and focused on three areas: prospective planning, market development, and finance. Working now in the financial field, he continues to try to better Mexico. By creating greater opportunities in Mexico, he hopes not only to curb illegal immigration to the United States but to attract human capital back into Mexico. In his words, "For many years, economic hardship, and most recently violence, have driven many great people away."

Jeff knows Mexico's violence and corruption personally. In 1998 men he believed to be police officers attempted to kidnap him and his brother, Kelly, apparently to collect money from ATMs. Feeling it would be better for his family to know he was dead than to live through a drawn-out kidnapping scenario, Jeff tried to break away and was shot three times.

Born and raised in "the colonies" in Nuevo Casas Grandes in northwestern Chihuahua, Mexico, Jeff graduated from Brigham Young University in 1982 and returned to Mexico. He professes a deep love for both his faith and his family. Today he travels between Mexico and Utah, where his wife, Michelle, and daughters live away from the recent increase of violence in Chihuahua, and to accommodate family health and educational needs. Despite the unrest, he spends most of his time in Mexico, where he feels a sense of mission. "I believe God puts us where He needs us."

• • •

IN TODAY'S POLITICALLY CORRECT SOCIETY, many people feel pressured to conform to commonly accepted beliefs and practices. One of the great things about Mormonism is that it teaches you to feel comfortable being different. After all, once you've shared the Joseph Smith story as a missionary, you can't help but become a bit more thick-skinned. And our primary mortal reference point, Jesus Christ, certainly stood against the political correctness of His time.

During my teenage years, in a group setting where alcohol was being served, I remember feeling that I, the non-drinker, was the one on trial. I became uncomfortable and sometimes defensive. The ensuing discussions usually began with a request to explain why I didn't drink, baiting me to argue about why alcohol was bad.

However, I soon learned to see this in a different light. Realizing that offering me a drink was many times a kind, heartfelt gesture, I would simply thank the person and politely say no. When pressed, I'd reverse my strategy and ask the drinkers to explain why they *did* drink, what they saw as the positive benefits of their drinking habit, and how they had gotten into it. While drinkers gave some creative and sometimes comical replies, their answers invariably involved the need to conform to social norms or practices.

Just after college, I started a new feed supplement business in my hometown in northern Mexico. Since molasses was one of our chief ingredients, I traveled frequently to Mexico City to deal with Mexico's then state-owned sugar industry. I quickly became friends with Don Luis Inzunza, a silver-haired, cigar-smoking executive who was a high-level government official. On one occasion he invited me to his cattle ranch near Tuxpan, Veracruz, for a couple of days, and upon our return to Mexico City, he took me to a luncheon at the prestigious *Club de Industriales*. In attendance were some of his lifetime friends, part of Mexico City's elite who either had been or were then leaders in government and business.

Don Luis introduced me to his friends as "my friend from Chihuahua who professes a religion with weird ideas." As eight or ten of us sat visiting around the table, a gentlemanly business mogul sitting next to me noticed that I did not drink alcohol. As the lunch progressed, he leaned toward me and quietly apologized for the group's drinking, commenting that personally he did not like to drink, but did so only for social reasons such as the setting we were in at the moment.

Sensing his discomfort in my behalf, I assured him that he should not be concerned about me, that although I didn't drink, I enjoyed very much being in the company of people who were drinking. He was taken aback by my response and, after taking a moment to process my comment, he asked why. I replied, "Because drunk people tell me all their secrets." At this he nearly choked on his mouthful of food and managed a heartfelt laugh. We had suddenly made a connection.

In 1995, when I ran for office for the first time, local members of my newly founded PAN party saw me, politically speaking, as the green-behind-the-ears candidate I was. Because they liked me, their protective instincts took over. On my first day as candidate for state legislator, the *panistas* (as members of the PAN party are known) took me out to make cold calls to constituents in their homes. They began my political training by giving me tips about how to approach people, what not to say, what to say, and how to say it.

I listened attentively and thanked them for their good advice. I then proceeded to organize them into two teams, explaining that each would take one side of the street. Thinking on my feet, I suggested that some of them should go out in front knocking on doors, thus avoiding waiting for people to come to their front doors. Others should then walk to the door with me, briefly introduce me as the PAN's candidate, and give a brief message. Finally, a few other people should follow up with brochures and stay with people to give closure while I went on to the next door to meet more constituents.

After a few hours of work, we stopped for a break at one of the many *changarros*—one-room, quick-stop stores usually inside or next to someone's home. The *panistas* were physically exhausted but exhilarated, having covered so much territory and contacted so many people. All were impressed by the overall success of our efforts. Surprised at my ease in the streets and convinced of the methodology, they asked, "Didn't you say that you had never been involved in politics?"

I answered, "Yes. It's my first day campaigning. What you perhaps didn't know is that I was a Mormon missionary when I was nineteen. If you think it's difficult getting people to change their votes, try getting them to change their lives. This is a piece of cake."

In 1997, just before I took office as a federal legislator at the *Cámara de Diputados,* the PAN party invited its newly elected and appointed members to a three-day retreat to consolidate what would become the PAN Parliamentary Group in the 57th Congress. Since Mexico's constitution does not allow consecutive terms for any public office, the PAN get-together was an opportunity for the entire body of newly elected legislators to meet one another and prepare strategies. This particular year would be the start of an exciting new legislature because the old-guard PRI party had finally lost their simple majority in the lower house.

A former legislator, Maria Elena Alvarez de Vicencio, was among those who addressed us at this retreat. She and her family were strongly connected to the leadership of the Catholic-leaning PAN party. She had come to give us some reminders on ethics and guidance about staying out of mischief for the next three years, the duration of our legislative term. I remember her warning us that during our time as federal legislators we would have more temptations than ever before, but that we should not yield. Instead, we should take advantage of the great cultural opportunities in Mexico City, such as the many theatres, museums, art displays, and cultural events.

Although I appreciated the advice, I soon came to wonder who of the legislators had any time to decide between temptations or good cultural events. After addressing issues in my district office each Monday, I would drive two or three hours to an airport to fly into Mexico City. I'd attend meetings and work all day Tuesday through Thursday, then fly out on Thursday evening or the next morning to address issues back in my district office on Friday and Saturday morning. I wondered how any of the legislators had time to do anything but work.

Much of the time crunch was due to lack of staff support. When we started our term, the only PAN staff for the majority of legislators in Mexico City was one secretary or administrative assistant for every twelve legislators. Eventually, one assistant was appointed for every four legislators. It was a frustrating experience just trying to keep up with all the legislation that was being presented. The fundamental problem was that Mexico's legislature, until the arrival of a new opposition majority, had been simply a rubber stamp for the government's executive branch. Before our arrival, the *Presidente* presented nearly 100 percent of all legislation approved. Assistants were needed only to make travel arrangements for legislators, who spent a lot of time in what was known as "parliamentary tourism."

I had befriended another legislator, Gerardo Buganza of Veracruz, from the first day the newly elected representatives met. Since I was a practicing Latter-day Saint and he was a Catholic who attended early-morning mass on a daily basis, we shared many of the same Christian values. Also, we lived in the same part of town, so we shared rides back to our respective apartments after long workdays. Juan Miguel Alcántara, who was part of the PAN's leadership, gave us the nickname *Los Abstemios*, or "those who abstain." At the time I thought it was simply that we didn't drink or smoke.

It was not until much later that David Atilano gave me a greater perspective on the reason for the nickname. David, a national oratory champion, had been an employee at the PAN group (part of our group leader's staff) and was aware of issues concerning the new PAN legislators. Toward the end of my three-year term, he converted to the LDS Church and became the campaign manager for my successful run for the federal senate. David revealed the nature of certain nocturnal activities some of the legislators were participating in at the time. I then had a much clearer idea of why they called us *Los Abstemios* and why Maria Elena had given her advice.

My twelve-year experience at the national level in the government of Mexico, and my observations of politics in other countries, have led me to believe that very few statesmen are left in the world. Many politicians, yes. However, I often remember the differentiation attributed to Winston Churchill: "A politician thinks of the next election; a statesman thinks of the next generation."

While I understand that in politics one cannot ignore the short-term perspective, we must not be so distracted by it that we take our eyes off the goal beyond the horizon. With this long-term perspective in mind, the great men and women of history had to stand alone at some point in their lives, many of them dying for their beliefs. For true leaders, the ability to stand alone, to stand for truth, is an essential quality to learn and to feel comfortable with. My LDS background, which teaches me to see things in a much longer time frame, has helped me to look further down the road, to work together with others to find common ground and build consensus whenever possible, and to feel secure standing alone when necessary.

Many commonsense aspects of Mormonism are rationally convincing and are part of why I am a member of The Church of Jesus Christ of Latter-day Saints. But my most fundamental reason is actually intuitive and the result of revelation. It flows from the quiet whisperings of the Spirit I have felt that tell me that the gospel of Jesus Christ is true, that He is my Redeemer. His Church has been restored upon the earth through His Latter-day prophet, Joseph Smith, and continues to move forward in open and active communication with the heavens through living prophets.

CECILIE LUNDGREEN

CECILIE "CC" LUNDGREEN was born in 1973 in the small town of Sarpsborg, Norway. She began playing golf at age eleven, inspired by her grandfather, her first coach. CC set a goal to become a professional golfer, and over the next several years she found herself representing Norway in Nordic, European, and World Championships. She was eventually ranked as Norway's top female golfer.

In response to her mother's advice that education is vital, CC moved to Florida in 1993 to attend Florida Atlantic University on a golf scholarship, playing on the FAU Golf Team while completing her degree. In 1998, she graduated with a bachelor of arts in education and a minor in German language and literature.

After going professional, CC joined the Ladies European Tour in 1999. On tour in 2001, she finished second in the Ladies South African Masters at Sun City, South Africa, and sixth in the French Open. She finished twenty-eighth on the overall 2001 European Tour Order of Merit.

CC's life changed greatly in 2002 when her mother passed away and again when she was baptized into The Church of Jesus Christ of Latter-day Saints. Of the latter, she says, "I have loved the changes, the peace, and the direction I have found within the gospel."

CC attributes much of her golf success as well as her feelings about life and religion to Reeve Nield, her coach and friend. She spends much of her free time in Zimbabwe helping with Eyes for Zimbabwe, a charity established in 1996 by Coach Reeve and fellow golf professional Laurette Maritz from South Africa.

As hobbies, CC enjoys listening to music, playing squash for exercise, traveling, tasting various foods, and watching good movies. Her favorite activity is attending the temple wherever she finds herself in the world. In her home ward, CC enjoys teaching the youth as she serves in the Young Women presidency.

• • •

I AM A MORMON BECAUSE SOMEONE CARED. Someone believed in me. Someone who had the faith, the knowledge, and a much greater understanding than I of our purpose on earth took the time to help me understand that the world didn't just happen with a random "big bang." Someone knew that the gospel of Jesus Christ would change my life forever and had enough love and concern to make sure I would stop and listen. That someone was my Heavenly Father, who sent into my life two amazing angels who turned everything upside down.

I grew up in Norway in a troubled home with loud voices, alcohol, and abuse. When I was eleven years old, my mother finally left my father. She realized that her two young children were better off without his alcohol problem and physical abuse. That summer I spent most of my time with my grandparents while my parents settled property issues, finances, and the like. My grandfather told me I'd better learn to play golf. He bought me a set of junior golf clubs, and off we went.

Golf changed my life. I loved spending time on the golf course with friends instead of being alone at home while my mother worked full time to support us. I quickly took to the sport and started to represent my club. By age fifteen, I was representing my country.

Through golf, I could bring a measure of pride and recognition to my family, since in my small hometown everyone knew our troubles.

I began to dream of life as a professional golfer. My mother let me spend summers without a job if I worked hard at golf, extended myself, and developed the talent others saw. She cheered me on as I strived to achieve my dream. Dedication, hard work, and a lot of practice finally paid off when I was granted a scholarship to Florida Atlantic University in America to further my education—and my golf.

It was hard, at age nineteen, to leave my mother and fly across the world to attend university. She had raised me with all the love she could give and had taught me to be levelheaded. But she was not religious. We never attended church, and religion was never spoken of, so I didn't really believe in anything or anyone. Most of my extended family were atheists, so no one spoke of religion or of Heavenly Father—except Grandma Lundgreen, who kept reminding us that the Lord is kind. At the time, I just laughed it off.

Over the next several years, life seemed to be made of tragedy. The grandfather who taught me to play golf died when I was seventeen, and I was angry. Then a young golfer I knew died from cancer, and a friend's seven-year-old daughter was struck by lightning while playing on the playground with her brother, suffering permanent physical damage. I was heartbroken. Life was not fair! During my first year in Florida, my father died after a battle with liver cancer caused by his alcoholism. I was angry with him and with the world in general. I struggled to find meaning in it all.

About a year later, my best friend died just before her twenty-second birthday from an undetected birth defect. I was furious! People I cared deeply about were dying all around me. I did not understand why, and I was desperate to find out what happened to them. Where did they go? Would I ever see them again? What was the meaning of all this? It seemed no one could give me the answers.

Meanwhile, I loved studying in America. I met many great people who taught me interesting things, but I stayed close to my mother's teachings: have respect for yourself and others; stay away from alcohol and drugs; don't go places you shouldn't go; behave like a lady. She was my hero! She worked hard to help me get through school with scholarships, student loans, and her extra savings. I was grateful for her sacrifices and felt her love all the way from Norway throughout my five years at the university. Her constant love and care and her ability to forgive and forget also helped my brother, who had made choices on the wrong side of the law as a result of my father's physical and emotional abuse.

After receiving my bachelor's degree, I pursued my golfing dream and joined the Ladies European Tour. I soon became the "famous golfer" in my country. I'll admit I loved receiving so much positive recognition from so many people.

On a golf course in Austria, I met my two Mormon angels, Reeve and Laurette. Laurette was a professional golfer from South Africa who had played on the Tour for many years, and Reeve was her golf coach from Zimbabwe. Every time I bumped into them on or off the course, I felt comfortable in their presence. We soon became good friends. When I started touring Europe, my mother and stepfather often traveled to watch me play. My mom saw Reeve giving Laurette a putting lesson one day and said, "Please teach my daughter how to putt! She is useless at it!" So, through my mother's inspiration, Reeve became my coach—another event that changed my life.

Reeve, Laurette, and I were sitting at a friend's kitchen table one day when the subject came up of faith and what we believed. I had quite a few things to say! I spilled out my feelings about how I didn't believe in anything, and how there was no God because if there was, how could He make such horrible things happen to me and my family, and by the way, where is my dad now and my best friend who died much too early?

Reeve listened patiently, and then she gently shared what they believed as members of The Church of Jesus Christ of Latter-day Saints. I didn't think much about it afterward. I knew very little about the Mormons and had no interest in learning more. But the first small seed was planted in my heart. Meanwhile, I was on my way to the top, or so I thought—playing great golf, making money, getting famous, and signing autographs. I was ranked twenty-seventh in Europe, slowly reaching my goals of fame and fortune. Since my childhood had been such a struggle, these goals had been my incentive. Silly me.

My friendship with Reeve and Laurette grew, and we started traveling together. They sometimes shared their thoughts, their feelings, and their faith with me. Reeve had served a Church mission in Utah and shared some amazing stories. I felt the Spirit strongly when she spoke, but I was too afraid to say anything. I began to feel remorse for some things I had done when I was younger, and my anger toward my father who had "ruined my life" disappeared as I heard about forgiveness and moving on. I also learned of God's great love for all mankind and about how He wants us to conduct our lives. It all made me feel so good, but fame and fortune were still at the top of my list.

I eventually visited Reeve in Zimbabwe. I felt something amazing in her home—a calm, warm feeling that was welcoming and peaceful. While there, I experienced, learned, watched, and felt. Family home evening was my favorite time. They enjoyed each other's company, shared spiritual thoughts, played, laughed, and were one big happy family. It was marvelous! During the first one I attended, Reeve's four-year-old niece was conducting and exclaimed, " . . . and CC is giving the opening prayer!" I panicked, not remembering having ever said a prayer before. I was saved when her three-year-old sister shouted, "No, I want to say it!" Little did I know there would also be a closing prayer. When I heard, "CC will say the closing prayer," I looked around for someone to rescue me. All I saw were folded arms and closed eyes. So I said my first prayer, amazed at the feeling that came over me as I did so.

I even attended the Mormon church and had to admit I began to enjoy it. Because I love children, I assisted in Primary on Sundays. I soon realized that the six- and seven-year-olds knew a lot more about God than I did. I began looking at life in a different light. Things seemed brighter. My past seemed to disappear as the anger I had inside slowly faded. I smiled more and became a kinder person.

When I returned to Norway, Reeve suggested that I invite the missionaries over for dinner. I enjoyed having them in my home and started attending church with them. I started to bless my food, say prayers, and keep the Sabbath day holy. My life was changing, and I wasn't sure how to deal with it. My mom eventually asked what I was up to. When I told her, her response was, "Well, Cecilie, I believe your head is on straight, so I will support whatever decision you make. I trust you." The rest of my family gave me a hard time, but Mom's words warmed and comforted my heart. How grateful I was for her!

One Friday morning, my stepfather called and told me to come quickly; something was seriously wrong with my mom. Within hours, she was on a respirator, unable to breathe by herself. After three days, she fell into a coma. My life was in turmoil. My mother, my best friend, was seriously ill, and I could do nothing!

During this time, I turned to the Lord. I had been taught about Heavenly Father. I had learned how kind He is and how we can always turn to Him since He always hears and answers our prayers. So I pleaded and prayed, begged and cried. I needed her here with me! I spent every day in the ICU, holding her hand and praying. I sang for her and told her how much I loved her. I also went to church and received blessings of comfort, and I prayed for hope. The doctors tried everything to help her, but nothing changed her condition. I prayed again and again for the Lord to grant me this one wish—to save my mother.

Then one day, as I knelt in prayer in my living room with Reeve, Laurette, and the sister missionaries, I knew that I had to let her go. With a broken heart and tears flowing down my cheeks, I told the Lord that if He really needed my mom more than I needed her, He could have her. The sobering reality hit me that my mother, whom I loved so dearly, was about to leave me! But instead of rage, my newfound knowledge of the restored gospel and its plan of salvation gave me a calm and peaceful feeling. I knew I would see her again one day. And so, four weeks after I received that terrifying phone call, I held my mother's hand as they turned off the respirator and she left us. She was fifty-seven years old, a victim of a brain aneurism.

I was mourning, I was distraught, and I felt lost in many ways. Yet I knew I had found the greatest joy in my life, the gospel of Jesus Christ. In this hard and humble time, I developed a strong testimony of the gospel—its power, its kindness, its perfectness. The Lord is always there when you need Him! I love Him! Two weeks after my mother's funeral, I was baptized—a day I will always remember.

Sadly, I lost contact with most of my remaining family when I joined the Church, due to their disapproval. I know that as I serve the Lord and become the example He needs me to be, things will improve with them over time. Meanwhile I was dedicated, obedient, and faithful. I worked on the things in my life that needed changing, and for the first time I felt peace, purpose, and a reason to live. I also found guidance and hope, and I found love and happiness in a completely different form. I loved being part of The Church of Jesus Christ of Latter-day Saints. Trials became easier, and I started welcoming challenges to my faith. I knew I had found the true church, and I knew I was happy. No one could take that away from me!

In July 2009 I went through the Stockholm Temple in Sweden and was sealed to my mother and father for time and all eternity, another day I will never forget. I knew then that the Lord's plan really is perfect. During my mother's illness, and while I was learning about the gospel, my heart and my mind changed—the way I looked at life, even the way I saw my father. We all have our struggles. We all make mistakes. And we all can turn to our Father in Heaven for help. Grandma Lundgreen was right. The Lord really is kind.

Now I live in a home filled with love, peace, happiness, laughter, and the Spirit of the Lord. Life has much more meaning when the Lord is the center of it! I am so grateful for my membership in The Church of Jesus Christ of Latter-day Saints and for what the gospel has brought to my life and what it teaches me daily. I might still travel from continent to continent as a professional golfer. I might still sign autographs and wave to a clapping crowd. But I do it with direction and purpose as a member of the Church and a representative of our Heavenly Father. I am proud to be His daughter.

LAURETTE MARITZ

Laurette Maritz, fondly known as Lolly, was born in Johannesburg, South Africa, in 1964. She began playing golf at age eleven and soon realized she wanted to play professionally. In spite of her small size, she became South Africa's top amateur golfer with a +2 handicap by the time she was seventeen, representing her country at tournaments throughout the world.

In 1983, she was offered a full golf scholarship in the United States at the International University in San Diego, California. During her time at the university, Laurette won numerous events and awards. The highlight of her college years was being presented with the United States Player of the Year award in 1987, making her the top collegiate player in the USA. She was inducted into the United States Hall of Fame as the first player to be chosen for the eight-player All American Team for four consecutive years while attending college. She graduated with a bachelor of arts in physical education in 1987.

In 1988, Laurette turned professional and joined the Ladies European Tour. She began by winning the Spanish Open, the first tournament she ever entered. Two weeks later she won the Portuguese Open. Subsequently, she has won numerous events worldwide and has had many top ten finishes on the Ladies

European Tour. She has been an example to many, including young aspiring golfers. Television commentators call her "the Lady of Golf."

To date Laurette has had eleven hole-in-one shots!

During her off-season, Laurette visits Zimbabwe, where she practices golf and enjoys the southern hemisphere's warm summer months. Her hobbies include playing squash (daily), making movies, going on safari, fishing, listening to music, and watching sports—especially rugby.

More than fifteen years ago, Laurette, together with her golf coach and manager, Reeve Nield, founded Eyes for Zimbabwe. This charity provides free cataract surgery to people of all ages by raising funds at charitable golf events for the medicines and supplies needed for these life-changing operations. Laurette personally packs and prepares the medicines and medical supplies for the eye camps and hospitals where volunteer ophthalmic surgeons operate, giving sight to an average of 120 patients in just five days.

Laurette feels blessed with her work, loves the people of Africa, and is willing to help anyone in need. She also loves the Lord and enjoys attending Mormon temples as she travels worldwide. Her favorite reading materials are her scriptures.

• • •

I CONSIDER IT A BLESSING and a privilege to have values and principles to guide me. Life is full of wonderful and not-so-wonderful experiences, and the gospel of Jesus Christ helps me to deal with unforeseen challenges. It gives hope, and hope is what we all need.

Certain challenges are put before us to strengthen us and prepare us for great things to come. I grew up in South Africa in a dysfunctional home with drugs, alcohol, and abuse. I did not know how to deal with this during my childhood and often wondered why a kind Heavenly Father would put me in such a family. But I always had faith that He would help my sisters and me. I remember one night hiding under my bed, fearing for our lives, pleading with Him to please protect us. I do believe that angels looked after us that night.

I was a dreamer as a child. I loved all kinds of sports and played most of them at school. At age eleven, I was introduced to golf and fell in love with it. I remember sitting at my desk in class, looking out the window and thinking about wanting a job that required me to be outdoors. I made up my mind at that moment to become a professional golfer. It was challenging because I was not very big, but I worked hard and got stronger and put all my energy and efforts into becoming the best I could be.

I nearly gave up when I was fifteen because I lost interest. My coach, who never really gave out compliments, said that I could not give up because I had too much talent. Having someone believe in me made the difference, and I started winning tournaments in my country. At age eighteen, I represented my country in the World Championships in Geneva, Switzerland.

Due to the travel involved, I did not receive a high school diploma. This bothered me because I knew that education is a key factor in life. Heavenly Father knew my desires and made a miracle come true for me. I was working at a golf course as an assistant in a pro shop. The Professional Golfers Association was having its championships at the course where I worked, and professional male golfers from all over the world were coming to compete. I thought it would be a wonderful opportunity to learn from these fine players.

One young man from California kept coming into the shop asking to leave his shoes or his golf balls there. When I mentioned the locker room upstairs, he admitted he wanted to ask me on a date. I said I would go on one condition: that he would play nine holes of golf with me and tell me if I were good enough to be a professional

golfer. We did, and he told me that I had a lot of talent and would one day make a fine professional. He also told me all about a university he attended on a golf scholarship, but I took no notice.

Later I received a phone call from a recruiter for the United States International University in San Diego, asking if I would be interested in a golf scholarship. I did not understand what that was. When he explained that I needed a high school diploma, my heart sank. I described my situation, and he said to take the SAT exam. I passed it and sent my portfolio to the university the scout had suggested.

The weekend my portfolio arrived, the golfer I had been on a date with was visiting his coach at her house and saw my portfolio on her table. He said, "You need to get her here! She's really good. I played nine holes with her!" Thanks to this divine intervention, the university offered me a full scholarship.

Upon arriving in the USA, I found the closest Mormon ward (congregation). I had been baptized at age thirteen, and I still remember how clean and elated I felt as I came out of the water knowing that my Heavenly Father loved me with a very special love. The

Church was something I wanted in my life, as the Lord had always walked by my side. I had attended LDS seminary in my teenage years, where my testimony of the gospel had grown.

During my four years of university, I won many college golf tournaments. I was the first woman in the history of collegiate golf to be a First Team All American for four consecutive years. I was ranked number one in the United States in 1987 and afterward was inducted into the hall of fame in San Diego.

My greatest achievement was receiving a bachelor of arts degree in physical education. I remember walking onto the podium feeling a sense of satisfaction that I had received my education not only in school but also in life. I learned that as I served the Lord, He would bless me. My peers knew that I was a Latter-day Saint, and I knew that I must live by gospel values and be a good example to those around me. My example eventually led to the baptism of my Swedish roommate. When the Lord says that He will pour His blessings upon us, He certainly keeps His promises. We also need to keep our promises to Him.

After graduating from university, I joined the Ladies European Tour as a professional. During my twenty-four seasons on the Tour, I have won ten tournaments worldwide, played in four World Cups, and traveled to many countries. I have had twenty-four seasons of absolute joy and success both on and off the golf course.

I met my golf coach, Reeve Nield, in 1994. She is also a Mormon and never does anything without asking for help from our Heavenly Father. Her example makes me want to live the gospel better. I have witnessed many miracles in our lives and in the lives of others while traveling every week with Reeve and another Mormon professional golfer, Cecilie Lundgreen. I did not serve a mission when I was younger, but I feel I am serving one now and feel honored to have such a great support group to lift and to love me. I love living the gospel and look forward to every opportunity to serve. As

Joseph Smith so aptly put it, "If you live up to your privileges, the angels cannot be constrained from being your associates."

Through Reeve and Cecilie, I am fortunate to be involved in a humanitarian project called Eyes for Zimbabwe. We felt inspired to start this organization in 1997 to perform free cataract operations for the blind. We assist in giving sight to approximately 4,000 Zimbabweans every year by raising money through golf to purchase medicines and medical supplies. Each time a person receives his or her eyesight, it is truly a miracle! And when an older person receives eyesight, the child responsible for caring for that person can then attend school and enjoy a normal life.

One elderly lady who regained her eyesight after ten years of blindness sang us a tribal song of thanks. It brought tears to my eyes. A song was what she had to give. As she sang from the depths of her heart in gratitude for getting her life back, I thought of how we need to be grateful for the blessings the Lord gives us and to share with others those things we hold dear to our hearts. What would have happened to her if we had not listened to the inspiration we received to serve the people of Zimbabwe?

The Lord inspires us so that we can make a difference in this world. Using the talents He has given us to touch the hearts and lives of others and to serve with all our hearts and minds is a privilege. I am grateful to a loving Heavenly Father who gave me trials in my early years to strengthen me so I could help other people. Let us live our lives with no regrets and with the energy to give others a future to look forward to.

Why am I a Mormon?

- Because I love the Lord with all my heart, and it makes me happy when I do right by Him. It gives me peace in my heart, and I know that when I serve others, I am serving God.

- Because our prophet and apostles live as they ask us to live, as examples of Christlike love and service. I have met and listened to President Thomas S. Monson, and I know he is truly the Lord's prophet who receives revelation for the Lord's children all over the earth. He is wise; he is inspired; and he is full of love.
- Because this church is the only one that has the priesthood of God, the authority to act on His behalf.
- Because God has encircled me with His love throughout my life. When I need direction, I go down on my knees to ask Him, and He answers me.
- Because being a Mormon has taught me to forgive. I have forgiven my parents for what they did to my sisters and me when we were children. If I am not willing to forgive, how can I in turn ask for forgiveness?
- I love life and the challenges that come with it. I am grateful to know that the reason we are on this earth is to learn from our experiences, to serve others with great passion and care, and to love without hesitation.

All in all, I love being a Mormon!

J. W. MARRIOTT JR.

J.W. MARRIOTT JR. is chairman and chief executive officer of Marriott International, Inc. His leadership, spanning over fifty years, has taken Marriott from a family restaurant business to a global lodging company with more than 3,700 properties in seventy countries and territories.

Mr. Marriott's vision for the company is grounded in his intense focus on taking care of the guest. He is also known for his hands-on management style, which has produced a culture that recognizes the value individuals bring to the organization. This "spirit to serve" culture is based on the business philosophy of his parents, J. Willard and Alice S. Marriott: "Take care of the associate, and they'll take care of the guest." Marriott International has consistently been on *Fortune*'s lists of most admired companies, best places to work, and top companies for minorities.

As a youth, Mr. Marriott developed a passion for the family business and worked in its restaurant chain during high school and college. He joined the company full-time in 1956 and soon took over management of Marriott's first hotel. He became executive vice president of the company, then its president, in 1964. He was later elected CEO (1972) and chairman of the board (1985).

Regarded as a lodging innovator, Mr. Marriott began shifting the company from hotel ownership to property management and franchising in the late 1970s, a transformation that accelerated its growth and culminated in the company's split into Marriott International, a hotel management and franchising company, and Host Marriott International, a hotel ownership company chaired by his younger brother, Richard Marriott.

Mr. Marriott currently serves on the board of The J. Willard & Alice S. Marriott Foundation and is a member of the National Business Council and the Executive Committee of the World Travel & Tourism Council. He has also served on the board of trustees of the National Geographic Society, as director of the United States Naval Academy Foundation, as chairman of the President's Export Council (PEC), and as a member of the Secure Borders Open Doors Advisory Committee (SBODAC) and the U.S. Travel and Tourism Advisory Board (TTAB). He recently served as chairman of the Mayo Clinic Capital Campaign.

Mr. Marriott earned a BS degree in banking and finance from the University of Utah and served as an officer in the United States Navy. He is married to the former Donna Garff. They have four children, fifteen grandchildren, and six great-grandchildren.

• • •

WHEN I WAS VERY YOUNG, my father and I left our home in Washington, D.C., to visit his boyhood home on a small farm west of Ogden, Utah. We walked over the dry and barren fields, past the irrigation ditch where he had learned to swim, and through the old brick farmhouse where he had lived. He told me about growing up there and about his parents' hard work as they struggled to raise eight children with few resources.

He also told me about his grandmother Elizabeth Stewart, who had sailed from Liverpool, England, to America in 1851. She was only nineteen years old when she arrived here. She had no money and hardly any clothing, but she went to work in St. Louis and saved enough money to buy provisions for her journey west. She joined a Mormon handcart company and pulled her handcart across the plains and over the mountains to the valley of the Great Salt Lake. When she arrived, she had no place to live, no job, and no hope of finding one. She went from door to door looking for work. Finally, someone took her in and offered to feed and house her if she would take care of their children and do the housework.

Later she met John Marriott. They were married and raised eight children who had been left motherless when his first wife had died; in addition, they had nine children together. When I asked my father why Elizabeth left England and came to America to endure such hardships and suffering, he said it was because she had joined our church and had a firm conviction that it was true. She wanted to be with other Church members where she could worship without persecution.

As I grew up attending an eastern prep school, I was frequently called upon to defend my religion to those classmates who made fun of it. I often thought about Elizabeth Stewart and her sacrifice for her beliefs. As I defended my church, I too came to believe it was true. To strengthen my convictions, I studied and tried to learn more about our teachings and doctrines. The more I learned and prayed about them, the more convinced I was that the church into which I had been born was indeed the Church of Jesus Christ.

When I graduated from prep school, I did not follow my classmates to the Ivy League but returned to my roots and attended the University of Utah. There I met and married a beautiful LDS girl, Donna Garff. We were married in the Salt Lake Temple and were promised that we would be together for eternity if we were faithful.

After serving for two years in the U.S. Navy (I was unable to serve a mission for our church, as the Korean War was in progress and no missionaries were being called), I returned to Washington and went to work in the family business. Soon our first child, Debbie, was born, and within a few weeks the doctors advised us that she had a serious congenital heart defect. It was 1957, and the doctors at the Mayo Clinic were just beginning to work with a new heart-lung machine. We were told that someday, perhaps, Debbie could be healed through open-heart surgery, but we should wait for the surgery as long as possible.

Finally, in 1962, Debbie became quite weak; she could not walk very far, and her lips were blue from lack of oxygen. The doctors said it was time to operate. We took Debbie to Mayo. She was given a priesthood blessing of healing that she would survive the operation and her heart would be healed. However, two days following the surgery, her little heart began to fail. As the doctors worked on her through the night, Donna and I stayed on our knees in prayer.

When we called the nurses' station at 4:00 A.M., we learned that Debbie had been close to death but somehow had rallied. Her heart was beating strongly and with a normal rhythm. We knew that our prayers had been answered and that the special blessing she had received had provided the needed power to heal her. Today she is the mother of five grown children and a grandmother of two. Her husband is a local Church leader (stake president) and all of her sons have served missions. Debbie served with her husband, Ron, when he was mission president in the Belgium Brussels Mission. That little five-year-old girl with not much chance of survival now runs our Government Affairs program at Marriott. Her miraculous healing was another experience that continued to prove to me that God lives and answers prayers.

In 1972, when Donna and I were busy raising our children, I was made chief executive officer of our company. Two years later, I was called to serve as the bishop of the Chevy Chase Ward in Washington—an unpaid position as minister over a flock of several hundred souls. My previous Church positions had been far less

demanding, and I felt inadequate for this new calling. However, my primary concern was where I would find the time to carry out my new assignment. I was working eighty hours a week, and any time left was for the family and a small Church assignment. But I accepted my new position and somehow found what typically amounted to an additional thirty hours per week to carry out my responsibilities.

Serving as a bishop was, perhaps, the most faith-promoting experience of my life. I performed marriages, conducted funerals, helped struggling families, and counseled teenagers with problems. I also worked to help an impoverished group of Hispanic members who somehow managed to pay a full tithe (10 percent of their income). Often, when they would make their $5.00 weekly contribution, I had difficulty holding back the tears. I soon realized that I was able to find the time to fulfill my calling because my Heavenly Father opened the way for me.

Some years later, when I was starting up an old boat and turned the key to see if the tanks were full, there was a terrible explosion. I was on fire, and I jumped into the lake to put it out. I had third-degree burns on my hands and on my legs. While at the hospital, I was given a priesthood blessing that promised I would survive the burns and that I wouldn't be disfigured. It also said there was a purpose in what had happened to me.

When you're lying in the hospital writhing in pain, to have someone say there is a purpose in it is hard to understand. However, fifteen years later, I was asked to participate in an interview with Mike Wallace for a *60 Minutes* program about the Church. Mr. Wallace asked me specifically if I attended church and why I believed in God. I told him about surviving the fire. I attributed my survival to the fact that I had been given a priesthood blessing and was told that I would survive. I had faith in that blessing and was able to bear my testimony to that effect. Afterward I remembered the part of the blessing that had said there was a purpose in the accident. I realized that I had just been given the opportunity to bear my testimony on national television to 30 million people that God lives and that Jesus is the Christ and that we are blessed when we're faithful.

My membership and activity in our church has provided me with balance and stability. It has been an anchor in a busy and sometimes overwhelming life. Through the example of many righteous people as well as through my own study and Church service, I have learned for myself that God lives and Jesus is the Christ. I have also learned that prayers are answered—perhaps not always in the way we would prefer, but they are answered. Above all, I know that life does not end with mortal death and that obedient Latter-day Saints married in the holy temple of the Lord will enjoy eternal life with their families.

Because of our family's membership, activity, and commitment to our church, we have enjoyed happiness beyond measure. The Church of Jesus Christ of Latter-day Saints has been the greatest blessing in my life.

KIETH W. MERRILL

KIETH W. MERRILL is a filmmaker, director, writer, and producer. A member of the Academy of Motion Picture Arts and Sciences and the Director's Guild of America, he has received an Academy Award (*The Great American Cowboy,* 1974) and additional nominations for an Oscar (*Amazon,* 1998) and an Emmy (*The Wild West,* 1993).

Mr. Merrill pioneered the commercial large-screen cinema industry. His Grand Canyon Imax Theater and film project introduced the concept now known as "destination cinema." His film *Grand Canyon—The Hidden Secrets* is one of the twenty-five most successful independent films in history and was the first film to be inducted into the Imax Hall of Fame. His other "destination film" projects include the Niagara Falls Imax Theater, Canada; Imax at River Center, San Antonio, Texas; and a large-screen film for the Polynesian Cultural Center in Laie, Hawaii. He also created the films *Legacy* and *The Testaments,* which run continuously at special venue theaters around the world.

Among Mr. Merrill's other successful works are *Olympic Glory,* the first Imax-format film of the Olympic Winter Games; *Yellowstone,* an Imax-format film for the Grizzly Bear Park Theater at West Yellowstone, Montana; *Treasure of the Gods,* an Imax-format film at Zion National Park; *Ozarks Legacy and Legends* in Branson, Missouri; *Passion of Life* for Valencia, California's Imax Dome; and *San Francisco Adventure* for the Cinemax Theater at Pier 39 in San Francisco.

Mr. Merrill is a founder of Audience Alliance Motion Picture Studios, which is currently developing several feature films including an Imax-format film at the Great Wall of China. He has served as a member of the board of trustees of Southern Virginia University and is past president of the Brigham Young University Alumni Association. He is a recent recipient of the Brigham Young University Distinguished Alumni Award.

Kieth Merrill, who grew up on a farm and loves country music, is a cowboy at heart. He is married to his college sweetheart, the former Dagny Johnson. They reside in the Sierra foothills of California's gold country, have been married forty-four years, and have eight children and thirty-three grandchildren.

• • •

I AM A MORMON BECAUSE . . .
I was born in a small, rural town in Utah to a mother whose great-grandfather was a friend of the Prophet Joseph Smith and to a father who shared a legacy of faith with pioneer ancestors and the bloodline of apostles, prophets, and patriarchs.

Because . . . I was baptized at the age of accountability and given the gift of the Holy Ghost. On that day I became an official member of The Church of Jesus Christ of Latter-day Saints, "the Mormons."

Because . . . Until the second grade at Farmington Elementary School, I thought everybody in the world was a Mormon. When I discovered Betty McDaniels was something called a "Catholic," I began a journey of religious curiosity, inquiry, study, and contemplation that has defined my life.

I am a Mormon because . . .

Mormons believe in the Bible and embrace all that is good in all other churches, circumscribing all truth into one great whole.

Because . . . For Mormons, the story of Jesus in the New Testament does not end with the Crucifixion but focuses—with an understanding enlightened by revelation—on where He went after he spoke to Mary at the tomb and what significant things happened during the forty days He spent with His Apostles after His return to earth as a resurrected being.

Because . . . Traditional Christianity is tarnished by an unholy history of apostasy, corruption, and horrific campaigns of violence carried out in the shadow of the cross. The Church of Jesus Christ of Latter-day Saints is the only Christian church that escapes the disturbing legacy of power, politics, and perversions during the Dark Ages.

Because . . . Mormonism (so-called) is the reestablished church of Jesus Christ brought back to the earth by divine manifestations in the early nineteenth century.

I am a Mormon because . . .

I believe Joseph Smith Jr. was a prophet in league with Abraham, Moses, and Elijah. I believe he received divine revelation. I believe he translated an ancient record by the gift and power of God. I know by my own experience and through the analysis by Mormon scholars more gifted than I that Joseph Smith did not originate the Book of Mormon nor plagiarize it from some mysterious source—an enigma that demands serious consideration. It is 531 pages of religious history in the context of ancient cultures, recorded by two dozen writers, and compiled over the course of one thousand years. It has withstood the onslaught of critics for nearly two hundred years.

Because . . . I feel linked to Joseph Smith in uncommon ways. My great-great-grandfather William Holmes Walker lived with Joseph and his wife, Emma, as part of their family. Of Joseph, Great-grandpa Walker said, *"The more extensive my acquaintance and experience with him the more my confidence increased in him."* Sometime in the summer of 1842, William recorded in his journal, *"The Urim and Thummim were placed in my charge for a time and many other important trusts were confided to me which I am happy to say were held sacred to myself."* William H. Walker was an honorable and honest man who spoke the truth.

I am a Mormon because . . .

I cannot comprehend a God that was invented and reinvented by men over the course of a hundred years of compromising councils that began a few hundred years after the death of Jesus Christ.

Because . . . The Church of Jesus Christ of Latter-day Saints is the only Christian church that does not cling to the creeds of men but understands the true nature, distinct personage, and majesty of God the Father, His Son Jesus Christ, and the Holy Ghost. They revealed themselves by direct and personal revelation to the Prophet Joseph Smith.

Because . . . John wrote, "And this is life eternal, that they might know thee the only true God, and Jesus Christ, whom thou hast sent" (John 17:3), and it is only within the doctrines of Mormonism that I have been able to find them.

I am a Mormon because . . .

The doctrines of Mormonism answer the four most important questions we can ask, and they do so with clarity, authority, scriptural verity, and the witness of the Holy Ghost.

Who am I?

Where did I come from?

What is the purpose of my life?

What happens when I die?

Because . . . Ours is the only Christian church patterned after the ancient order established by Jesus with twelve apostles, along with seventies, pastors (bishops), and evangelists (missionaries).

Because . . . That pattern, now a worldwide church, is miraculous. The fact that it functions on principles of service and sacrifice without paid or professional clergy is evidence of divine direction.

Because . . . The Mormon church is the only church with claim to the Melchizedek Priesthood after the holy order of the Son of God in a clear, unbroken chain of ordination.

Because . . . It is the only Christian church with temples where members can participate in sacred ordinances and make covenants consistent with the timeless order established by God.

Because . . . Only in a Mormon temple was I able to marry my darling wife "for time and all eternity" rather than "until death do you part."

Because . . . Life as a Mormon is about as good as life can get in all the things that matter. The pattern for living, emphasis on family, laws of health, service to others, and consistent encouragement to be kind, helpful, charitable, unselfish, forgiving, loving, and virtuous while endeavoring to follow the example of Jesus is a wonderful way to spend the only mortal life God has granted us.

Because . . . Raising children in the confidence of everlasting family associations amplifies love in our lifetime and adds joyous expectations for our everlasting lives beyond the grave.

Because . . . Members, teachers, and leaders have been and are an extension of our family in raising our eight children and thirty-three grandchildren.

Because . . . I am part of a worldwide brotherhood and sister-hood of members that is impossible to describe to one who has never experienced what Jesus meant when He said, "As I have loved you, . . . love one another" (John 13:34).

I am a Mormon because . . .

In a lifetime of study I have never found—beyond the boundaries of Mormon doctrine—an acceptable theology, philosophy, doctrine, ideology, or scientific explanation for the universe, the origins of life, the purpose of existence, or what happens when we die. None that I have considered comes close to the logic, symmetry, and sensibility of the doctrines, scripture, and revelations of The Church of Jesus Christ of Latter-day Saints.

Because . . . I believe God is the same yesterday, today, and for-ever. Therefore, I believe He continues to reveal His will to prophets. I have the great privilege of knowing most of the men called to serve as prophets, seers, and revelators in our time—the First Presidency and Quorum of the Twelve Apostles who lead the Church by the inspiration and revelation of heaven. They are brilliant. They are sanctified by service. They astound me. I trust them. They are spe-cial witnesses of Jesus Christ in the world.

Because . . . The Lord has said, "To some it is given by the Holy Ghost to know that Jesus Christ is the Son of God, and that he was crucified for the sins of the world. To others it is given to believe on their words, that they also might have eternal life if they continue faithful" (Doctrine and Covenants 46:13–14).

I am twice blessed. It is given to me to believe on the words of apostles, prophets, and others who know that Jesus is the Son of

God by the power of the Holy Ghost. Their voices resound and the Spirit burns the truth of their testimonies into my soul. I also know by a personal witness of the Holy Ghost that Jesus is the Christ.

Because . . . Within the scriptures, revelations, and doctrines of Mormonism I have found my belief in Jesus Christ and an abiding faith in His matchless life and the infinite virtue of His atoning sacrifice. I believe He is the Son of God, that He died for us, and by His grace and Atonement we shall live forever and be given the opportunity of eternal life. Because I am a Mormon and a student of the fullness of the gospel reestablished by Christ Himself, I am blessed to understand Him in all His majesty as Firstborn Son of God, Creator, Jehovah, the Only Begotten, Messiah, Jesus, Savior, and Redeemer of the world.

I am a Mormon because . . .

Any of the reasons given above are sufficient cause for membership, adherence, and participation in the Mormon church. Taken together and validated by a lifetime of experience, it is impossible to imagine any other course.

I am a Mormon because . . .

I believe that The Church of Jesus Christ of Latter-day Saints embraces the fullness of the gospel of Jesus Christ.

This hope in "things which are not seen, which are true" (Alma 32:21) brings a joyous confidence in the purpose of our lives and enlivens each precious day of our sojourn here.

JOY MONAHAN

JOY MAGELSSEN MONAHAN was born and raised in Hawaii. She started surfing at the age of eight. At thirteen, she began surfing competitively and still loves to do so. Her surfing achievements include two Hawaii state championships, two national championships, and being named the 2008 ASP Women's World Longboard Champion.

In 2006, Joy married her high school sweetheart, Drew Monahan. She graduated from Brigham Young University–Provo in 2010 with a bachelor's degree in accounting. She and Drew currently live in Hawaii and love spending time with their first child, Jackson, who was born in August 2011.

• • •

FROM THE BEGINNING, surfing has been a special part of my life. My father taught my three sisters and me to surf when we were young, and as I grew, my love for the ancient Hawaiian sport grew. I spent as much time in the water as I could. Since the day I told my mom I would rather go surfing than go to soccer practice, I haven't looked back. I started surfing up to six days a week and eventually began competing in local and national competitions. By all accounts, I was a "surfer."

If you had asked me then if surfing was in any way related to my religious beliefs, I might have told you that I was a Mormon who happened to surf and that no correlation whatsoever existed. If you were to ask me that question now, however, I would tell you that I am a Mormon first and foremost. I would also say that surfing has helped me become a better Mormon than I otherwise would have been. Three lessons I learned from surfing have solidified the way I think about my membership in The Church of Jesus Christ of Latter-day Saints: knowing what my priorities are, keeping the proper perspective so that I can keep those priorities in order, and having the faith to allow God's hand to guide and nurture me. These three lessons have continually taught me why I am a Mormon.

The summer before my freshman year of high school, I decided I wanted to start competing in local surf competitions. My sisters and I would have small, private, friendly surfing competitions among ourselves, and the competitiveness was something that I enjoyed. My sisters would tell you that I was overly competitive; my sense is that those competitions were preparing me for official competitions to come.

My father recognized how important surfing was to me. He also knew how detrimental it could be for someone my age to devote too much time to only one thing. He decided to assemble our family in our living room for one of the most important meetings I have ever attended. The topic was my decision to surf competitively. He taught me the importance of priorities. He told me that church, family, and school came before surfing. I would need to attend church meetings, do my chores, and get good grades in order to have the privilege of surfing on weekdays. This is the first lesson that taught me why I am a Mormon. He wanted to make sure my life priorities were in order if I wanted to surf competitively. I am a Mormon because my father taught me the proper priorities.

That day, my dad helped to strengthen my testimony of Jesus Christ by teaching me the importance of putting my Savior first. He also set up a structure that allowed me to realize the blessings of the gospel. There were times when it would have been much easier to switch my priorities and put surfing first. At these times, however, I remembered the important lesson taught by countless scriptures and summed up by Elder Neal A. Maxwell, one of the Apostles of our church: "If you have not chosen the kingdom of God first, it will in the end make no difference what you have chosen instead." I learned that I was not as happy when I lost sight of the priorities my dad set out for me.

It was during that first summer of competing that I learned two things in such a clear and concrete way that I have never forgotten them. First, I realized that my Heavenly Father and my family are more important than anything else. Second, I learned that I *love* to compete. As the summer's contests ended, I wrote in my journal that I wanted to become a world champion surfer. I had no idea how closely intertwined my goal and these two lessons would become.

Over the years, surfing provided me with some great experiences, all of which were enhanced because of my faith and the lessons I had learned about priorities. I was able to compete and travel all over the world. Still, after eight years of competing, my ultimate goal of becoming a World Champ eluded me. I had participated in the World Championships but had always come up short.

In 2006, I married my high school sweetheart, and we decided to attend Brigham Young University in Provo, Utah. At this point, I thought my surfing days were over. I felt okay with it because I knew I was putting family and education first. I quickly realized, though, that my Heavenly Father was mindful of my desires. I was able to continue competing during the summer months that we spent back

home in Hawaii. In 2007, I went to France to compete in the World Championships and again fell short of my longtime goal, placing fifth.

In 2008, I was working on getting accepted into the accounting program at BYU. I realized I would need to stay in Utah for spring semester in order to finish the prerequisites for when I applied that fall. The semester would end just two weeks before the World Championships in France. I could either focus on school and not worry about the contest or work really hard and try to do both. I chose the latter.

My husband and I spent that semester running between the accounting lab and the gym. I knew I couldn't waste any time or I wouldn't be prepared. When the semester ended, I had ten short days to practice after having surfed only a handful of times over the past eight months. At this point I began to understand the meaning of this scripture: "Therefore . . . let us cheerfully do all things that lie in our power; and then may we stand still, with the utmost assurance, to see the salvation of God, and for his arm to be revealed" (Doctrine and Covenants 123:17). I had prioritized my life correctly; I had done all things that lay in my power (as cheerfully as one could when learning accounting!); and I was able to "stand still, with the utmost assurance" that my Heavenly Father would bless me with what He saw fit.

Time seemed to fly once I got to Biarritz, France. The night before the quarterfinal heats, I was still in the competition. That night, surfing taught me the second lesson that makes me a better Mormon. While I was saying a simple prayer of thanks, I learned the lesson of perspective. I was thanking my Heavenly Father for allowing me to surf well enough to make it this close to my childhood goal. I had been working hard for so many years to achieve this goal, but I was afraid that winning could change who I had become. In that prayer, I asked Heavenly Father to help me maintain perspective. I wanted to be a Mormon first, and then a surfer. I didn't want to win and accomplish my goal if it meant giving up my perspective on life and losing what is most important. I am a Mormon because of a simple prayer that put things in the appropriate perspective.

When the final buzzer sounded, the announcer was yelling, "Joy Monahan is the 2008 Longboarding World Champion!" I remember each detail of that great moment. Most of all, I remember how grateful I was that I knew Heavenly Father wanted this for me. He trusted that I would maintain the proper perspective after achieving such a lofty goal. Later that same day, I found out that I had also been accepted into the accounting program at BYU. That was one of the best Tuesdays of my life!

After that summer, I thought I had it all nailed down: Maintain your priorities, keep things in perspective, and your childhood dreams will come true. It is as simple as that! I am glad to say that I was mistaken. While keeping priorities and maintaining perspective are great lessons, they do not guarantee that our goals will be achieved.

That brings us to the third lesson that I learned from surfing, perhaps the most important of the three. I think this lesson is best explained by Elder Hugh B. Brown, another Apostle: "God is the gardener here. He knows what He wants you to be." I am a Mormon because I have strived to allow God to be the gardener.

I learned this lesson one short year after achieving my goal. I was working on becoming the first female to win back-to-back World Championships while also trying to get the grades to get into the masters of accounting program at BYU. This time I was more prepared for the contest than the year before. I was able to go home to Hawaii after winter semester, giving me two and a half months to practice my surfing instead of just two weeks. I had my priorities straight. I had things in perspective.

I traveled all the way to France and lost in the very first round, my worst showing at a World Championship. Then, not too long after, I found out that I was not accepted into the master's program. Needless to say, that summer was not as fun as the previous one.

I thought I had done everything I needed to do in order to achieve success. I thought, *If there is anything in my life that I have control over, it has to be surfing.* I had been surfing since I was eight; surely I could determine my own success. I forgot only one thing. I forgot that God is the gardener. He knows what He wants me to be, better than I myself know. He knew that winning and getting into the program were not what I needed at the time.

If I were not Mormon, I might have taken these failures (however small they might be) as signs that God was not concerned with my success. Luckily, being a Mormon has prepared me to understand these failures. I know what I saw as failure was actually my Heavenly Father shaping me to become a better version of myself.

Although I do love to surf and compete, I don't let being a surfer define who I am. I am a Mormon first, and only then a surfer. I am a Mormon because every time I have followed correct principles, I have seen God's hand revealed in my life. I rest assured that God is in charge. He knows what He wants me to be.

BRANDON MULL

BRANDON MULL is the #1 *New York Times* bestselling author of the *Beyonders* and *Fablehaven* series. Ever since C. S. Lewis's Narnia books inspired his love of reading as a child, he has spent much of his life crafting fantasy adventure stories that children and parents can enjoy together.

Millions of copies of his books are now in print. *Fablehaven* has been published in twenty-seven languages.

Brandon served an LDS mission to Chile from 1994 to 1996 and graduated from Brigham Young University in 2000. He currently resides in Utah with his wife and four children.

• • •

SINCE THE TIME I GREW old enough to wonder about the meaning of life, I've had a strong desire to find answers. Is God really there? Does He care about me? Is there more to mortality than being born, reacting to stimuli, and dying? I was taught by my parents that God is real and that He loves me, but I wasn't willing to believe blindly. I didn't have a lot of interest in just pretending that God was real.

I knew there might not be any definitive answers. It could all be relative. Life might only hold as much meaning as we each decide to impose. Then again, what if concrete truths are awaiting those willing to seek them? What if an actual God exists who has created everything for a reason? Either way, I wanted to explore the possibilities and discover as much as I could.

I had some reasons to suspect that God might exist. It was hard for me to imagine a universe as orderly as ours without an architect. Left to itself, it seemed to me that the cosmos should be a meaningless void: no matter, no energy, no space, no particles, no natural laws. Let alone vast systems of stars and planets. Let alone the infinitesimal complexity of atoms and molecules. Let alone life. Let alone intelligent life.

I also found it interesting that so many people throughout history had professed to see God or communicate with Him. In the scriptures, individuals testified that they had interacted with angels. Signs and wonders had supposedly followed certain ardent believers. Observers had documented the miracles that Christ performed. And although many of these witnesses were hated and even faced death for their testimonies, they did not back down. That didn't seem like the behavior of liars.

My parents also seemed convinced that God was real based on personal experience. Many other friends and relatives felt likewise.

None of this evidence really proved anything, but it motivated me to keep exploring my questions with an open mind. I wanted God to be real. I wanted life to have meaning. I wanted my existence to continue beyond this life. I wanted my loved ones to continue existing with me. But I didn't want to fool myself. I wanted to find the truth of the matter.

This is where my religion became helpful. My parents are members of The Church of Jesus Christ of Latter-day Saints, commonly called the Mormons. My dad joined the faith in high school, and although my mom was born into the religion, her immediate family didn't take it very seriously until around the time she reached high school as well.

At church I always heard that God is living and real. My religion didn't talk about God as somebody who used to communicate with humankind thousands of years ago and had now become silent. He also wasn't discussed like a personage from a fairy tale who lived long ago and far away. I wasn't told I had to place all my trust in some specific preacher or even in the words in the Bible. My teachers and parents claimed that just as God spoke to prophets in the past, He still speaks to prophets in our day. They emphasized that since God is really there and really cares about us, anyone with enough faith and sincerity could reach out to God and get answers. Anyone could learn for themselves that He exists—straight from the source.

Thirteen articles of faith summarize the beliefs of The Church of Jesus Christ of Latter-day Saints. One of my favorites is the ninth: "We believe all that God has revealed, all that He does now reveal, and we believe that He will yet reveal many great and important things pertaining to the Kingdom of God."

I don't think a religion that views God as inaccessible could have motivated me even to try to believe in Him. If God had spoken to humankind for centuries, as described in the Bible, guiding people with both their immediate problems and their more far-reaching spiritual issues, why would He stop? God either exists or He doesn't. He either interacts with humankind or He doesn't. Would a perfect, all-knowing Being change? Would He take a break? Biblically, God only stopped responding to nations and individuals when they turned away from Him. My religion assured me that the best way to learn of the reality of God is to ask Him directly. I had the same right to know for myself as any ancient figure in the Bible.

This idea appealed to me, partly because I had doubts. What if God were a myth? What if the Bible were fiction? What if people had lied about miracles and angels and such? What if believers were

simply good people deluded into sincerely believing a comforting lie? Could religion exist only to offer consolation to the doomed citizens of an uncaring universe? Any of these doubts seemed plausible. But if God told me directly that He lived, then I'd know with surety that I should learn more about Him. If prolonged attempts to communicate with Him yielded nothing, I'd eventually have a pretty good reason to stop trying.

Plenty of scriptures encouraged me that if I asked I could receive, if I sought I could find, if I drew near to God He would draw near to me. And it made sense that we could only know God through revelation. Guessing or wishing or imagining would be useless. For humankind to know God with any confidence, He would have to reveal His existence to witnesses, like the prophets of the Bible. For an individual to fully trust those witnesses, he or she would need some kind of personal, recognizable confirmation that the testimonies were valid.

My answer didn't come all at once. I read the scriptures. I pondered what I read. And I prayed. I prayed sincerely, on my own, asking straightforward questions as if I were actually talking to somebody. At times I felt a confirming feeling in response to certain questions, especially when I asked God if He were real and if He loved me. At their strongest, these answers were felt both physically and emotionally.

Over the years I have received a lot of help from God. I have brought Him problems in personal prayer, and sometimes He has answered, especially when I asked earnestly and the need was great. He has confirmed certain choices I have made. Twice He has nudged me to change major decisions I had made, to my benefit. He has brought me comfort and a quiet certainty that death is not the end of existence.

I have never seen angels. But I have felt answers so strongly that I am certain God exists. I have had many experiences where I've been absolutely positive the communication was more than wishful thinking. I feel strongly that anyone who seeks God diligently and sincerely can achieve the same knowledge. I can't prove what I know, but I do urge anybody who wonders to experiment and prove it to themselves.

Why am I a Mormon? I'm a Mormon because the way I was taught to communicate with God works. I'm not sure I could believe in a religion that offered less than a personal relationship with my Heavenly Father.

Mormons believe that the accounts in the Bible are true. Those records tell mostly of God's dealings with the descendants of Abraham in the Middle East thousands of years ago. We also believe that God interacted with some of the ancient inhabitants of the Americas, and that some of those records were compiled into the Book of Mormon. This book of ancient scripture was translated by a modern prophet, Joseph Smith, less than two hundred years ago. Like the Bible, the Book of Mormon testifies of Christ and lets us know some of what God expects from us. We believe the Book of Mormon was prepared for our day to serve as a confirming witness that the Bible is true and that Jesus Christ really is the Son of God and our Savior.

Either the Book of Mormon is a true account of prophets receiving revelation in the Americas, or Joseph Smith or other unknown parties somehow made it up. I write fiction for a living. I've read the book several times, and I can't see how anyone could have made up the Book of Mormon, let alone a young, relatively uneducated farmer over two hundred years ago. The book is complex, deep, wise, and good. The book bears powerful witness of God and Christ and clarifies some of the doctrines that seem open to interpretation if one is relying solely on the Bible. It feels authentic. But most important, the book invites readers to ask God if it is true. I did. It is.

The point of this essay is not to explain everything that Mormons believe. But I can say we believe that God is alive, that anyone can talk to Him, that He continues giving the world evidence of His existence through recent and living prophets and apostles, and that after years of prayer, study, and personal revelation, I sincerely believe this is true.

I can also say that I enjoy how Mormons live. We place a huge emphasis on family and relationships. One of my favorite quotes from a modern prophet is, "No success in life can compensate for failure in the home." Think how much better our world would be if everyone believed and lived that simple statement!

Mormons value free will. Many of the commandments we follow help protect our ability to remain in control of our choices. It is a big part of why we avoid drugs, alcohol, and tobacco. We even avoid some mildly addictive drinks like coffee and tea. It's also why we're counseled to avoid excessive debt and gambling.

Mormons are searching for lasting happiness. We try to base our joy on meaningful relationships with friends and family and on a real relationship with God. We try to give service and treat others how we would want to be treated. Even if I didn't believe this church was true, I would know from experience that the commandments we live help people avoid a lot of the pitfalls that can interrupt happiness.

Sometimes when I'm on the road as an author and people hear that I'm Mormon, they ask about polygamy. Having multiple wives has not been allowed in The Church of Jesus Christ of Latter-day Saints for a long time. In the early days of our church, God asked some of the members to live that law for a time. Before anybody throws too many stones at us for it, keep in mind that all Christians, Jews, and Muslims revere prophets who had multiple wives, such as Abraham, Isaac, and Jacob. I'm glad the law existed anciently, because it makes it seem a little less weird to me that some of the pioneers in our church felt God asked them to live like that for a time.

Those are a few basics about why I'm a Mormon. Nobody in our church is perfect, especially me, but I've found that Mormons who are trying to live their religion tend to be good friends, helpful neighbors, devoted Christians, and sincere believers in God.

REEVE A. NIELD

REEVE ALLISON NIELD is a professional golf coach on the Ladies European Tour. For the past eighteen years, she has assisted players like Laurette Maritz, South Africa's top women's golf professional. Many of Reeve's golfers have gone on to achieve great success on various professional golf tours world-wide. Reeve explains, "If I believe they can, one day *they* will believe they can—and they *will!*"

She was born in Salisbury, Rhodesia (now Harare, Zimbabwe), the fourth of six daughters of Reginald Joseph Nield, a Rhodesian sports hero, and his wife, Iris Merle Nield (née Devine). Sports were a major focus in the home of the two-time captain of Rhodesia's national rugby team, so Reeve was a natural in her youth. She represented her school in swimming, field hockey, basketball, tennis, and squash.

At nineteen, Reeve embraced fast-pitch softball and represented Zimbabwe at the World Series in the USA and in numerous other international events. At the peak of her softball career, her pitching was observed by a golf coach who decided that if she could throw a ball with that strength and speed, she could certainly hit one. Reeve was introduced to golf, and "two lessons and eight blisters later I was hooked!"

In 1992–1993, Reeve was privileged to serve a full-time mission for The Church of Jesus Christ of Latter-day Saints in the Utah Provo Mission.

In 1996, Reeve and Laurette Maritz founded Eyes for Zimbabwe after meeting a twelve-year-old girl who had been blinded with bilateral cataracts for four years. Twenty U.S. dollars for medical supplies and a fifteen-minute operation restored the girl's sight. Reeve realized that, with the necessary supplies, thousands of people could be relieved of the same debilitating infirmity. Eyes for Zimbabwe (www.canon.no/e4z) sponsors golf events to raise money worldwide to purchase the much-needed medicines and medical supplies, annually restoring sight to more than four thousand cataract patients of all ages.

Reeve's hobbies include family, sports, photography, cooking, fishing, and helping others along their way.

• • •

M Y PARENTS, REG AND IRIS NIELD, were each raised by religious mothers who taught them to pray. Once married, they felt an urgency to find a religion for their own young family. They attended various congregations and asked their leaders, "Where were we before birth?" "What is the purpose of our lives?" and "Where do we go when we die?"

No one could answer these three basic questions until one afternoon in 1962. My father was home resting after contracting bilharzia (a parasitic disease), and two young Mormon missionaries knocked on the door. The missionaries' message that day was: "Where do we come from? What is our purpose here on earth? and Where we will go when we die?" At the end of the lesson my parents were overjoyed, and my father told the missionaries, "You have taught me more in one night than I have known my whole life!" Almost fifty years later, my parents still love to go to church.

I grew up in the war-torn country of Rhodesia. I don't think

anyone in that country at that time had the courage *not* to believe. Daily we turned to our Heavenly Father in prayer for guidance, for direction, and for the safety of our families and friends. We watched them leave home each day and prayed fervently that they would return. Throughout this trying time, I witnessed my parents serving, sharing, and uplifting those around them—bringing peace and comfort to many disheartened souls through the gospel's message.

When I was eight years old, I had two experiences that changed my life forever. First, I had the wonderful opportunity of being baptized. After years of waiting for my eighth birthday, I entered into the waters of baptism, and my heart leaped for joy as I experienced an overwhelming feeling of the Lord's love and care for me. Afterward, my father, with other worthy Melchizedek Priesthood holders, laid his hands upon my head to bestow the gift of the Holy Ghost upon me. The most amazing feeling of warmth filled my entire body, and I knew for a surety that my Heavenly Father was with me, a spiritual experience that I will forever treasure.

Second, my father announced that our family would be sealed (bound together for eternity) in the Salt Lake Temple. At that time, Rhodesia had worldwide sanctions imposed against it. No Rhodesian was allowed to enter the United States. The visa consulate at the U.S. Embassy in South Africa was absolutely exasperated with my father and let him know that regardless of whether they issued the visas, we would never be allowed to enter the United States. My father shared that we were Mormons and that he wanted to take his family to be sealed in the house of the Lord. The consulate eventually conceded and issued our visas, but she told my father that he was wasting his time and a lot of money.

We arrived in New York extremely tired after the long flight and waited our turn in the U.S. Customs and Immigration line. The man ahead of us was caught smuggling watches by the officer, who was absolutely infuriated and immediately deported the man. Our turn was next! As we stepped up to be served, my mother asked us each to smile. At that exact moment, the shift changed. A new officer came in to serve us. He looked over our passports and asked, "Where are you going?"

My father replied, "Salt Lake City, Utah."

The officer then asked, "Are you Mormons?"

My father said, "Yes."

Then he asked, "What have you brought with you?"

My father answered, "A zebra skin and a few other gifts." The officer hesitated slightly, then stamped the passports and wished us all a good trip.

As we walked through the doors, tears rolled down my parents' cheeks. They fully appreciated the miracle that had just transpired. On April 8, 1975, our family knelt together in the Salt Lake Temple, and we were sealed as a family for time and for all eternity. I will always be grateful for my inspired, faithful parents.

I love my family. While we are far from perfect, being members of The Church of Jesus Christ of Latter-day Saints has given us some great direction and guidelines. As the saying goes, "Families that pray together stay together." There is something unique about kneeling together as a family in prayer and feeling of our Heavenly

Father's love. It seems to settle unresolved disputes and brings a feeling of unity and love.

For Mormons, Monday nights are reserved for family home evening. It is a wonderful time to spend together, regardless of what we choose to do—oftentimes a short gospel lesson followed by playing some games and eating treats or going to see a movie or whatever the family might enjoy doing together. As a family of six daughters, we never had a dull moment. Many of our friends would "just happen" to visit on Monday nights, and they were always welcome to join in.

I love Sundays. My mom would play music from the Mormon Tabernacle Choir, and my parents were always excited to go to church. Two bathrooms available for seven women to get ready presented challenges, but once we were there, a feeling of peace, love, friendship, and direction descended that I have never experienced elsewhere. Church was fun because we were invited to participate and share our opinions while we were taught simple gospel truths, all of which seemed to recharge my soul's "batteries."

As a professional golfer, I travel the globe for most of the year. Thanks to www.lds.org, I am able to locate and attend the closest Mormon chapel, where I join in singing the hymns I love (usually in a foreign language). Since a worldwide curriculum is used for Sunday School, the same lesson is taught, regardless of which country I am in.

I love to read the scriptures. When I was a child, our family would often wake early to go running, then come home to read the scriptures together and finish with family prayer. During this time, I learned of the sacrifices that righteous men and women in other times made to obey God's will. I gained a greater understanding of the Lord's will for each of His children. The Book of Mormon is an amazing book in which prophets of old share with us the miracles that filled their lives and truths that should still govern our lives today. I have witnessed how my life and the lives of those around me have been blessed, guided, strengthened, and changed for the better by reading and pondering its words.

I respect priesthood authority. When I was three years old, I had a seizure that left me unconscious for many hours. A number of medical specialists were called in to assist during this time. Our country's top neurosurgeon conducted a number of tests and came to the conclusion that I was brain dead. He told my father that he was very sorry, as there was nothing else that he could do to help, and he had no idea how long I would live. At that time my father placed his hands on my head and gave me a priesthood blessing. He promised the Lord that if my life were to be spared, he would serve the Lord for the rest of his life and would encourage me to do the same. Shortly thereafter I began to speak. At every one of my birthdays, my father recalls that experience with tears in his eyes. For years I was a "medical wonder" to the physicians involved. I am grateful for my father's faith in his priesthood authority that enabled me to be healed.

I love guidance from the Lord's commandments. My parents love playing sports. My father captained Zimbabwe's national rugby team, so it was inevitable that we would follow our parents' lead. I pitched at the fast-pitch Softball World Series, played once every four years in competition with countries like the United States, China, Japan, Australia, and New Zealand. For the past eighteen years, as a scratch golfer myself, I have coached professional golfers, mostly on the Ladies European Tour.

Being a professional athlete presents challenges, the greatest being health concerns and injuries. Mormons live by a health code known as the Word of Wisdom. We abstain from tea, coffee, alcohol, tobacco, and harmful drugs, and we are counseled to eat healthy and in moderation. Throughout my sporting career I have reaped health benefits by keeping this law. I have always avoided cola products, and over the last few years I have excluded all caffeine from my diet, including chocolate, which I loved. I have experienced a vast improvement in my health, with far fewer aches and pains.

Keeping the Sabbath day holy has also been important to me. My greatest challenge in doing so was when, two months prior to attending the Softball World Series, I was told by the team selectors that if I refused to play at the series on Sunday, they would not select me for the team. When I shared my concern with my parents that day, they said it was my choice to make. I told them I had already decided not to play. Two weeks later, the selectors reconsidered their decision. I was selected for the team, and I was not required to play on Sunday.

I love missionary work. Matthew 28:19 reads: "Go ye therefore, and teach all nations, baptizing them in the name of the Father, and of the Son, and of the Holy Ghost." Missionaries have always frequented our home, and from childhood I wanted to be a full-time missionary. In 1992, my wish came true when I received my mission call to serve for eighteen months in the Provo Utah Mission. I have never been so busy, so tired, so poor, so inspired, or so happy.

I worked mostly with foreign college students. It was a privilege to introduce our Asian friends to Christianity, sharing with them simple gospel truths regarding our Heavenly Father, our elder brother Jesus Christ, and their plan of happiness for each of us. At the baptism of our dear Japanese friend Chieko, she asked me with tear-filled eyes, "What would have happened if you had never come on your mission?" At that moment, my eyes also filled with tears. I knew that if I only came to find Chieko, it was worth it.

I love being a Mormon and always have! My heart rejoices to know that our Heavenly Father truly loves and appreciates each of His children, and that He wants us to be happy. I am a Mormon because I know that the principles this church teaches are true—and because it makes me happy!

GIFFORD "GIFF" NIELSEN

GIFF NIELSEN was the sports director and anchor on KHOU-TV in Houston, Texas, for twenty-five years and now serves on the board of directors at Houston's Memorial City Bank.

He has an extensive sports background, having played professional football as well as college football and basketball. Giff attended Brigham Young University on a football and basketball scholarship. During his junior year, he turned his full attention to football and played quarterback for the BYU Cougars. The Football Writers of America named him an All-American.

The National Collegiate Athletic Association chose Giff as one of the top five scholar athletes, and he recently received the NCAA Silver Anniversary Award signifying success in his profession and in the community after his playing days.

Giff graduated from BYU with a bachelor's degree in communications in 1977. The Houston Oilers drafted him in May 1978. He played quarterback for the team for six years before retiring in May 1984 to join the 11 News anchor team.

He has been inducted into the BYU Hall of Fame, the Utah

Hall of Fame, and, in 1994, Giff was inducted into the College Football Hall of Fame.

Among the highlights of his extensive service in the community, Giff sits on the executive board of the Boy Scouts of America, Sam Houston Area Council. He hosts an annual golf tournament in Houston that benefits local children's charities and has raised over $5.5 million since its inception in 1986. Some of the beneficiaries include The First Tee of Houston, the YMCA after-school program, and Kids Way of the United Way.

Gifford Nielsen now serves as an Area Seventy in The Church of Jesus Christ of Latter-day Saints. He and his wife, Wendy, reside in Texas. They have six children and fourteen grandchildren.

• • •

MY CHILDHOOD WAS ANY LITTLE BOY'S DREAM. I grew up near the foothills of the Rocky Mountains in the university town of Provo, Utah, where my parents ran a boardinghouse for dozens of male college students. Even though I was the youngest child after five sisters, I felt that I had countless big brothers. We played football, basketball, golf, or whatever sport was in season, and, to top it all off, my best friend, Jeff Smith, lived around the corner and had a huge backyard and four older brothers to join in the fun. We all dreamed of becoming professional athletes.

My parents were hardworking, loving people who always made me feel I was on top of the world. My sisters adored me yet kept me humble by expecting me to do my own housework. My life was one continual round of eating, sleeping, and playing sports. I didn't often think about being a Mormon until I got a little older, but the Church was as much a part of our life as was the clear mountain air I breathed.

I don't remember the exact moment that I gained a fervent testimony of my own, but I do remember thinking seriously about my religion as the result of a pointed question a reporter asked me during my junior year as BYU's starting quarterback. After the usual questions about the upcoming Tangerine Bowl game we were to play in Florida, this man looked me in the eye and said with authority, "I don't see how your religion can help you in playing football."

Then he held the microphone very close to my mouth and turned up the volume on his recorder. I believe that during that brief pause between question and answer, my idyllic life flashed before me, and I pondered deeply just what being a Mormon had meant to me.

I said without equivocation, "My religion gives me direction, purpose, and joy. I love football, but it isn't the most important thing in my life. I'm going to go out and play a game on Saturday, and I'll fight harder than anyone out there to win because I'm a competitor and I hate to lose. But win or lose that game, I'll still get up the next day and go to church. I'll still have everything that is most important to me and I'll know where I came from, why I'm here, and where I'm going when I die. That's how my religion helps me in football."

The reporter put the microphone down and asked, "How's your offense looking for the big game?" And I smiled inside, knowing that, win or lose that game, I was winning in life because I truly knew who I was and Whose I was. That kind of victory is the foundation and structure of my entire existence. The gospel of Jesus Christ has grounded, shaped, and enriched my life beyond all else.

Later a knee injury ended my college career, dashing my hopes of being a top contender for the Heisman Trophy (college football's premiere award) and changing my future professional football paycheck from over a million dollars a year to less than fifty thousand. This life-altering injury invited me to think deeply about what was most important to me. I sat down and wrote a list of what I most valued, and it looked like this:

1. My Heavenly Father, my Savior, Jesus Christ, and their gospel as found in The Church of Jesus Christ of Latter-day Saints
2. My family
3. My friends
4. My health
5. My education
6. My future career—how I would make a living for my family
7. Athletics

When I looked at the list and realized that six of the seven things I most cherished remained unaffected by my injury, sports took its proper place in my priorities. I knew the Lord's will would be done, and I could accomplish whatever He wanted me to do.

It is impossible to estimate just how the fruits of the gospel have shaped and enriched my life through the ensuing decades. I have felt constant love and support from my Heavenly Father and Jesus Christ. I know that my Savior personally atoned for my sins and that the priesthood keys of His restored gospel make it possible for me to spend eternity not only with Him but also with my entire family. This knowledge blesses my life daily.

Faith in my all-knowing, unconditionally loving Father in Heaven—who listens to every prayer and knows what I need even before I ask—brings "the peace of God, which passeth all understanding" (Philippians 4:7) and reduces tragedy to technicality. The gift of the Holy Ghost as my constant companion renders decision making a delight as I heed and follow the whisperings of that familiar and beloved still, small voice. And communion with my brothers and sisters at home and around the world reminds me that we are all connected as part of God's treasured family.

My wife, Wendy, and I cannot comprehend how we would have had the courage even to begin the awesome task of parenthood without the wisdom, assurance, and experience of loving parents, the scriptures, the prophets, and myriad Church leaders and teachers. They blazed the trail and lit the pathway for us to follow as we prayerfully brought six magnificent children of God into this often confusing world. Our desire and hope has been to guide them back to the presence of their heavenly parents, and through the gospel's inspired doctrines, ordinances, and programs we have had help every step of the way.

Our children have found the balance, the knowledge, and the inspiration they have needed to guide them through this life. From learning about God when they were toddlers to serving Him on missions, they have come to know for themselves the truth of the scriptures, the light of the gospel, and the peace of a sure testimony of their Lord and Savior Jesus Christ, who atoned for their sins.

Through the light of the gospel, I have learned the meaning of love, compassion, courage, integrity, virtue, and steadfastness, and I have had many opportunities to plant seeds of faith and nurture them to full fruition. The Church of Jesus Christ of Latter-day Saints contains God's truth upon the earth today—the power, authority, and light of Heavenly Father, Jesus Christ, and the Holy Ghost. Without its all-encompassing illumination I would feel lost. With its inspired influence I can "press forward with a steadfastness in Christ, having a perfect brightness of hope, and a love of God and of all men" (2 Nephi 31:20), to fulfill my earthly mission and say with Paul, "I have fought a good fight, I have finished my course, I have kept the faith" (2 Timothy 4:7). Indeed, my boyhood dreams can and will come true because I am a Mormon—one who loves the Savior and basks in the light of His love through the good news of His restored gospel found in The Church of Jesus Christ of Latter-day Saints.

STEPHANIE NIELSON

STEPHANIE NIELSON was born, raised, and married in Provo, Utah. She is the eighth of nine children born to Stephen and Cynthia Clark. She is a popular blogger and author of nieniedialogues.com. She began blogging in 2005 while living in New Jersey as a way to keep her and her husband's family informed about their life in the East.

From 2005 to 2008, her blog steadily grew in popularity and readership. Her blog entries are a natural portrayal of life as a wife, mother, Mormon, daughter, sister, and citizen. They are filled with pictures and images that represent the common joys in the roles of her life.

In the summer of 2008 she and her husband, Christian, were involved in a serious airplane accident. A close friend perished from his injuries and Christian and Stephanie survived the crash with burns covering Stephanie's arms, legs, face, and hands.

She has been featured on *The Oprah Winfrey Show, The Today Show with Matt Lauer,* and the *Glenn Beck* program. Recently *20/20* did a one-hour special highlighting her story and recovery process. In these interviews she explains why she believes she beat the odds of surviving their tragic accident and what life is like with her new appearance and physical limitations.

Stephanie, age twenty-nine, lives in the "tree street" area in Provo, Utah, with her four beautiful children—Claire, nine; Jane, eight; Oliver, five; and Nicholas, four—and her handsome husband, Christian, with whom she is madly and relentlessly in love.

Before the accident, Stephanie was a yoga instructor in Arizona and an avid runner. Stephanie also loves to ski and has been a ski instructor at Sundance Resort in Utah. Last winter, Stephanie began skiing for the first time since her accident. Skiing came back to her with triumphant ease!

She and her family are frequently seen on Utah Lake on their sailboat, the *AuroraMark* (the name came from Stephanie's and Christian's middle names).

Stephanie is healthier and happier than ever. She has begun doing yoga again and plans to run in races next year if all goes well. She will have frequent surgeries to release and rebuild areas on her burned skin for most of her life. She is upbeat and is thrilled to be expecting another child.

Although reconstructive surgery is an ongoing requirement, Stephanie maintains a joyful attitude for life and living the roles she loves.

• • •

I HAVE ALWAYS FELT CLOSE TO THE SPIRIT. Ever since I was young, I remember feeling the Spirit. I felt it in my heart, which is why I cried a lot when I was young, especially when I was at church, singing hymns or listening to beautiful music. It moved me even though it was unexplainable. After my baptism I felt the Spirit in my life more than ever, and I was finally able to identify what it was. I enjoyed its constant companionship and the positive effects I felt and loved.

I am so happy to have felt that early in my life. It has blessed me throughout my hardships.

When I had three small children under five years old and was pregnant with my fourth, my father called me his "pioneer girl." I have always loved that. My heritage and ancestry is enormously rich in pioneer history. It was a real honor to be likened to those pioneer ancestors, and I live each day to be just that.

When times are tough, I think about my pioneer forebears, and that gives me immeasurable strength that keeps me moving through the hard times. I think, "If they did it, I can certainly overcome these challenges." That helps me face trials with heart and with a clear mind as to why the Lord has placed them in front of me.

I am who I am because of the women in my life. They have given me great strength and courage and shaped my perspective of what motherhood is all about.

When I received my patriarchal blessing at age sixteen, I was promised that if I learned from my mother and the women of the scriptures, motherhood for me would be a blessing. I will never forget that. It has always stuck with me. I believe it is true, and I hold those women high and would never want to do anything to disappoint them.

I also understand the value of children, who they are, and who I am to them. Being a mother is the greatest job of all. In fact, I wouldn't call it a job; it is an opportunity, an honor to be a mother, especially in this day and age.

I also feel that following the whispering of the Spirit in my life as a mother has helped me enjoy and feel fulfilled being the one whom the children rely on.

Being a Mormon means that I know who I am, I know where I am going, and I know, understand, and love the plan that has been laid out for families, particularly mine.

The Mormon church helps us understand that living as a family

is God's plan, and we are taught how to rear our children in righteousness, following the Savior's example. This knowledge has changed the way I teach my children, how serious it is to me that they know and understand good choices versus bad ones and the consequences of each.

I also want my children to understand that it takes hard work to keep going in life sometimes, but there are sweet rewards that we will enjoy—not just in the end, but during the pain and suffering—that will come and give us that extra push we need to keep going.

My husband and I have had so many amazing experiences together that all started in the temple when we were sealed. And they have never stopped. They have blessed our life beyond words and continue to do so.

On August 16, 2008, my husband and I, along with a good friend, were in a Cessna four-seater aircraft to travel home from a trip to our family ranch in New Mexico. On takeoff, the plane crashed and burned. My husband had a broken back along with burn injuries to 30 percent of his body. I was trapped in the airplane and was burned over 80 percent of my body, and our friend and pilot, Doug, died. I was placed in a medically induced coma for more than three months to help me try to recover and heal.

From the moment the airplane went up in flames, I was praying. I knew God would *never* leave me. I knew it then and I still know it now.

I never lost my faith in God or blamed Him, even through my struggles to heal, my multiple surgeries, my physical changes, and the role these all play in my children's lives (and mine). In fact, I am thanking Him every day for this trial. I feel honored to carry it, and I hope I am doing it in a way that is pleasing to Him.

I know the plan. I know what we are doing, and I understand the seriousness of rearing my children in the way the Lord has set for His children. The end, the reward, is worth doing anything and everything I can to make sure my family gets there. Without this knowledge from the Church, it would be unreachable. That is why I'm a Mormon.

ROBERT C. OAKS

GENERAL ROBERT C. OAKS was born in Los Angeles and grew up in Provo, Utah. He graduated from Brigham Young High School in 1954 and entered the first class of the U.S. Air Force Academy after attending Brigham Young University for one year. After graduat-

ing from the Academy in 1959 and undergoing pilot and fighter gunnery training, he flew combat missions in Vietnam. He also attended the U.S. Naval War College and received an MBA degree in personnel management from Ohio State University in 1967. Throughout his thirty-five-year career, he consistently returned to fighter flying and was still flying F-16s in Germany at the time of his retirement in 1994.

General and Mrs. Oaks have moved thirty-three times in their married life and have lived in Japan, Germany, Italy, and South Africa, as well as in most parts of the United States. General Oaks served twice as a Pentagon staff member and once on the staff at the Air Force Academy. He has commanded units at all levels of the Air Force. At Ramstein Air Force Base in Germany, he commanded the 86th Tactical Fighter Wing and later was commander of U.S. Air Forces Europe. He also commanded allied NATO air forces in Naples, Italy, and Ramstein, Germany.

General Oaks relinquished command of U.S. Air Forces in Europe in 1994 and retired from the United States Air Force as a general after more than thirty-five years of service. Following his retirement, he moved to Pittsburgh, where he became senior vice president for operations at US Airways. He was awarded the Distinguished Flying Cross for his Vietnam service and two Distinguished Service medals.

In 2000, General Oaks was called to serve as a General Authority for The Church of Jesus Christ of Latter-day Saints and assigned to Johannesburg, South Africa, where he became the area president, presiding over Church operations in southeast Africa. After an additional four-year assignment at Church headquarters in Salt Lake City, Utah, Elder Oaks was assigned to serve as president of the Europe area, presiding over Church operations in forty-four countries. He was released as a General Authority in October 2009 and returned to his home in Utah.

Elder Oaks has been married to the former Gloria Mae Unger since 1959. They are the parents of six children and have sixteen grandchildren.

• • •

PERHAPS THE IMPORTANT QUESTION is not why I am a Mormon, but why I stayed a Mormon. The answer has to do with a series of commitments I made to the Lord and with my seeing and feeling His hand in my life at a number of important junctures.

I felt His hand guiding me even as I made the decision to join the charter class of the Air Force Academy. My cousin, Elder Dallin H. Oaks, had urged me to join the Utah National Guard while I was in high school. I went on to Brigham Young University thinking I would major in engineering and then go to law school. As part of my law school plan, I enrolled in a political science class taught by the legendary Stewart Grow. I began to feel that I could enjoy a number of disciplines.

At about that time, I learned that a test would be administered to students who might be interested in attending the newly announced Air Force Academy. I was in some turmoil about which direction to go academically and decided to take the test. Although it was quite competitive, I was selected for the starting class.

The more I learned about the Academy, the more interested I became. I could study engineering and political science as well as a number of other disciplines. The Academy had the perfect curriculum for me to follow my interests, and I could become a fighter pilot, too.

I got to play football for the Academy for two years, but my playing time was cut short by a severe knee injury. This injury almost kept me from being commissioned. In fact, if I had gone through the normal commission process, I never would have made it. But since I was at the Academy, and they had already lost 100 of the first class of 300, they decided to graduate and commission me.

I was troubled about not going on a Church mission, though, and thought that maybe I should leave. I took my concern to my commanding officer, perhaps the best leader I ever had in the military. It was Christmastime, and I told him I needed to go home and serve a mission for my church. He said, "Well, come here and get in my car."

We drove around the old Lowry Air Force Base, the first home of the Air Force Academy. As we passed airmen shuffling here and there, my commander said, "Do you think they need leadership? Do you think they need Christian guidance?" I said yes. "Well, you can provide that leadership in your military career. You don't have to stay here. You can go home and go on a mission for your church, but your mission could be here, too."

I had a great deal of respect for him. I was impressed that he cared about me and my future and that he would take so much time with me. I said I would stay.

Once I made that decision, I never thought about leaving the military for the next thirty-nine years.

I went into the military with a testimony. I wasn't searching. I had always tried to live the gospel and keep the commandments. My resolve was strengthened and deepened during my career as an officer.

One of my early assignments was to Cannon Air Force Base near Clovis, New Mexico. During that assignment, I received word that I would be stationed at Misawa Air Base in Japan. My squadron commander called me in to say good-bye.

"Bobby," he said, "you've done a good job for us. Now, you are a Mormon. You don't drink. I am religious and don't believe in drinking, but I have felt that sometimes a drink just helps move things along, especially in a social situation."

I said to him, "If I ever have to do that, I will get out of the Air Force." I had always been committed to the Church, but in that moment in the presence of that squadron commander, I made a firm, renewed commitment to the Church and to the Lord. And that commitment is why I stayed a Mormon.

One of the beauties of life in the military is that you are on either one side or the other, and everyone knows it. At the time I made that commitment, my friends knew that I was a non-drinking fighter pilot, a Latter-day Saint who was going to work to live my church's standards. There had never been a doubt in my mind, but now I was committed openly.

The commitment was important to me personally, but how I lived it was important to my career. For example, one of my commanders called me in one day. He was a hard-drinking fighter pilot who told me that he wouldn't harass me for my non-drinking if I didn't harass him about his drinking. There is an important principle here, and living it strengthened my success in the military. I worked to stick to my commitments, but I didn't wear them on my sleeve.

I don't think any of my peers ever felt I looked down my nose at them. I could go to beer call and to their happy hours with them; however, I was "in the squadron but not of the squadron." When I went to their homes, they always had apple juice or something for me. My friends took care of me in that way because, although they knew my commitment, they did not feel any condescension from me.

A number of times I felt the Lord's hand in my life directly and immediately. The only time that the Word of Wisdom became an issue again was during a high-level Soviet Union–United States military conference on "Incidents at Sea." I was on the United States negotiation team as a colonel with three navy admirals. This was during the Cold War. Though we were enemies, no one wanted to inadvertently start a war. The idea of the negotiations was to develop protocols to follow when our respective ships encountered each other. Our countries agreed that this could better be worked out among military men at the sub-political level.

After these successful negotiations in Moscow, our Soviet military hosts took us on a tour to Leningrad (now St. Petersburg). It concluded with a dinner, and naturally there were toasts. After turning down vodka and white wine, I found a glass of pink lemonade. Fifty to sixty people stood between our high-ranking host and me when he lifted his glass of vodka in a toast. Yet, through the crowd he saw me holding aloft my glass of pink lemonade. He glowered and instructed me to get vodka. Through my interpreter, I said I was fine. "You're a pilot, aren't you? All pilots drink. Get your vodka. We are not going on until you get your vodka."

My interpreter, an NKVD agent, told me to pick up the vodka quickly. He whispered to me that if I didn't, he might end up in

Siberia. At times like this in the past I had been able to diffuse the situation with humor. That clearly wasn't going to work here.

With great seriousness I offered up a very short silent prayer, "God, help me." The next instant, the Soviet admiral's interpreter touched his arm and whispered in his ear, "It's because of his religion." The admiral, just as abruptly as he had started, simply moved on with the toast. As it happened, the admiral's interpreter had been with me in a delegation to the United States the year before. We had become friends and talked a lot about religion, including our views on alcohol. The Lord had the answer to my prayer in place a year before I needed it.

It is interesting to me, as I get older, to look back on my military life and see how often the Lord intervened to save my life. Once He saved my life when my parachute initially failed to open. I should have died, or at least had a crushed pelvis, but I walked away.

Another time I was flying a night mission over the Mekong Delta. My altimeter malfunctioned. I was above a cloud bank and, certain I was much higher than I actually was, I thought, "I only need to punch through this cloud bank, and I can hit my target." Just as I was about to execute that maneuver, I saw the reflection of the moon. It wasn't a cloud bank; it was the Mekong River.

I knew the Lord was with me then, but I really knew it when I was shot down over enemy territory. I was able to fly another ten miles past the antiaircraft placement that shot my plane. I landed in the middle of a rice paddy, surrounded by a herd of water buffalo. As it happened, an Army helicopter was passing by and was able to pick me up. I escaped injury and avoided the Viet Cong prison camps.

When we weren't flying, we lived in a compound in Saigon. One day one of the house girls, who seemed like a nice person, said she had a little shop downtown and invited me to stop by sometime. Sometime later, I decided to visit her shop. I put on my helmet, opened the gate, and started the 90cc Honda. Instantly I had a strong feeling, "Don't go." I shut off the Honda, closed the gate, and went back to my quarters.

I didn't think much more about it. Thirty years or so later, as I was reflecting on the Lord's hand in my life, this incident came back to me. The Lord was talking to me. I don't know what would have happened, and I don't care. I just know it wasn't something good and that the Lord intervened to protect me.

Those small things go on and on—the little close calls, whether flying or in other difficult situations. I just knew that the Lord was there.

Our family has moved many times. We have lived several places in the United States, but also in Europe and Asia. We always found the Church and served.

None of this would have been possible without my wife, Gloria. Together with our six children, the Church was at the center of our lives.

Somewhere along the line, we all need to decide whether we are in or out. Our family decided we were in for the long haul, and that decision has been like a gyroscope for us during this long odyssey. Being Mormons has given us true bearings.

R. Craig Poole

Since taking the helm of Brigham Young University's women's track team in 1980, Coach Craig Poole has built a program that is consistently among the best in the nation. Under his guidance, the Cougar track team has posted an almost perfect record on conference and regional levels and has consistently been a contender at the national level. Since 1983, his teams have won all eight HCAC crowns, seventeen of eighteen WAC titles, nine of ten MWC indoor titles, and seven of eight MWC outdoor titles.

Awarded the 2006 Cougar Club Dale Rex Memorial Award for his success as a coach, Craig Poole has coached six individual national champions. During his thirty years at BYU, he has coached eighty-one athletes to All-American status.

Coach Poole's athletes have earned a total of 165 All-American honors, including eighteen national champions. He has been honored as the MWC Coach of the Year seven times, including the 2009 season, and the WAC Coach of the Year ten times. He also received HCAC Coach of the Year and IAC Coach of the Year awards. He was inducted into the USTFCCCA National Coaches Hall of Fame in 2011.

In 2004, Coach Poole was the head coach for the United States at the World University Games in Beijing, China. He also served as coach and advisor to the Taiwan national team at the Asian and World Championships in 1987 and as technical coach for Taiwan at the Asian games in 1991. He served on the coaching staff for the West Team at the 1989 Olympic Festival, as head coach for the U.S. National Team vs. Great Britain in 1990, and for the IAAF U.S. World Indoor Championships Team in 1993.

He was named to the 2004 Olympic coaching staff for the 2004 Summer Olympics in Athens, Greece. He coached the U.S. athletes in the heptathlon, long jump, and triple jump.

Coach Poole is a respected force in USA Track and Field, where he has been the National Broad Events Chairman for four years, responsible for the national development of the long jump, triple jump, high jump, pole vault, and heptathlon. He has had additional roles as the Multi-events Chairman responsible for the development of the heptathlon, a position he held for ten years. He was a member of the NCAA Rules Committee. In 1993, he was the Head USA Women's Coach at the World Indoor Championships in Toronto, Canada.

Coach Poole received an EdD in Physical Education and Educational Administration from the University of Utah in 1970. He was a full-time Athletic Professional at BYU, where he taught Sports Psychology/Performance. He is married to Sharon Woodland. The couple has four children.

· · ·

I HAVE ALWAYS BEEN ACTIVE in the Church, for as long as I can remember. When I was a youngster, my parents made sure that I went to Primary and that I was in Scouting and that I attended Mutual (for teens) and so forth. When I went to high school, I was in the early-morning seminary program, and in college at Utah State, of course I took institute classes.

My dad was my coach from the time I was a small kid, so I had a great association with my father while growing up. He believed in playing a lot of sports, and I enjoy and believe in playing sports because that's about all I ever did. The sport we played depended on what season it was. I ended up being a fairly decent athlete. I was coached by my father in high school and was therefore expected to perform on a higher plane in order to justify my position. I had to be a little bit better—or else.

I played football for one year at college, but I wasn't big enough. They eventually advised me not to come out for football anymore— maybe they were afraid I'd be like a bug on a windshield. Instead I got into campus politics and into fraternity life. I was very much involved with that part of the university and fought a hard-won battle to become junior class president.

At that time young people did not assume they would go on missions; they were asked. So young men were not necessarily prepared to go. My bishop had sent most of the boys in our ward who wanted to go, but I had not been asked. When the bishop walked across the street to where I was washing my car one day and asked me if I would go on a mission, I was not mature enough to say yes. I just told him that because I was involved with campus politics and had just won this office, I didn't think it was right for me at that time. I had already made another commitment. But my bishop was wise. He kept me involved in the Church and kept me active in the auxiliary programs.

So as far as my Church experience, I've never had an inactive day in my life. I've always held one leadership position or another. I met most of my challenges while going through college. There were people and teachers who challenged what I believed. It's a time when young people find out about what is right and what is not right, and I had some classes that challenged me that way.

What first converted me to the Mormon church was an experience with my next-door neighbor, my closest friend, who had just

returned from a mission. We were asked to administer priesthood blessings to sick people in the hospital. One of the women was very ill. In fact, she was probably not even conscious of our efforts, but we gave her a blessing anyway. We had fasted for two or three days. We walked out of that hospital knowing everything was well. We had the most beautiful, warm feeling that you could ever imagine. That was the first opportunity I had to know that something existed beyond us that was warm and true. From then on it was a matter of maintaining activity in the Church, doing those things that you are supposed to do.

Of the many good things that happened later, I would say the Lord was more aware of my possibilities than I could have been. I started my athletic coaching career as a junior high school coach, and during those six years I completed my master's degree and my doctoral degree. I was invited to Skyline High School in Salt Lake City, Utah, where I was the head men's coach until they began their women's programs, which I became responsible for in the early

1970s. I was also a biology teacher, a physiology teacher, and a science teacher for ten years. Our Skyline teams won over 96 percent of our meets, including seven state championships, three of them consecutive, both men's and women's.

Coach Robison at BYU suggested that I apply there, and since coaching in college was my goal, I did. I had previously interviewed for jobs at Stanford and the University of Utah and didn't get either one of them. Coach Robison helped me get into BYU, where I coached for thirty years. He also set up a relationship with a senator from Taiwan who was a former athlete at UCLA and an Olympic silver medalist in the hurdles. Through her, Taiwan sent athletes to the United States to train prior to the Los Angeles Olympics, and BYU began recruiting some of them.

A couple of the Taiwanese athletes who came to BYU did very well. When they became All-American, they invited me to be their advisor for the 1987 World Championship. I toured with them one year and went around the world, literally. In every country we visited during that period, we would be invited to the embassy. So lots of alcohol flowed. There would be toasts to the health of whomever and, of course, in my lifestyle that's not something I do. I had my glass of water or my Sprite. My most famous drink was the Fanta orange drink.

When we got to Germany, the ambassador invited the whole delegation to a dinner at the embassy. When we all sat down, I noticed a glass of grape juice on the table. One of the athletes who could speak English stood up and said, "Coach, tonight we drink grape juice in honor of you. No alcoholic drinks will be served because we noticed that you don't drink alcohol." People often do understand that we are a little bit different.

After thirty years at BYU, I had planned to retire in 2012. But in 2010, the people at USA Track and Field came to me and asked if I would be interested in running their program at Chula Vista. I wasn't interested at first, but they kept pressing me to accept their invitation. Eventually, because there are many very fine coaches out there with excellent credentials, I asked, "Why have you chosen me for this position?"

The interviewer thought for a moment and said, "Because you're honorable." I thought that was an interesting statement and a testimony to what we try to espouse, what BYU stands for. It strikes home for me, the value of what we represent as members of The Church of Jesus Christ of Latter-day Saints. If I do my job the way I'm supposed to and live the lifestyle I believe in, it is a compliment to our Church.

So why am I a Mormon? First of all, there is enough LDS history in my family tree to suggest that the Spirit has spoken to many generations of my family positively. Some of my mother's ancestors came across the plains by handcart, and one was sent back to help other handcarts come across. On my father's side, converts from a large family in South Carolina came west to Franklin, Idaho. I've experienced those whisperings of the Spirit myself, creating a very strong belief in the hereafter and in Jesus Christ and His salvation.

I have also had a lifetime of learning and experience, much of it firsthand experience. Secondhand experience is important as well; people play a role in our lives. My conscience is the guardian of my spirit and my soul and my mind, and some things ring true and some things do not. Some things I experience seem sour, and happiness is a matter of filtering out the sour to come up with the sweet taste of those things that add substance and value to my life.

In any environment, you have to be true to yourself. You can't become something that you're not. When you become LDS, and you are totally committed, you have to be on guard not to slip; you have to be aware of who you are. Let me put it this way: When I was coaching in high school, I always used this statement with the young people, which I believe is based on a Chinese proverb: "Honor your father and your mother and bring them no shame."

Whatever you do reflects by name association not only on yourself but on your spouse, your children, your ward "family," even on your friends and the greater community. You have a real responsibility to be honorable in all you do and to be the best you can be while being yourself. So I am a Mormon through the LDS lifestyle that is my heritage. But I also have a testimony of the gospel from many, many spiritual confirmations that I have experienced personally.

BRUCE REESE

BRUCE REESE is president and chief executive officer of Hubbard
Radio LLC, a position he has held since Hubbard Radio's purchase of seventeen radio stations from Bonneville International
in April 2011. Hubbard Radio operates twenty-one radio stations in Chicago, Washington, D.C.,
Minneapolis/St. Paul, St. Louis, and
Cincinnati.

Prior to joining Hubbard Radio,
Mr. Reese worked at Bonneville for almost twenty-seven years, first as general
counsel, then as executive vice president,
and, since 1996, as president and CEO.
Before joining Bonneville, Mr. Reese
practiced law with firms in Washington,
D.C., and Denver. He began his legal career with Department of
Justice in Washington, D.C.

His community activities include the United Way of Salt Lake
Board of Directors, Intermountain Healthcare Board of Trustees,
Primary Children's Medical Center Board, and Pioneer Theater
Company Board. Professionally he has served as chair of the
Joint Radio and Television Boards of the National Association of
Broadcasters and as a director of the Associated Press.

Mr. Reese was raised in West Lafayette, Indiana. He attended
Princeton University and graduated from Brigham Young University
with a BA in 1973 and a JD in 1976. He and his wife, Lu Anne,

live in Sandy, Utah, and are the parents of seven children. They also have four daughters-in-law, two sons-in-law, and nine grandchildren (with three more on the way).

Mr. Reese served a mission in the Germany North Mission of The Church of Jesus Christ of Latter-day Saints from 1969 to 1971. Subsequently he has served in the Church as bishop, high council member, stake mission president, Young Men's president, Sunday School teacher, and ward music chair.

• • •

D O YOU HAVE A TRULY embarrassing moment in your life? Not the funny embarrassing kind, like getting sick at the top of the Ferris wheel on a blind date. (I actually did that.) I'm referring to a memory of an important event that is so distressing that you wish you could erase it from your own memory as well as the memories of all the witnesses. This is, in part, a confession.

I was raised in a wonderful and caring Latter-day Saint family outside of Utah. My father was a professor at a major midwestern university, my mother a well-educated woman who cared for me and my brother and sister at least full-time. Education was important in our home, as were our neighbors and the Church. We were at church every Sunday, which in those days meant three meetings. Mom and Dad fulfilled every Church calling given them, and we children held all of the offices and received all the awards that Mormon kids got in those days.

I look back on my growing-up years with great fondness and love. But, if I were to characterize my youth in the Church, I would say that it was focused on obedience and compliance and not on things of the Spirit. Although I was nurtured and taught right from wrong at home, I don't think of it as a "faith-full" home. If the concept of "the arm of flesh" ever has positive connotations (and I think it does), our home had a heavy influence of self-reliance.

I was also blessed to grow up in the decade of the 1960s, with all of its turmoil. Undoubtedly owing to the household in which I was raised, many of the temptations of that era didn't affect me much. But I did fall prey to the so-called intellectual freedom and the optimism of the age. In a community where almost all my classmates were children of university faculty members, we believed "smarts" and idealism could solve all the world's problems. I graduated from high school and headed to a storied Ivy League institution. After a year, I transferred to Brigham Young University. (I wish I could ascribe a deep spiritual experience to the decision, but it was mostly that I was tired of being at an all-male school.)

I had a great academic experience at BYU and ended up being part of the first class at the law school when it opened in 1973. But BYU will always be dear to me for the other experiences I had there. Certainly the most important was meeting my wonderful wife, Lu Anne. It was also at BYU that I met the first young men my age who had served missions. I had never considered serving a mission. Perhaps because most of my Church leaders had themselves not served missions, due to World War II and the Korean War, I don't think I had ever been asked about a mission. However, my bishop at BYU asked me whether I planned to go. So, at the end of my first year at BYU, I put in my papers and got a call to the North Germany Mission.

Here's that embarrassing moment I wish I could erase. At my missionary farewell, in front of families that had known me from my earliest years, I had the opportunity to share my testimony of the gospel and say why I was going on a mission. I told all of these friends that I didn't know if the Church were true or not. But, I said, even if it were not, I was glad to be going on a mission because the Mormon lifestyle was worth sharing and spreading.

From that starting point, even I am amazed that I'm still a Mormon.

What has happened in my life to convert me from one who admired a lifestyle to one who has a conviction that the gospel of Jesus Christ has been restored in these times? As is the case with many Mormons, I can't point to a specific experience that marked a turn. But the fact is that I have been blessed to see the fruits of Mormonism manifest in its adherents. Their examples have led me to find in the Church so much more than a nice way to live.

Those experiences began for me on my first night in the missionary language training facility in Provo. I said my perfunctory prayers and hopped into my upper bunk. I then watched as one of my fellow missionaries-in-training knelt for thirty minutes in fervent personal prayer, seeking the strength and skill to learn a new language. The language was not intimidating to me, but it dawned on me that I was wholly lacking in another type of knowledge that I would need as a missionary. Meaningful prayer was a completely new experience for me. Henry was a remarkable example.

All of us worked on our German together, and I was paired with a missionary who had a serious speech impediment. As we practiced the language, he would frequently come to a word that he just couldn't get out. After struggling, he would almost always have to go back to the beginning of the thought and start again. What had been a difficult problem in English became painful in a non-native language. Persistence, patience, and prayer sustained a faith that I had never seen before I met Karl.

Most of the missionaries I knew were like me, in pretty early stages of developing faith and testimonies, learning on the job. About a year into my mission, I was assigned to work with a young man who had come into the mission field with a rock-solid testimony built on study, practice, faith, and prayers. As missionaries, we frequently talked about "knowing" the truth of a particular principle, but for me (and most others, I believe) such statements were expressions of faith and hope. But when Larry said, "I know," it wasn't just an expression of faith. He had studied and prayed and lived the principles. I saw for the first time in a peer someone who *knew* the truth of the doctrines he was teaching—knew them with the same conviction that my father might hold a principle of aerodynamics to be true or that I might be certain of the dates and locations of a Civil War battle.

I've been blessed with many great examples of faith and service. Some of them are individuals known to many in the Church. Because of my job, I had the opportunity to meet with our late prophet, President Gordon B. Hinckley, for a couple of hours every month for a twelve-year period and then four or five times a year for the last ten years of his life. Our conversations were usually about business, and I don't know that I've ever met a faster study or better decision maker in my life. But his faith in the Father and the Son and in their power to make our lives more fulfilling and meaningful, along with his relentless optimism about the goodness of men and women in this life, were even more remarkable than his intellectual skills.

I had great teachers in college—Terry Warner, Neal Lambert, and Arthur Henry King come to immediate mind—who combined great minds and deep faith. I was recruited to and taught in law school by the incomparable Rex Lee, a great teacher, a remarkable lawyer, a man with the ability to be a friend to all. I have also had the privilege of the example and mentorship of others who might not be so well-known in the Church who have taught me the depths of the gospel: Rod Brady, Bob Johnson, Bob Barker, Steve Snow, Joe Cannon, Jim Jacobson, Brent Black, and so many others. Their examples of excellence in their professions combined with deep faith and requisite actions have helped me understand the power of Mormonism.

What is that power? The gospel teaches us about the great rewards that await us in the next life if we are obedient to the Lord's laws in this life, if we keep the covenants we make as active members of the Church, if we serve our fellow men and women as we should. I know all that to be true. But, those are not the motivating factors in my testimony. What moves me is, oddly enough, similar to the embarrassing farewell talk I gave when I left on my mission. However, it's not about a nice lifestyle anymore. What I have come to love about the gospel is its power to make this life so much more meaningful, rich, and fulfilling. The knowledge that we can change, the knowledge of the eternal nature of families, the sense of shared heritage that we have with all mankind—these are the reasons I am a Mormon.

One of my dearest friends and very best examples, Kem Gardner, talks often about the blessings of being born with "believing blood." I think he means both a family line reaching back to the early days of the Church *and* the gift of a willingness to try to believe, as the Book of Mormon prophet Alma teaches us (see Alma 32). He has that gift. My wife has that gift. I'm not sure I was born with it, but I am grateful that wonderful examples led me to seek the gift and learn it. I pray that our children and their children will find "believing blood" part of their Mormon heritage.

HARRY REID

UNITED STATES SENATOR HARRY REID (D-NV) was born in the small mining town of Searchlight, Nevada, in 1939. He graduated from Utah State University in 1961 and earned a law degree from George Washington University. His law school years acquainted him with Capitol Hill, where he worked nights as a police officer to pay for school.

Harry Reid married Landra Gould, his high school girlfriend, in 1959. The Reid family eventually grew to include five children and now includes sixteen grandchildren. Senator Reid was first elected to the House of Representatives in 1982. In 1986, he was elected to the United States Senate, where he became the Senate Majority Leader in 2007.

• • •

I WAS BORN AND RAISED in Searchlight, Nevada, a mining town of about two hundred people. However, mining was not the main industry in Searchlight when I grew up; the number-one business was prostitution. At one time in my youth there were thirteen separate bordellos in town.

I went to a two-room school, and most of the time one teacher taught all eight grades. I grew up thinking our family had one of the best homes in Searchlight. But on reflection, I realize that it had no hot water, only an outside toilet, and was heated by a wood-burning stove.

During all the time I spent in Searchlight there was never a church or, as I remember, even a church service. So when I went away to high school in Henderson, some forty-five miles away, it was a real adjustment. I hitchhiked or obtained rides in other ways to and from Basic High School. I would stay with people during the week and go home on weekends.

My first boarding site in Henderson was with my father's brother, Uncle Joe. His wife was Aunt Rae, who many in the family thought was a little strange because she was a Latter-day Saint.

Aunt Rae was very good to me. She was strict but fair. One thing she suggested was my going to something called seminary. A boy named Ron was nice to me, and she said he also went to seminary. I thought it unusual to go to class before school started, but because of Ron and Aunt Rae I agreed to try this thing called seminary.

The seminary instructor was Marlan Walker. He was also a high school Spanish teacher and, as I learned later, an LDS bishop. To say he was a good teacher is a gross understatement. He was mesmerizing. For the first time in my life, I heard the message of Jesus Christ.

In my high school years, I took two years of Spanish from Marlan Walker, as did my wife-to-be, Landra Gould. Marlan went out of his way to be kind to everyone, especially to me and my Jewish girlfriend, Landra. He set an example in kindness that was impressive.

I obtained an athletic scholarship to attend the College of Southern Utah, where I lived in a dormitory with two of my Nevada friends. It was a room for four, so we were assigned a roommate named Larry Adams, who was a Korean War veteran and a returned

Mormon missionary. He always acted as a returned missionary should.

Because Landra's parents did not want her to marry a non-Jew, we decided, following my sophomore year in college, to elope. Our former Spanish teacher, still a bishop, heard of our secret marriage plans and said he would save us the twenty-five dollars for a justice of the peace and would himself marry us—in his LDS chapel, no less.

After he married us, we two nineteen-year-olds went to Utah State University to complete our education. My brilliant wife sacrificed her remaining college education in order to work so I could become a lawyer.

Landra rose before dawn each day to take a bus to Thiokol Chemical Company about fifty miles distant, where she worked to pay for me to attend college. The bus driver, Mr. McPherson, was an LDS stake missionary. Because of his teaching and his patience, we were baptized into The Church of Jesus Christ of Latter-day Saints.

After more than forty years, Landra and I believe our joining the Church to be among the best decisions we ever made. We accepted the Church and a new life because of the power of example. Many contributed to the change, from Aunt Rae to Marlan Walker, from Larry Adams to the stake missionaries. They were effective because they lived their lives as shining representatives, even models, of the life of Jesus.

Our blessings are many. We have five children and sixteen grandchildren. All five of our children have attended Brigham Young University, and all have been married in the temple. Each child has been a positive example for us.

After these many years I believe that the Church has been a steady, positive blueprint for my life. Without the direction of the Church, I would have been without a compass.

So you see, I am glad I believed. I am glad I became a Mormon.

BLAKE M. RONEY

BLAKE M. RONEY was one of the founders of Nu Skin
Enterprises, serving as its president and CEO from 1984 until 1996,
when he became the company's
chairman of the board. Today Nu
Skin Enterprises is one of the largest direct-selling companies in the
world, and its products are sold in
more than fifty countries throughout the Americas, Europe, and the
Asia Pacific region. The company's
stock is publicly traded on the New
York Stock Exchange.

Mr. Roney's business and civic
achievements include recognition
by International Business Awards as 2009 Chairman of the Year, a
2004 honor as one of the 100 Most Influential People in Utah, and
the Utah County Chamber of Commerce 2011 Pillar of the Valley
Award. He has also been honored as Chief of Mtalimanja Village in
Malawi, Africa, and with an honorary doctorate of humane letters
from Salt Lake Community College.

Mr. Roney earned a degree in business finance from Brigham
Young University's Marriott School of Management in 1983. He
currently serves on several community and university boards and is
active in civic and religious organizations. He is the father of eight
children.

. . .

I AM A MORMON BECAUSE I was born a Mormon. I have stayed a Mormon because The Church of Jesus Christ of Latter-day Saints makes me happy. It offers the true teachings of the Savior.

I have a pretty simple view of the world. It seems clear to me that I have a Heavenly Father who loves me beyond comprehension and desires my happiness most of all. This loving Heavenly Father provided a plan that I could follow to become completely happy. The key to His plan is His Son Jesus Christ, our Savior. I think the most important sentence ever uttered was from Heavenly Father, who said upon several occasions, "This is my beloved Son: hear him" (see Mark 9:7; Luke 9:35; and others). This tells me that the way to happiness is to learn what the Savior taught and to obey it and share it with others.

It is clear that the Savior's teachings are simply instructions to achieve happiness. Some of them I understand. Others I may not recognize as contributing to my happiness, but prior experience with

Christ's gospel assures me that they do. His teachings mostly promote loving others—being kind to them and serving them. I have tried to live the teachings of the Savior my whole life. As I have aged, it has become clear that His teachings are a source of goodness and peace in my life as opposed to a set of oppressive rules. I often observe that all of the positive elements of my life come from living these teachings. I have also noted that, for the most part, the level of happiness I observe in others' lives seems to be proportionate to the percentage of eternal truths that they live, knowingly or not.

I am certainly not perfect, and I assure you that Mormons in general are not perfect. We do, however, have the perfect plan to achieve peace and happiness forever. That is exactly what anyone can have, to the degree that they follow the plan.

I want my family to be happy. I want to help everyone become happy. So I choose happiness. I have experienced spiritual confirmations that are undeniable testifying that the teachings of the Savior are true. I have no choice but to make them part of my values. I intend to keep trying to live the Savior's teachings to the end of my days and to repent quickly when I don't.

I am a Mormon because I know that The Church of Jesus Christ of Latter-day Saints provides the most complete knowledge of our loving Heavenly Father's plan for our happiness—a plan that explains what all of us on earth are about and that so clearly delivers the peace and joy it promises. I am a Mormon because it makes me happy.

DAVE ROSE

SINCE BECOMING HEAD COACH of the Brigham Young University men's basketball program in 2005, Dave Rose has guided the Cougars to an array of on-the-court awards and accolades. With 159 wins and 45 losses, Rose currently holds the BYU record for career winning percentage (.779) and the Mountain West Conference (MWC) record for winning percentage in league games (.813). At the same time, Rose's basketball program ranks in the top 10 percent nationally in academic progress made by its athletes. The NCAA honored the Cougars with Public Recognition awards for four straight seasons  (2007 through 2010) for high academic achievement, the only Division I program to earn both this recognition and a bid to the NCAA Tournament each of those years.

Also excelling off the court, Rose was honored by the National Association of Basketball Coaches with its 2008 Game Pillar Award for Service, one of four Pillar Awards (Education, Leadership, Service, and Advocacy) that the Association gives annually.

Rose returned BYU to the national stage with five straight seasons in the top 25 polls and five consecutive trips to the NCAA Tournament. In his first season, he and his staff produced the nation's second-most improved team by turning a 9–21 squad (tied for last in the MWC) into a 20–9 NIT qualifier, finishing second at 12–4 in the MWC. From 2007 through 2009, the Cougars won the MWC league championship three years in a row, tying for the title the third year.

This past season, Rose and the Cougars set numerous program records with 32 wins and an .865 winning percentage, a fourth conference title in five seasons, and nine straight weeks ranked in the top ten. Both the AP and the ESPN/USA Today Coaches Polls ranked BYU number 3. Wins over Wofford and Gonzaga in the first two rounds of the NCAA tournament put BYU into the Sweet 16 for the first time since 1981. Rose also coached the nation's player of the year and NCAA Division I scoring leader, Jimmer Fredette, who averaged 28.9 points per game and earned numerous player of the year honors in 2011, including Naismith, AP, Oscar Robertson, and *Sporting News*.

Rose, a native of Texas, and his wife, Cheryl, have three children and six grandchildren.

• • •

I GREW UP A MEMBER of The Church of Jesus Christ of Latter-day Saints. My parents are lifelong members, as were their parents and their parents before them.

Although I've never known anything different, I do know that being a member of the Church has had a positive impact on my life in every way.

Being a Mormon gives me greater purpose and direction. It helps my wife and me in raising our family. Basically, it guides me in every decision I make. Many good things happen in my life because of my belief in the gospel of Jesus Christ, but most significant is the help that has come during the most difficult moments in my life. At such times, my faith helps me overcome the pain and fear. The resulting knowledge and assurance move me forward into the unknown, to do things that are unfamiliar and difficult. This faith even makes it possible for me to do the impossible.

As a freshman at Dixie College, I excelled in both basketball and baseball and was voted all-conference in both sports. A few Major League Baseball teams even contacted me and had some interest in drafting me. I had worked hard to be successful in sports and felt I was finally reaping the rewards. While at Dixie, I attended a meeting where the prophet of The Church of Jesus Christ of Latter-day Saints spoke to the students. In his address, President Spencer W. Kimball said that every worthy young man should serve a mission for the Church. I felt he was talking to me personally, but I was nervous about leaving so many opportunities behind. If I went on a mission, I knew I would have to start from scratch in two years. But I also knew it was what the Lord wanted me to do.

As a child, one of my favorite scriptures had always been Doctrine and Covenants 82:10: "I, the Lord, am bound when ye do what I say; but when ye do not what I say, ye have no promise." I decided at that moment that I would go on a mission. It was a difficult decision that many people did not understand, but I knew it was what I wanted to do. My mission to England was a monumental factor in my life. It set a precedent that I would always try to do what my Heavenly Father wanted me to do.

Three years later, as I was nearing the end of my junior year at the University of Houston, I injured my knee during a game against Villanova in the first round of the NCAA tournament. Following the game, the doctors who examined my knee determined that I would need surgery. I was scheduled for a scope, but as the operation progressed, the surgeon realized that my patellar tendon needed to be rebuilt. After the surgery, the doctors told me that this injury would end my career. It was unlikely that it would heal well enough that I would ever be able to play basketball again.

I was devastated. Everything I had worked toward for so many

years disappeared in an instant. I found it hard to believe that all I had done to get to this point would end this way. After the surgery, I was in tremendous pain. The news that I might never play basketball again was devastating, and I was at one of the lowest points of my life. The pain and fear led to a lot of thought and prayer, and over time I felt an answer to my prayers. I came to the conclusion that if I did my part and worked hard enough, I would indeed be able to play and fulfill my lifelong dream. I knew I couldn't do this on my own; I needed the Lord's help.

My surgery was in May, and for the next sixteen months, I worked hard every day to get my knee strong enough to play again. I had to redshirt the next season and watch as my team made it all the way to the Final Four of the NCAA Tournament. My recovery was long and difficult, but I had faith and believed that I would get better. The days I spent in rehab were incredibly painful, but I didn't worry about how much it hurt that day; I just believed that it would feel better the next day or the next month. Not until school started my senior year did I finally feel confident that I would be able to compete at my previous level and finish my college career at Houston. My prayers were answered. I was able to play with my team during a terrific season that ended at the NCAA Championship Game.

Almost thirty years later, I found myself in a similar situation, but with drastically higher stakes. I was in a hospital in Las Vegas fighting for my life. Only days earlier I had been at Disneyland with my family, and only months earlier I had been coaching my team at Brigham Young University to its third consecutive conference basketball championship. But at that moment I was lying in bed recovering from major emergency surgery, weak from the loss of blood. The doctors had removed a tumor, my spleen, six lymph nodes, and a portion of my pancreas, plus given me ten units of blood.

Two days later, my surgeon gave me the grim news that I had pancreatic cancer. At that point I was scared, and I knew my family was scared. I remember thinking, "How can this get any worse?" and that's when it did. Two days following surgery, I was hit with a pulmonary embolism or a blood clot that lodges in the lungs. This was the most painful and terrifying thing I had ever experienced. As I struggled with every breath, I knew I needed a miracle.

My sister-in-law came to the hospital and left me a plaque that reads "Miracles Happen" and a book entitled *The Healer's Art* by Lloyd D. Newell and Don H. Staheli (Deseret Book, 2006). The days in the hospital were very long, and the nights were even longer. I asked my wife to put the plaque in a spot where I could see it. The words "Miracles Happen" helped me believe that I could get better and kept my mind off all the horrible possibilities.

During one of those endless nights, my wife read to me from *The Healer's Art*. These powerful words were exactly what I needed to hear:

"Of all the miracles of Jesus recorded in the New Testament, three-fourths of them are described as healings. With all the affectionate sympathy of a devoted parent (for their spiritual Father He was), and with perfect confidence in the height and depth of His power, His heart was drawn out over and over again to bring the joy of health and wholeness to many of the sickly lambs of Judea's fold. Even with His knowledge of the schooling that comes through suffering, He sought to ease the pains of the innocent. *In His infinite mercy, He righted the apparent wrongs of nature, smoothed festered flesh, cooled the fevered brow, bade the parting spirit to return, and restored the deceased to the arms of sorrowing loved ones. That He should have been able to do so should be of little wonder. As President Boyd K. Packer has so aptly observed, 'Christ is the Creator, the Healer. What He made, He can fix'"* (2–3; emphasis added).

As I listened to these words, I felt like there was no difference between me and these people healed by Jesus Christ. Was it possible that I could receive a miracle just like those in the New Testament? The following days were extremely difficult, but I believed that I would get better. I understood that there was not much room for hope with this diagnosis, but I knew deep inside that somehow my body would heal and I would recover. Just as with my earlier knee injury, I believed that the present situation, however bleak, did not matter. Things would be better tomorrow or the day after that.

My players had received news of my condition. As a team they made the decision to fast and pray for me. This had a very powerful effect on me during some of my most difficult and painful times. I knew that each of them was praying for me, and this gave me greater physical and spiritual strength. I cannot express the deep admiration and respect I have for my team. These young men are dedicated, service oriented, and intelligent people (as well as very talented players) who are willing to live their faith at BYU. Their faith and prayers built mine, giving me the strength and faith I needed to heal.

A week later, I was transferred to the Huntsman Cancer Institute. My family and I were still reeling from the original diagnosis when we were told that there was a chance that this tumor was different from the typical pancreatic cancer. I was given a more specific diagnosis that, unlike the usual aggressive pancreatic cancer, mine was a slow-growing, nonaggressive form. This new diagnosis gave everyone hope that I could get better and continue living as a husband, father, grandfather, and coach. I continued to believe that I would heal and be able to do all those things I desired to do in my life.

I received a miracle. I don't know in what form the miracle took place, but I do know it was required of me to believe it was possible. A scripture in the Book of Mormon says, "For behold, I am God; and I am a God of miracles; and I will show unto the world that I am the same yesterday, today, and forever; and I work not among the children of men save it be according to their faith" (2 Nephi 27:23).

I believe that the faith and prayers of others, including many people I didn't even know, helped me to survive those frightening days in Las Vegas in order to heal and finally to recover that summer. A power comes from believing. Faith is the first and most important step to witnessing amazing things, even miracles. I know that my faith is a gift from God, and it is the key to everything good in my life. My belief in God and my faith in Jesus Christ have carried me through the most amazing and the most difficult days of my life. For these reasons I am grateful to say, "I am a Mormon."

JAN SAUMWEBER

JAN SAUMWEBER is senior vice president, global Wal-Mart team, for Sara Lee Corporation. She leads a team of more than a hundred professionals in managing a $2 billion worldwide business. Prior to her current assignment, she served in leadership roles in both sales and marketing at Sara Lee. Before joining Sara Lee, Jan was an executive with ConAgra Frozen Foods and the Minute Maid division of the Coca-Cola Company.

Jan is currently a member of the board of directors for Students in Free Enterprise and BYU's Marriott School of Management National Advisory Council. She has also served on Western Michigan University's Food Marketing Advisory Board and on the board of the National Frozen Food Association. She was a founding member of Hands for Honduras, a nonprofit organization that funds projects to improve the lives of the impoverished.

Jan earned a bachelor of arts degree in business from North Central College in Naperville, Illinois. She and her husband, Les, have four children. They enjoy sailing, scuba diving, and waterskiing.

• • •

L IFE AS LES AND I PLANNED it changed with one sentence: "You can't work and treat this disease," the Mayo Clinic doctor told my husband. It was 1983. I was a twenty-four-year-old college student, and we had just had our first child. I would now need to be the one in the workforce supporting our family.

I had always expected to be home with our children, to be there when my children arrived from school as my mom had been for me, making our home the place kids would want to hang out. Most of my goals centered on creating a strong family that would love spending time and having fun together.

This yearning for a close-knit family led to my initial interest in the Mormon church. A few years earlier, we had found a pamphlet from The Church of Jesus Christ of Latter-day Saints inserted into our apartment mailbox. It mentioned a free manual with ideas about family togetherness. I ordered it, and the missionaries delivered it a few days later.

That same month we moved to a new apartment building, and my statistics professor, Dr. Ray Littlejohn, showed up with his two small children to help us move. I noticed the special way he treated his children. It turned out he was a Mormon. His relationship with his children reflected his belief that families are eternal units that remain together after this life. He was leading by example, teaching his children to serve others. He invited us to go to church with his family, beginning our investigation of and ultimate conversion to The Church of Jesus Christ of Latter-day Saints.

As I learned more about the Church, additional things became important. For example, I came to love serving others as a lifestyle. The Church encourages members to participate in a "family night" every Monday evening, and some of our most memorable ones have involved service. One week we chose the topic "gratitude."

Following a family discussion, each of us wrote a thank-you note to someone who had helped us. We delivered one to my son Joe's Little League coach, along with a plate of cookies. When he answered the door and saw one of his players with treats and a note of thanks, he choked up and said, "Wow, in my twenty years of coaching, no one has ever thanked me." A life lesson for our family: to serve and be served.

I believe that children raised with a focus on serving others are less likely to get involved in the trappings of self-absorption. Recently, I helped to plan a pool party for a group of Latter-day Saint teenage girls. The day before the party, we learned that a young family had moved into a nearby vacant home that needed some serious attention. When the girls were asked whether they wanted to continue with their party plans or to scrape paint off of tile and paint walls, they unanimously voted to serve this family. They worked enthusiastically while singing Disney tunes and Church hymns.

On the way home, a chorus arose of, "When can we do something like that again? That was so FUN!" I thought of what teens across the country might be involved in doing that night. How many were selflessly helping others and calling it fun? These girls had been taught to serve. The LDS Church creates an atmosphere that facilitates raising children who realize the difference it can make to practice Christianity, not just believe in it.

I know well what it feels like to be on the receiving end of this process! We moved into a new home when I was eight months pregnant. As the moving van was being unloaded, three LDS women showed up, placed a chair in the kitchen for me to sit on, and declared that they were going to unpack my kitchen. I was allowed only to direct where things should go. They taught me to be served.

Another of the greatest benefits I've enjoyed from my membership in the Mormon church is what we call the gift of the Holy Ghost. Undeniably, I have been prompted by the Spirit, and I pray regularly for that continued guidance in my life. Let me share an example that took place over ten years ago that I still think about with emotion. It concerns a young lady with whom I was especially close, who had gone through some challenges not of her own making during her teen years.

I met Amber when she was five. We ended up in the same ward (congregation) again when she was sixteen, and we instantly clicked and became close friends. Amber exudes life, energy, and fun—as on the evening she phoned to say she was going to make cinnamon rolls and bring them by. An hour later, she called to tell me she had just reached the part of the recipe where the dough has to rise for a few hours. When we stopped laughing, I told her I'd be asleep on the couch, and she could come in and wake me up whenever she arrived. We had a fabulous early-morning chat over cinnamon rolls!

Amber went to Utah for college, and I was excited when I received the telephone call saying that she was engaged. A Latter-day Saint marriage is a sacred ordinance performed in a small room in a Mormon temple with family members and a few close friends. (The wedding reception, often held afterward, is usually a larger, more general celebration.) I received an invitation to Amber's temple wedding in Utah and to her reception in Chicago. Since I lived in Chicago, I assumed she had invited me to the wedding as a courtesy, knowing she would see me at the Chicago reception.

One day, while working in my home office, I got a strong prompting: "You need to be at Amber's wedding." I logically thought it through: The wedding was in two days; Les was out of town; I had young children at home; and I would see her at the Chicago reception a few days after the wedding. I went back to work. A few minutes later, I again felt, "You NEED to be at Amber's wedding." I called to check on flight prices. They were exorbitant, given that it was just days away, so I talked myself out of it again. A few hours later, I felt these words so clearly I almost heard them:

"YOU NEED to be at Amber's wedding." Clearly, I wasn't going to get my work done until I relented, so I booked a flight, found places for my children, and headed to Utah the next day.

Since this took place before cell phones, and Amber was already in transit, I could not let her know I was coming. I walked into the temple still not sure why I was there, and hoping it would not be disruptive to have me attend unplanned. Amber's father was standing near the entrance alone. He stared at me in disbelief, then explained that he had just finished breaking the news to Amber that her mother was not going to be able to attend the ceremony. He asked me to join Amber in the bride's room. When I walked in, she and I stood for a few seconds staring at each other. Then, as we hugged, she said words I will never forget, "How do you always know when I need you?" To serve and be served.

I love how our wards are structured to facilitate serving each other, functioning much like an extended family. The whole system just "kicks in" when you move to a new place. For example, on our first day at church after a move to St. Louis, a gentleman with children the same ages as ours introduced us to his family and invited us over for dinner that night—Easter Sunday. He did not mention that he held the busy Church position of stake president, presiding over ten local wards, and was a retinal surgeon with a full schedule. The time he took to help us in our transition meant that our children would "know someone" on that scary first day of school. What a gift!

Two weeks later, I was called to be president of the ward's Young Women's organization. Through this assignment, I came to know Katrina. She was twelve, the same age as our daughter, Jackie, and had some challenging circumstances in her family life. Her grandmother brought her to church, and in my capacity as her youth leader, I came to understand her situation.

Despite her troubled home life, Katrina radiated innocence and

sweetness. We began inviting her to join our family for visits and sleepovers, and eventually for family vacations. She knew if she were having a bad day, she could call. We would come get her, no questions asked. Katrina became a regular addition to our family.

When the girls were fifteen, we received unexpected news that we had to relocate. We couldn't bear the thought of leaving Katrina. She had learned she could count on us. How could we tear that apart? Surely God had put us in each other's paths for a reason. I couldn't sleep.

When we went house hunting in our new town, Katrina came along, unaware that I hoped to have her move with us. I wanted her to see the area, schools, and church in case she would be able to accompany us. The hurdles were big. Would her family agree to let her, their youngest, move away? Would a school system allow us to enroll a child with whom we had no familial or legal connection? Les and I stopped by the school to explain the situation. The wonderful administrator responded, "If you can get her here, she can go to my school." His school of more than three thousand students was bursting at the seams, and he could understandably have said no.

As we walked out of the building, the tears started. I knew God was clearing the way.

Next we met with Katrina's mother and asked if she would consider allowing her daughter to spend the next semester with us. She thought about it, then posed it to Katrina. What a big decision for a fifteen-year-old who had lived in the same house her whole life, to choose whether to move out of state and leave everything familiar behind. Katrina's biggest concern was whether things would further deteriorate for her family if she were not there, and whether she would be at fault if they did. Weighty issues for a teenager. She decided to move with us, and the semester turned into a permanent arrangement. My quest to have a close family became complete in a way I had not anticipated.

The past six years having Katrina in our family have been wonderful and rewarding. It was not always easy. Over the years, she and Jackie—who shared her brother, parents, and friends—transitioned from being best friends to the close bond of sisterhood. Katrina graduated from high school with a high GPA, earned her LDS Young Womanhood achievement award (comparable to an Eagle Scout), and attended religion classes with Jackie for an hour before high school each day. She is now a senior at BYU's Idaho campus, a few hours from Jackie at BYU in Utah. Her family has made progress addressing their challenges. Katrina is studying psychology and wants to work with troubled youth. To serve and be served.

I am deeply grateful for my membership in The Church of Jesus Christ of Latter-day Saints. This decision, more than any other I've made, has shaped my life, my relationships, my values, and my closeness to my Savior.

HANNAH CLAYSON SMITH

HANNAH AND HER HUSBAND, John, live near Dallas, Texas, with their three children. Hannah does legal projects part-time from home as senior counsel for the Becket Fund for Religious Liberty, a public-interest law firm based in Washington, D.C. She has served as law clerk to two U.S. Supreme Court justices—Justice Clarence Thomas and Justice Samuel A. Alito, Jr. She litigated trial and appellate level cases at large law firms in Washington, D.C.

Photo by Scott G. Winterton, *Deseret News*

Hannah graduated from the J. Reuben Clark Law School at Brigham Young University. She served as executive editor of the *BYU Law Review*, as an assistant to Professor W. Cole Durham Jr., organizing international legal conferences at the BYU International Center for Law and Religion Studies, and as a teaching assistant for now-Utah Supreme Court Justice Thomas R. Lee in his civil procedure class.

Hannah graduated from Princeton University, where she majored in the Woodrow Wilson School of Public and International Affairs, focusing on education reform policy with a minor in the teacher preparation program. She was a student teacher at Princeton High School teaching courses in U.S. history and A.P. comparative government. As a college student, Hannah served as president of the LDS Student Club and music director of an a cappella singing group, and she played violin in the chamber orchestra. She worked as a summer counselor at Especially for Youth at Brigham Young University.

She currently serves in her local congregation as an early-morning seminary teacher for a class of high school juniors and seniors. She served a full-time mission in France and Switzerland, teaching the gospel, performing community service with local relief groups, and teaching English classes. Previously, she served as the president of her congregation's women's organization; as president of her congregation's ministry for teenage girls; as teacher of the adult Sunday School class; as teacher of the class to prepare members to enter the holy temple; and as a cultural arts director, conducting an oratorio for the two-hundredth anniversary of the Prophet Joseph Smith's birth.

Finally, she volunteers as a board member of the international LDS attorneys association—the J. Reuben Clark Law Society—and as a member of the *Deseret News* Editorial Advisory Board.

• • •

I AM A MORMON, FIRST, because my ancestors were Mormons. Born into a faithful Latter-day Saint home, I was taught from a young age about our Mormon pioneer ancestors. My family's legacy of faith extends back seven generations to the foundation of The Church of Jesus Christ of Latter-day Saints. Both my mother's and my father's ancestors followed the call of conscience to become members. They sacrificed what faith required, sometimes at great cost.

One ancestor, Parley P. Pratt, was called by God in 1835 as an original member of the Church's Quorum of Twelve Apostles, which, together with the Church's presidency, serves as its senior leadership. A fearless and inspired missionary, Pratt preached the gospel of Jesus Christ with power and eloquence that still resonates in the extensive

records that remain. He taught and baptized many, several of whom became Church leaders, including a future Church president, John Taylor, and a future mother of another Church president, Mary Fielding Smith. Pratt authored many of the Church's first missionary pamphlets and hymns. While on a mission to England, he reached a broad audience by founding and editing the *Millennial Star,* the Church's main publication abroad.

Fleeing religious persecution in Missouri and then Illinois, Pratt led his family and others to resettle in the Salt Lake Valley in present-day Utah in 1847, part of the first wave of Mormon pioneers who blazed trails across the Great Plains. His team surveyed and built the road that would bring many through the last line of Rocky Mountains into that valley through what is now called Parley's Canyon. On yet another long-distance journey to preach the gospel, this time in Arkansas, Pratt paid the ultimate price for the cause of Christ.

As a child, and still now, I marvel at the character and devotion my ancestors displayed to remain true to their faith. I am a Mormon because they first led the way.

I am a Mormon because my earnest mother and father, as the parents of three of God's children, taught my brother and sister and me about Jesus Christ. I am forever grateful to them for their love and devotion to us. In an age when some advocate that children should be unguided and "free" to discover what they want to believe, I am thankful that my parents taught us to love Jesus Christ, to cherish His teachings, and to strive to be an example of Him in all that we do and say. When I reached the traditional age of accountability for my decisions (age eight), I chose to be baptized. Dressed in white, I was briefly immersed in water to wash away my sins and signal a new life and commitment in Christ. My father baptized me because he, like all worthy adult men in our church, was ordained to the priesthood of God. The baptism followed the example of Jesus Christ, who said to John the Baptist that to fulfill all righteousness, even He, the perfect Son of God, must be baptized to obey God's law. I am a Mormon because Christ first was baptized to heed Heavenly Father's commandment.

I am a Mormon because as a young adult far from home attending college at Princeton University, I chose to study the scriptures and gain an independent and firm belief in the truthfulness of the gospel of Jesus Christ as restored through modern prophets, starting with Joseph Smith. While studying at Princeton, I encountered for the first time friends who actively challenged my faith or vocally disagreed with LDS teachings. For example, I recall studying in my dorm room the New Testament epistles alongside the words of modern LDS prophets, so I could respond adequately to my friends' questions about what Mormons believed about salvation: did it come by faith or by works? For four years, challenged by such probing questions at a place where everyone questioned everything, I studied and prayed to be able to answer those who questioned what I believed and why. I am a Mormon because, through study and prayer and confirmation of the Holy Spirit, I became personally convinced of the truthfulness of Christ's gospel.

I am a Mormon because, as a missionary in France, I saw how the teachings of Christ blessed and transformed the lives of those who heeded them and joined His Church. Following graduation from Princeton, I was called by God through a living prophet, Church President Gordon B. Hinckley, to share the gospel of Jesus Christ with Heavenly Father's children in France and in French-speaking Switzerland. After two months of intense preparation in the Church's Missionary Training Center in Utah, I served the French people in Lyon, Saint-Étienne, and Besançon. As missionaries, we taught complete strangers that Heavenly Father loves them and wants them to return home to live with Him after this earthly life. In order for any of us to do that, we taught that we must make and keep promises to strive to become like our Heavenly Father by following the example of His beloved Son, Jesus Christ.

Time after time, I saw our friends respond to the influence of the Holy Spirit and take steps closer to Christ: reading the scriptures, praying to Heavenly Father, participating in church meetings, and serving others with love. One time, we were teaching a woman in Lyon about the Prophet Joseph Smith's humble prayer for spiritual guidance in 1820 that was answered by the appearance of Heavenly Father and Jesus Christ. She put her hand over her chest and told us she felt a warm burning in her heart. We explained that she was feeling the Holy Spirit who confirms the truthfulness of the gospel. She was baptized a few weeks later, and her life was forever changed. The gospel of Jesus Christ transforms people's lives for the better. I am a Mormon because, as a missionary, I saw the fruits of the Mormon faith bless the lives of those I taught and loved.

I am a Mormon because Heavenly Father has enabled us to be with our families for eternity if we make and keep sacred covenants in temples of the Lord. After I returned from my mission, I was "sealed" through temple marriage to my husband, John, in the LDS temple in Oakland, California. We believe this sealing makes our family an eternal unit, allowing us to live together forever if we remain faithful. The person conducting our sealing ceremony (Elder David B. Haight, one of the Twelve Apostles at the time) expressed his belief that our deceased family members were celebrating with us in the temple on that special day and rejoiced in our decision to unite our lives there. The act of sealing binds my husband and me together, our children to us, and our family with our ancestors' families in a chain that links our family through the centuries. I love this beautiful doctrine. At a time when the institution of marriage is increasingly questioned and undermined, I am grateful for a church that teaches the divine origins and sacred purposes of marriage. I am a Mormon because I believe in the doctrine of eternal families through eternal covenants we make in sacred temples.

I am a Mormon because I believe in the divine calling of mothers. After my husband and I were married, we graduated from law school and returned to the East Coast for clerkships and for positions in private practice and government service in Washington, D.C. After we practiced law full-time for several years, Heavenly Father blessed us with three children, all named for honorable ancestors: Gladys Woodruff, Lucy Pratt, and George Albert. The gift of these three beautiful children has graced our lives immeasurably. I am grateful that I can learn the lessons of mothering unique to raising children. I feel the inspiration of my Heavenly Father every day as I nurture, teach, guide, and love them. It is an awesome thing that our Heavenly Father allows us to become more like Him through parenting His spirit children on this earth. I believe that no calling brings us closer to that ultimate goal than the divine calling of motherhood. I am a Mormon because I know my Heavenly Father delights in my being a mother.

I am a Mormon because I believe in doing good and being

an example of Christ's goodness in an increasingly secular world. After I became a mother, I was approached by the president of the Becket Fund for Religious Liberty, a public-interest law firm based in Washington, D.C., that defends religious liberty for people of all faiths. I was invited to do legal projects part-time from home while being a mother to my children. After prayer and discussion with my husband, we saw the hand of the Lord in this opportunity, and I accepted. At the Becket Fund, I have worked shoulder to shoulder with people from many different faith communities, defending clients from diverse religions. It is a special blessing to work with such good people in such an important cause. I am regularly impressed by the goodness and sincerity of these true believers. Although our beliefs may diverge on points of doctrine, we strive to worship freely in our own way the God we love.

In today's discourse, we often see religious ideas or religiously grounded positions discarded as unreasonable or irrelevant. I think it is important that like-minded people of faith everywhere seek opportunities to stand up for those who seek to honor God as they feel called to do. Latter-day Saints understand what it means to be persecuted for religious belief. When we see religious bigotry anywhere, we should be the first to defend the rights of our fellow believers to practice their faith. This is what the God I believe in wants us to do. I am a Mormon because I believe that "all men" should have the "privilege of worshiping Almighty God according to the dictates of [their] own conscience . . . let them worship how, where, or what they may" (Articles of Faith 1:11).

I am a Mormon because, along my life's journey, my soul responded to the call of the Holy Spirit to be a follower of Jesus Christ. I know that my Heavenly Father lives and that He has a divine plan of happiness for my life and for all His children who have ever lived on the earth. I believe in His Son Jesus Christ and in His divine mission to atone for our sins so that each of us can return to live eternally with Heavenly Father. I believe in the calling of modern prophets, who proclaim that God continues to speak to men and women today as He did in times of old. I know that we can find the everlasting gospel of Jesus Christ in His holy word, including the Bible and the Book of Mormon and the writings of prophets alive today who receive revealed truth to guide us. I am a Mormon because I believe these truths.

JOHN M. SMITH

JOHN M. SMITH lives near Dallas, Texas, with his wife, Hannah, and their three children.

John is a lawyer with expertise in national security issues. He works for Raytheon, a U.S. defense company, as the lawyer for its cyber security division.

Previously, John served as associate counsel to President George W. Bush. At the White House, he was the primary legal advisor to the Homeland Security Council staff. With senior lawyers across the national security and intelligence communities, he worked on counterterrorism, cyber security, intelligence, privacy, disaster response, and WMD defense.

John clerked together with his wife for then-Judge Samuel A. Alito, Jr., on the U.S. Court of Appeals for the Third Circuit. John then practiced international, regulatory, and white-collar criminal defense law at Covington & Burling in Washington, D.C.

John graduated *magna cum laude* from Princeton University, where he was elected Phi Beta Kappa and senior class president. He authored a public policy thesis on the post-Soviet transition in Russia, Ukraine, and Belarus. During summers, he worked in those countries to facilitate humanitarian aid to hospitals and training to medical professionals through the Children of Chernobyl Relief Fund and the American International Health Alliance.

He received his law degree *magna cum laude* from Brigham Young University's J. Reuben Clark Law School, where he was lead articles editor of its *Law Review* and authored articles on religious liberty.

John served a decade as a U.S. Army reservist, as an intelligence specialist and JAG officer. He was decorated for his service in a NATO Partnership for Peace mission in Eastern Europe and briefly supported the 101st Airborne Division at Fort Campbell, Kentucky.

In the LDS Church, John has served as a counselor in three bishoprics, elders quorum president, ward mission leader, and Young Men's counselor. He served two years as a missionary in Russia and Ukraine, including nine months as assistant to the mission president. He remains fluent in Russian and Ukrainian and has interpreted for senior Church leaders.

John's other international experience includes working on legal matters in Georgia, Russia, and Ukraine; teaching seminars sponsored by the American Bar Association for Ukrainian judges and lawyers; monitoring the presidential election during Ukraine's Orange Revolution with former members of the U.S. Congress and European Parliament; and speaking at international legal conferences promoting religious liberty, co-hosted by the BYU International Center for Law and Religion Studies.

• • •

I T WAS MY FIRST DAY of a new job. As the newest lawyer for the president of the United States, I was finding my way around the White House. I entered a room with dark blue curtains and American flags to hear my new boss address the nation about a policy involving three causes I care deeply about: morality, religion, and the law.

Two of the honored guests in the front row were familiar. I had previously seen them in action advancing these causes. The president was now honoring and meeting with them. For me, the two guests also represented two turning points in my path to becoming a Latter-day Saint.

The first was a professor at Princeton University, the place where I had embraced the restored gospel and decided to be baptized into The Church of Jesus Christ of Latter-day Saints. He taught my first course in constitutional law, which pointed me toward my profession. Also in that class was my future wife, Hannah Clayson, who pointed me toward an eternal family.

The president's other familiar guest was an Apostle, a senior leader of the LDS Church whom I had last seen in Ukraine, where I had served as a missionary. In these two places, Princeton and Ukraine, I came to "walk in newness of life," learning and sharing the Truth that sets us free (Romans 6:4).

Between my American father and my Ukrainian-born mother, my boyhood bridged two religions, languages, and cultures. Born in New York and raised in New Jersey, I attended my mother's Ukrainian Catholic Church, serving in the choir and as an altar boy. For a decade, my loving mother taught me a Ukrainian language lesson every morning before school, and I attended a weekly Ukrainian school, religion class, and Scouting activity. I questioned sacrificing so much free time to study a heritage that appeared doomed under endless Soviet repression. But my faithful parents encouraged me to persist, expressing confidence that it would lead to something good.

Then the unforeseen intervened. Gorbachev's era of reform loosened the USSR's totalitarian grip, giving hope to its people and those abroad who prayed for their liberation. In 1988, my family traveled to Washington, D.C., to join a march commemorating the 1,000-year anniversary of Christianity coming to Ukraine. We

demonstrated in front of the iron-fenced Soviet Embassy, chanting, "Free Our Churches in Ukraine!" I remember feeling very passionate, even then, about confronting the evil of denying others the right to worship God freely. As I took my final set of Ukrainian-school exams in Ukrainian history, geography, literature, culture, and language, the walls of Communism were being torn down across Eastern Europe.

Preparing for college, I wrote in my applications my goal to bring "the best of the land of my father to the land of my mother." My appreciation for America's contributions to the world—liberty, a moral force, and the rule of law—was already deep. But practically, I had little idea how to reach my goal.

In September 1991, I arrived at Princeton and soon happened upon a pair of LDS missionaries standing near the main campus library. I wanted to know more about their faith. Since I had heard as a boy from my parents the stories of Jesus Christ, I wanted to be more like Him. I was looking for a people who could show me how. I wanted to learn more about the Lord and His will for me.

From what I knew of Latter-day Saints, they took Jesus Christ seriously. They did not shy away from His hard commandments that I had read in the New Testament: turn away from sin and temptation; love your neighbors, even your enemies; forgive others their wrongs; give generously to the poor and needy; trust God always, even through suffering and injustice; and go tell friends and strangers the Good News of eternal life.

The Latter-day Saints I knew were earnest about living the Lord's teachings, even when that demanded moral courage, sacrifice, and social ridicule. They were organized to facilitate direct, personal Christian service toward each other, their neighbors, and others far away. Their Church had a pioneering role in American history, and I was aware that my father's family had been among those pioneers.

Could this church be what I had been seeking? Could it help me do the Lord's will?

Soon missionaries began to meet with me regularly, and they invited my two LDS classmates on campus to join us. One of them was Hannah. She and I had several sincere and profound conversations about faith. Then she asked me two questions that altered the course of my life:

1. Do you want to know if this church and the restored gospel are really from the Lord? (Yes, but now is not a good time.)

2. Will there ever be a perfect time?

Hannah was right. I was mindful of Jesus' invitation: "If any man will do [God's] will, he shall know of the doctrine, whether it be of God" (John 7:17). It was time to start doing, so I could know. I prayed and studied and began attending church services. My discussions of faith with Hannah became regular. She understood her faith with a keen intellect, believed it with conviction, lived it with integrity, and could explain it to someone with probing, nuanced questions. I had never met such a powerful combination, all in one Christian.

After several months, I focused on a story in the Book of Mormon about an ancient group of believers in the wilderness, led by the prophet Alma, who invited them to commit to the Lord:

"As ye are desirous to come into the fold of God, and to be called his people, and are willing to bear one another's burdens, that they may be light; Yea, and are willing to mourn with those that mourn; yea, and comfort those that stand in need of comfort, and to stand as witnesses of God at all times and in all things, and in all places. . . . Now I say unto you, if this be the desire of your hearts, what have you against being baptized in the name of the Lord, as a witness before him that ye have entered into a covenant with him, that ye will serve him and keep his commandments, that he may pour out his Spirit more abundantly upon you?" (Mosiah 18:8–10).

This question penetrated my soul. This was the desire of my heart. I was soon baptized. A year later, as Hannah was called to serve as a missionary in France and Switzerland, I was also called to bring the best thing from my father's country to my mother's country. I had listened to those who taught me how to become a Latter-day Saint. Now I would learn more by inviting others to come unto Christ.

When I arrived at Princeton in September 1991, the Soviet Union was unraveling. The people of Ukraine were literally tearing down the false idols of atheist communism. About the time I had first approached those two missionaries at Princeton, two LDS Apostles ascended a hill in Kyiv, Ukraine, that overlooks the river where the city's population entered the water to be baptized a thousand years earlier. There, one of the Apostles offered a dedicatory prayer that Ukraine would embrace missionaries of the restored gospel. He prophesied that "the spires of temples will be seen across this great land."

When I arrived in Kyiv as a missionary several years later, the Kyiv Mission president told me he was sending me and my companion to establish a permanent missionary presence in a "new" region of the country, western Ukraine, starting with its largest city (L'viv). Until that point, LDS missionaries called to Ukraine had been taught Russian and thus deployed only to several Russian-speaking cities, and not to the Ukrainian-speaking western region (roughly the size of England and Scotland combined). Carrying a short list of L'viv residents who had somehow expressed interest in the Church, and draft translations of the Book of Mormon and Church hymns (not yet published in Ukrainian), we headed out to establish the Church in the west.

We could sense immediately the Lord's help in sharing the gospel in western Ukraine. Through a modern prophet, the Lord has promised that every person will hear the gospel "in his own language" (Doctrine and Covenants 90:11). Our very first listener in L'viv helped explain why that promise mattered so much to Ukrainians: "When you teach me these things in Ukrainian, I can believe you. It was in Russian that we were taught that God did not exist." We soon needed a place to conduct our first baptism and found a swimming pond in a park—near KGB headquarters. When the park manager queried why we wanted to rent it early on a Sunday morning, I explained. Silence. Would he refuse, or even turn us in to hostile authorities? Then he replied, in essence, "You are doing God's work. The water belongs to Him, so I cannot charge you for it. Use the pond whenever you need it."

In the following months, I witnessed many miracles that enabled us to spread the gospel into four other large cities of western Ukraine. From the city closest to my Ukrainian relatives, a father journeyed hours to L'viv in search of the LDS missionaries once he heard we had arrived. Having no other way to contact us, he wandered the streets, asking if anyone had seen missionaries. In a city of almost a million people, before we even began wearing name tags, this seeker of truth found us. We followed him back to his city and established the first LDS congregation there around his small family. I saw this pattern repeated in the other Ukrainian cities we opened. I marveled how precisely the Lord's ancient promise was being fulfilled in modern Ukraine: "I will take you one of a city, and two of a family, and I will bring you to Zion" (Jeremiah 3:14).

I knew from my studies how much the Ukrainian people had suffered through the centuries as they struggled "against the rulers of the darkness of this world" (Ephesians 6:12). I saw in person how this evil still burdened Ukraine. So I felt real joy in punching holes through such darkness every day—teaching the doctrines of free will, faith and redemption in Christ, eternal family relationships—and then watching Ukrainians step into the light. The gospel teaches that each individual is a unique child of God, of infinite and eternal worth—not a fungible, disposable labor asset of the state. It teaches trusting in God and giving freely, not fear and compulsion. It teaches love and devotion toward family as a virtue, not a threat to state allegiance. Learning why family history research was so difficult for Ukrainians motivated me all the more: not only had Soviet atheism destroyed so many churches and clergy, but the KGB method for destroying believers and other so-called "enemies of the people"—by persecuting their whole families—meant that knowing to whom you were related could be fatal. To protect their children, parents and grandparents kept them in the dark about God and their relatives. Today, with a temple of their own, the Ukrainian Latter-day Saints are connecting their families eternally and healing their land.

In 1944, my infant mother and her parents fled Ukraine for the

West, a day before the reinvading Soviets captured and persecuted their village. My grandfather saved his family by escaping to the United States and won for them the freedom to worship God and to cherish their Ukrainian heritage and language. He was never able to return to his homeland, but he taught those values to me.

In 1945, as my Ukrainian grandparents were reaching safety just ahead of the Communist "Iron Curtain" descending across Eastern Europe, my paternal great-grandfather, LDS Church President George Albert Smith, addressed the whole Church about missionary work and "Russia," whose Soviet empire then included Ukraine. He foresaw that land "as one of the most fruitful fields for the teaching of the gospel of Jesus Christ." He prophesied that its people would soon "desire to know" of the Lord's work.

I have personally witnessed that prophecy fulfilled. I have seen how the restored gospel has transformed my life and those I taught as a missionary. I know our Father in Heaven loves all His children here on earth and calls us to serve each other. His prophets continue to lead us in the way of Christ, back to the Father in one eternal family.

WENDY ULRICH

WENDY ULRICH holds a PhD in psychology and education from the University of Michigan and an MBA from the University of California, Los Angeles. She has been a practicing psychologist for over twenty years and is a former president of the Association of Mormon Counselors and Psychotherapists. She is the founder of Sixteen Stones Center for Growth (sixteenstones.net), a small group of mental health professionals committed to enhancing the spiritual and emotional resilience of LDS women and their loved ones. She has authored several books, including, with her husband, Dave Ulrich, the *New York Times* bestseller *The Why of Work: How Great Leaders Build Abundant Organizations That Win* (McGraw Hill, 2010; thewhyofwork.com). They have three children.

• • •

A GOOD FRIEND WHO IS ALSO a member of The Church of Jesus Christ of Latter-day Saints visited me recently, and her visit happened to fall on what members of the Church refer to as Fast Sunday. On the first Sunday of each month we are encouraged to fast—to forgo food and drink for approximately twenty-four hours—and to donate the money we would normally have spent on

food to those in need. We are also encouraged to use this period of fasting to petition God on behalf of those we love and to draw closer to Him. As my friend and I approached the end of our fast, a bright contentment and stillness settled in my soul. My friend, acknowledging a similar feeling, said, "I'm so grateful to have been taught to fast. I never would have thought this up on my own."

I too would never have thought up fasting on my own. In fact, I fasted many times before I saw any spiritual benefit in the practice. I can still go through the motions of fasting without feeling much of anything except hungry. But increasingly I notice that sincere fasting and prayer brings a particular peace into my life that seems to come in no other way. I feel more fully myself, more grounded in my relationship with God, more sensitive to spiritual impressions, more genuine in my relationships with others.

Like exercise (something else I never would have thought up on my own), fasting can be difficult for me and doesn't necessarily yield immediate results or satisfaction. A non-LDS acquaintance, a spiritual woman, decided to try it. Her assessment was, "I'll never do that again! That was ridiculously hard, and all I got out of it was cranky and hungry." So fasting is definitely an acquired "taste." It helps to have social support—like an expectation from an early age that one can succeed and testimonials of the spiritual benefits fasting brings—to help a person persist long enough to contact the finely tuned spiritual experiences that can come once the hurdles of physical discomfort are cleared. Fasting in such a way as to allow these experiences to surface is still challenging to me, but I am grateful to have been taught to fast.

People from many faith traditions fast and pray; these are hardly unique ideas. But they are one very small part of a broad lifestyle of spiritual commitment that has led me to feel, recognize, value, and receive the Spirit of God. The teachings and stories of the LDS Church awakened me to the possibility that a fallible, ordinary woman can come to know God, and these teachings have shown me a path to get there. That path includes many practices and doctrines that, like fasting, I never would have thought up on my own. In fact, some of those elements have been not only unlikely but at times unsettling. I have had to remind myself that Jesus' teachings were also unsettling at times, even to those who knew Him best. But I have been on the path long enough now to say with confidence that it has led me to the One I have sought. I have experienced His humility, His wisdom, His goodness, and His love, beyond my power to describe them.

Like many people who have longed for a close and loving relationship with God and more regular access to spiritual comfort or direction, I used to wonder why God seemed so distant when I wanted so much to be close to Him. In recent years I have increasingly realized that I am the one who has kept Him far away, not so much by my disobedience as by my restlessness, my distractibility, my impatience, my blindness, and, especially, my fear. Intimacy is hard enough to tolerate in human relationships, where closeness reminds us of just how vulnerable we are, how often we have been disappointed and hurt, how much we have to lose. God, for me at least, has been even harder to let close than people. But I am learning that He can be trusted to tell me the truth about myself and the world, even when the truth is hard, and He does so with a love and kindness that leave me wanting it more instead of wanting to push it away.

The Mormon church teaches without apology that God can be found, that He wants to be found, and that ordinary people can find Him. Fasting, praying, studying and pondering scripture, paying tithes and offerings, ordering my time and relationships, serving other people in systematic ways, and a host of other aspects of what it means to try to live as a disciple of Christ, a saint—these are the spiritual disciplines that have helped me gain the spiritual stamina I needed in order to tolerate the closeness to God I have sought (and feared).

Whether as a Mormon, a Christian, or simply one who believes in God, I acknowledge struggling with many challenges to my scientific and scholarly training, my somewhat liberal inclinations, and my personal comfort. I have experienced periods of doubt, dissatisfaction, disillusionment, and disapproval with God, Christianity, and the LDS Church. Still, I have come to deeply love the Lord, and I have come to love The Church of Jesus Christ of Latter-day Saints. Specifically, I love the comprehensiveness of its doctrine, the scope of its charitable service, the beauty of its stories, and the quiet, dignified goodness of so many of its people. But I especially love the hope that it holds out to me that sincere people who are willing to submit to the Lord's tutoring can receive the Holy Ghost and be changed and sanctified by His influence. I have felt that influence teach me, change me, lead me to understand and receive the Atonement of

Jesus Christ, and prepare me to seek and endure the consuming fire of God's love.

It seems most reasonable to me that if there is a God, we will not come to know Him through scientific reasoning, argument and debate, historical treatises, or social programs. As others have noted, either He reveals Himself to us or He will remain unknown. I continue to find credible the witness of the young Joseph Smith that he saw God the Father and His Son Jesus Christ. In his words, "They did in reality speak to me. . . . I knew it, and I knew that God knew it, and I could not deny it, neither dared I do it; at least I knew that by so doing I would offend God, and come under condemnation" (Joseph Smith—History 1:25).

Among the hundreds, maybe thousands of impressions, helps, and ideas that I believe have come to me from God either in answer to prayer or "out of the blue," perhaps many could conceivably be written off to coincidence, messages from my subconscious, or wishful thinking. However, a few are so tender, so powerful, or so utterly unlikely that I would have to say with Joseph Smith that I know they are from God. And I know that God knows I know, and I cannot walk away. I believe that all people of every nation, family, language, race, and religion are His children. He knows us by name, loves us beyond measure, and reaches toward us in whatever way we will receive.

Undoubtedly, sincere people may follow many paths to increase their spirituality and faith. My experience has been with this path, and it has led me to my Father in Heaven. Because I believe Jesus Christ's teaching that He is the Way, the Truth, and the Life, and that no one comes to the Father but by Him, I trust this path to be of Christ, my Savior.

BUNDIT UNGRANGSEE

BUNDIT UNGRANGSEE is a highly sought-after international conductor, with a career spanning five continents. He has conducted more than five hundred symphonic and operatic performances with more than forty orchestras worldwide, including the Los Angeles Philharmonic Orchestra, the prestigious La Fenice Theatre in Venice, and the Mormon Tabernacle Choir. Recent engagements include concerts with orchestras in Italy, Japan, Thailand, Singapore, South Korea, and Denmark.

In November 2005, Bundit was one of three international conductors invited to take an active part in the historic development of the Seoul Philharmonic Orchestra into a world-class musical institution. In June 2007, he invited the orchestra to give a concert tour in his home country of Thailand.

A Thai conductor of Chinese descent, Bundit is the first Thai to have won awards in many prestigious international conducting competitions. In September 2002 he was named Laureate and Co-Winner among 362 competitors from forty countries in the inaugural Maazel-Vilar International Conductors' Competition, held at Carnegie Hall in New York City. The Thai government has recognized his achievements with the titles of "National Artist" (*Silpathorn*) and "Cultural Diplomat."

Among the world-class artists with whom he has worked are Maxim Vengerov, Julia Migenes, Joseph Alessi, the LaBeque Sisters, Paula Robison, Christopher Parkening, Christine Brewer, and Elmer Bernstein. In April 2004, Arabesque Records released an album of Mozart flute concertos conducted by Bundit, featuring renowned soloist Paula Robison and the Charleston Symphony Orchestra.

In 1998, he received the Leonard Bernstein Conducting Fellowship and was invited to be one of only three Conducting Fellows at Tanglewood Music Center, where he was mentored by Jorma Panula and Seiji Ozawa. Earlier in the same year, he was among nine young conductors from around the world to participate in the Sibelius Academy Conducting Masterclass at Carnegie Hall led by Esa-Pekka Salonen, Music Director of the Los Angeles Philharmonic. Another teacher he recognizes as greatly influential is Maestro Lorin Maazel, Music Director of the New York Philharmonic Orchestra, who privately trained him over a period of three years.

The *Los Angeles Times* has reviewed Ungrangsee as "commanding calm and poise . . . exhibiting impressive assurance on the podium . . . His reading unwound unhurriedly and clearly, the patchwork drama made cogent and all the details noted, including pianissimo dynamics." The *Charleston Post and Courier* reviewed Ungrangsee as "display[ing] a sure touch . . . leading a glorious performance—a model of rhythmic drive, dynamic control and pinpoint accuracy . . . delivering a truly thrilling performance that left the audience breathless. . . . His reading, from beginning to end, was filled with deft touches that bespoke much attention to detail and phrasing."

Bundit has also become a respected author and speaker in his native Thailand. His books on leadership, self-development and music have sold several hundred thousand copies, and he is in demand as an inspirational speaker.

• • •

I WAS BORN INTO A TYPICAL Buddhist Thai family. My parents were not extremely devout, but they observed the basic tenets of Buddhism, as is expected of good Thai people. They had a shrine in their home and occasionally used amulets or prayed to different statues to ask for good luck and other blessings.

Ever since my childhood, these things bothered me. I knew in my heart that there was no way a wooden statue or a bronze amulet could help me. What power could it possibly have? It wasn't alive. It couldn't have any control over my life.

I felt the same way about Buddha. He had never in his lifetime claimed to be anything other than a man. Perhaps he was a good teacher who was able to help some people find peace. But he never claimed to be a god. I could respect him, but how could I pray to him for help? He was dead.

When I learned about Jesus Christ it was as though a new world of possibilities had opened up to me. Christianity hinges on Christ being exactly what He claims to be—that is, the Son of God. If Christ is not the Son of God, as He claimed to be, then He was just another man and a liar at that. But if He is what He says He is, and if He truly was resurrected as He testified He would be, then Christianity is the only true and living religion on the earth.

So at the age of fourteen, I converted to Christianity. I started attending a Pentecostal church. While I enjoyed learning about Christ, I was uncomfortable with other parts of the services. I soon stopped attending altogether, although I never lost my faith in Jesus Christ.

Years later, while following my dream to become a symphony conductor, I had moved to California in the United States and eventually won the position of Associate Conductor of the Utah Symphony. Friends in California warned me about moving to Utah; they said I should be wary of the Mormons. My interest was piqued, and so almost as soon as I got to Utah I started studying with the missionaries. When I heard the story of Joseph Smith, I felt that same stirring that had caused me to become Christian back at the age of fourteen. I had found Christ, and now I knew I had found Christ's true church. A few months later I was baptized, and a year later I married my wife in the Salt Lake Temple.

When I was a child, my family didn't have a lot of money. All seven of us slept in one room each night. The bathroom in our apartment was especially frightening. It didn't have any windows, and at night it was pitch black. I hated to have to go to the bathroom at night because it was terrifying to go into that damp blackness. But if I had even the smallest light—a flashlight or a flicker of daylight—then that bathroom wasn't so scary anymore. It took only a small light to chase the darkness away.

Finding Christ was like finding a light that dispelled the darkness out of my life. I finally found someone that I could pray to and feel as though my prayers were actually being heard. I finally discovered a living and breathing faith. I have never seen Jesus Christ, but I have faith that He lives today. Even though I have never heard His voice, I can feel His love for me. I can feel His love for my family. I know that God answers our prayers. He has answered many of my prayers in ways that I never dreamed possible.

I would like to share a brief passage from "The Living Christ," which was published by the First Presidency and Quorum of Twelve Apostles of The Church of Jesus Christ of Latter-day Saints in 2000:

"As we commemorate the birth of Jesus Christ two millennia ago, we offer our testimony of the reality of His matchless life and the infinite virtue of His great atoning sacrifice. None other has had so profound an influence upon all who have lived and will yet live upon the earth. . . .

"We solemnly testify that His life, which is central to all human history, neither began in Bethlehem nor concluded on Calvary. He was the Firstborn of the Father, the Only Begotten Son in the flesh, the Redeemer of the world. . . .

"We bear testimony, as His duly ordained Apostles—that Jesus is the Living Christ, the immortal Son of God. He is the great King Immanuel, who stands today on the right hand of His Father. He is the light, the life, and the hope of the world. His way is the path that leads to happiness in this life and eternal life in the world to come. God be thanked for the matchless gift of His divine Son."

Just over two thousand years ago, Jesus Christ was born on earth. What He accomplished in His thirty-three short years on earth is the single most important event in the history of the world. We should become familiar with every aspect of His unique and remarkable life. We should remember that His life did not begin in Bethlehem nor did it end on Calvary. Christ lives today. He atoned for my sins. He atoned for your sins. Because of His Atonement, I can be with my wife and children for eternity. I hope to teach my children to love Him as I do.

Our Savior chased away the darkness in the world when He was born. He is the light and life of the world. I love Him and am grateful to have found Him.

Bradford D. Waldie

Born in Arizona, the second oldest of eight children, Bradford Waldie entered the United States Air Force Academy after graduating from high school in 2004. Following his freshman year, he left the Academy to carry out two years of missionary work for The Church of Jesus Christ of Latter-day Saints in Ontario, Canada. There he learned Mandarin Chinese and was privileged to serve among and learn from a very diverse population.

Following his return to the Academy in 2007, Bradford declared Foreign Area Studies as his major, with a second major in Humanities and a Chinese minor. Over his years at the Academy he enjoyed participating in diverse activities, including running with the Academy triathlon team and cohosting a classic rock radio show. Most of all, Bradford enjoyed and appreciated the opportunities the Academy provided to explore the broader world. While a cadet he participated in research internships and cultural immersion trips to Israel, India, Brazil, Italy, South Africa, Egypt, and China. He was selected to participate in the Academy's study abroad program and spent fall semester 2008 at Nanjing University in China.

At the Academy Bradford also served in several leadership positions, such as the wing director of operations and chief of

training for Squadron 8. During the final year of his undergraduate work, Bradford was selected as a Truman Scholar and received
the Holaday Scholarship. He also received several awards, such as
2010 Outstanding Cadet in an East Asian Language Minor, 2010
Outstanding Cadet in the Humanities, and 2010 Outstanding
Cadet in Foreign Area Studies. He received his commission as a
Second Lieutenant and graduated first in his class in May 2010.

Bradford recently earned a master's of science in African Studies
at the University of Oxford, where he is currently studying for a
second master's in Global Governance and Diplomacy as a member
of Exeter College. In his research he has focused on security and
development in the eastern provinces of the Democratic Republic
of the Congo as well as Chinese diplomatic engagement in Africa.
He continues to enjoy a wide range of activities, such as rowing
for the Exeter College boat club, and pole vaulting for—and serving as captain of—the Oxford University Athletic Club. After the
completion of his graduate studies, Bradford will enter pilot training
at the Euro-NATO Joint Jet Pilot Training (ENJJPT) program in
Sheppard, Texas.

• • •

I STARED DOWN THE ENDLESS ROW of cadets wearing dark blue
hats on my first day of a new phase of basic training. As my eyes
focused on my destination, my hands began to tremble. The only
remaining place at the lunch table was the "hot seat," where basic
trainees undergo a seemingly endless barrage of verbal abuse before each meal while attempting to recite a cumbersome collection
of mandatory statements. Until that moment, I had successfully
avoided it, but now all I could do was prepare myself for a world of
trouble.

The new cadre member took his place at the head of the table.
His eyes surveyed my eight terrified classmates, finally resting on

Photo by Bill Evans

me. I kept my eyes locked in their mandated position, staring at the eagle insignia on the top of my plate, while I desperately attempted to review mentally the compulsory recitations. The cadre cleared his throat, and I prepared for a verbal beating, trying not to cringe as the upperclassman threw out his first question: "Who here knows Captain Moroni?" At that moment, I was grateful to be a Mormon.

Unbeknownst to my classmates—who had become accustomed to on-the-spot trivia questions about famous captains, colonels, and generals—our new cadre member had just asked the table to identify a famous hero from the Book of Mormon. I threw my arm straight out in front with my hand in a tight fist, indicating that I knew the answer. I heard audible exhaling and looked around to see my classmates' relief. For a fraction of a second, the eyes of my cadre member softened as we exchanged a look of tacit understanding of shared faith. In a flash, my nerves were eased, and though our common religious beliefs did not stop him from berating me for the smallest mistakes, I felt strengthened by the knowledge that I was not alone.

My first year at the Air Force Academy provided a proving

ground for my faith. I grew up in a family that regularly attends church meetings and is active in the Latter-day Saint (LDS) community. Under the protective umbrella of a faithful family and loving parents, I had slowly developed a testimony of the truthfulness of the gospel of Jesus Christ and of the blessings that come from living in accordance with His teachings. However, my nascent testimony had never been tested. That would change. When I left home to enter basic military training, after a tearful good-bye and a barbershop buzz cut, I found both my scalp and my soul exposed to the harsh elements of everyday reality in a very unfamiliar setting.

During the first days of basic training, I was instructed to march around endlessly with my eyes focused directly ahead. I was not permitted to speak freely, so I had plenty of time to think about my situation. I wondered why I had chosen the Air Force Academy; I wondered who I really was; and sometimes I struggled to find the desire and energy to continue studying the scriptures and praying as exhaustion and frustration began to take over. I wondered what good came from being a Mormon. I came to the conclusion that the only way to find out the depth of my faith and beliefs was to test them. I had arrived at the Academy expecting physical and mental challenges, but spiritual challenges were also on the horizon.

Immediately following basic training, as our academic year began, I discovered one way to test my faith. From my earliest Sunday School lessons as a youth, I had been taught the doctrine of keeping the Sabbath day holy. The Lord promises great blessings to all who keep one day of the week set apart for rest and worship. Despite having previously spent many Sunday evenings doing homework and catching up, I committed to completing all of my assignments earlier in the weekend so that I could set aside Sunday as a day of rest.

At the Academy, more than at most institutions, time is precious and cadets are purposely scheduled with more demands on their time than they have hours in the day. My vow to honor the Sabbath was intense since I had only six days in which to complete my work while other cadets had seven days to study, exercise, and prepare for military inspections. Completing my responsibilities while meeting my commitment was not easy; many times I awoke at three or four o'clock in the morning on Monday to study or to finish a paper. But I managed to complete all four years at the Academy without wavering from my goal.

My devotion to the Sabbath day commandment eventually brought many blessings. The Lord both strengthened my resolve and lengthened my stride. With the added vigor that came from my weekly respite, I found greater success in the classroom, on the athletic field, and in military training. Through that initial commitment early in my schooling, I learned for myself, independent of the influence of family and friends, that "all things work together for good to them that love God" (Romans 8:28).

While the Sabbath day commandment is common to many faiths, Mormon attitudes toward using clean language and avoiding movies that depict excessive violence, profanity, and vulgarity set us apart from most other denominations. For this reason, despite the fact that I was surrounded by many classmates devoted to their faiths, my decision to test my beliefs by refraining from swearing or watching R-rated movies caused me to stand out from most in my squadron. Opportunities to join friends in watching inappropriate movies or to use questionable language abounded, and my restraint often made me feel like an outcast. But I managed to move forward with faith and maintain the standards I had set.

Before long, I began to see a change in the way my classmates treated me. Their attitudes progressed from challenging me openly to ignoring me and finally to supporting my efforts to keep my mind and language clean. By my senior year, many who initially tested my resolve had become my strongest supporters. My good friends of other faiths would alter their vocabulary or turn off inappropriate entertainment when I was around. I remember one Friday night walking into a room to find a group of friends watching a movie. As soon as I came through the door, the DVD was paused and a friend said, "You probably shouldn't watch this. I'll come find you when it's over, and we'll all go out together." I learned from that and many other experiences that my friends respected my chosen lifestyle. I consider the respect they gained for my beliefs as a great example of the blessings that come from maintaining high moral standards. I will never forget their efforts to help me maintain my standards.

The most unexpected challenge to my faith came while I was traveling abroad on programs sponsored by the Air Force Academy. I had entered the Academy with little international experience, but with a strong desire to learn about the broader world. Naturally, I pursued every opportunity that arose to travel and soon found myself flying from one end of the globe to the other. During these travels, it would have been easy to miss Sunday meetings and distance myself from the Church. But, having learned in my youth that the Lord will provide a way to keep His commandments, I diligently sought out the Church no matter where I went.

The Lord blessed me for my determination and provided miraculous opportunities to allow me to stay close to the Church. On a trip to Israel after my freshman year, two other Mormon friends and I were touring the city of Jerusalem with a larger group of cadets early on a Sabbath morning. We had discussed possible ways we might attend church, but, without any access to transportation, decided we had no option but to remain with our group. First on the morning's agenda was a visit to the upper room where Christ and His disciples had shared the Last Supper. As we pondered the significance of our surroundings, perhaps in the very place the sacrament was instituted, I felt burdened by the fact that I was missing my own opportunity to partake of the sacrament.

Suddenly, I heard a familiar sound coming from a group of

travelers on the other side of the room. They were gathered in a circle softly singing. I walked toward the group, and as I approached I recognized the beautiful song "Come, Come, Ye Saints," a well-known LDS hymn. I tapped one of the gentlemen on his shoulder, and as he turned I noticed a small card around his neck that read "Latter-day Saint Tours." I relayed to him the fact that my friends and I were also Mormons and were looking for a way to get to a meeting. He instantly welcomed us into their group and invited us to join them for the remainder of their morning tour, which would conclude at the local LDS meetinghouse. After obtaining approval from our understanding commander, we left the cadet group and spent the remainder of the day with our newfound Mormon "family." As promised, the Latter-day Saint tour group, plus the three Mormon cadets, later gathered in a meetinghouse and participated in a beautiful and powerful sacrament meeting.

This experience of finding the Church and an instant circle of friends happened all over the globe. Whether running into missionaries in St. Peter's Basilica in Italy, seeing a Young Men's group cleaning a park in northern India, walking into a chapel in South Africa, or finding branches of the Church in Nanjing and Beijing, I learned that the Lord would provide a way for me to stay close to the gospel. Not only did these experiences show that the Lord is able to attend to my needs through members of His Church, no matter where I am, but they also taught me the simple truth that there is "One Lord, one faith, one baptism" (Ephesians 4:5). The Church of Jesus Christ of Latter-day Saints is truly a worldwide church, containing truths meant to bless the lives of all mankind.

I could recount many other stories to help explain what it means to me to be a Mormon. Yet, even the sum of all these experiences does not paint the whole picture. While each experience, each test of my faith, has brought answers to my prayers and proved my faith true, when I wake up early on a Sunday morning, exhausted from a long week, these stories are not what propel me out of my comfortable bed and off to church. Nor when I face a trial and am tempted to lower my standards does the thought of these experiences alone give me sufficient strength to overcome.

For me, the gospel is simple. The benefits of my belief come when I listen to a sacrament meeting talk and feel something inspire my soul to be better. The blessings of my faith come in quiet moments of reflection when a gentle whisper to my heart and mind directs me to change my path to the slightest degree. The brightness of my hope comes from the assurance that the trials of today will slowly transform into the blessings of tomorrow.

I am a Mormon because I know in my heart that when I stay close to the gospel, the Lord will never let me go astray. I am a Mormon because I know that no matter what challenges lie ahead, the Lord will give me the strength to overcome all adversity. To put it simply, I am a Mormon because being a Mormon brightens my perspective, calms my fears, and brings me joy.

MARK H. WILLES

MARK H. WILLES was appointed president and CEO of Deseret Management Corporation in March 2009. In addition to those duties, in May 2010, he was appointed president and CEO of KSL Television and Radio. He retired as chairman, president, and chief executive officer of Times Mirror in April 2000.

Mr. Willes joined Times Mirror as CEO in June 1995. In addition, he served as publisher of the *Los Angeles Times* from October 1997 to June 1999. Prior to joining Times Mirror, Mr. Willes was vice chairman of General Mills, Inc., Minneapolis, Minnesota. A fifteen-year veteran of the company, he served as president and chief operating officer from 1985 to 1992, when he was named vice chairman. He was executive vice president and chief financial officer from 1980 to 1985.

Mr. Willes previously served with the Federal Reserve System. He was president of the Federal Reserve Bank of Minneapolis from 1977 to 1980 and first vice president of the Federal Reserve Bank of Philadelphia from 1971 to 1977, having joined the Federal Reserve System in 1969. He began his career as an assistant professor of finance at the Wharton School, University of Pennsylvania, from 1967 to 1969.

Born in 1941 and raised in Salt Lake City, Utah, Mr. Willes received his AB degree from Columbia College, New York City, and his PhD from the Columbia Graduate School of Business. As an active member of The Church of Jesus Christ of Latter-day Saints, among other Church assignments, he has served as president of the Minneapolis Minnesota Stake for nine years and as president of the Hawaii Honolulu Mission for three years. He and his wife, Laura Fayone Willes, are the parents of five children and grandparents of twenty.

• • •

W E ALL MUST DECIDE, at some point, who we are and what we believe to be true. I was lucky. My journey of faith started before I remember. My parents were fully engaged members of The Church of Jesus Christ of Latter-day Saints. They taught me, and because I loved and trusted them, I believed. Actually, it was more than that. When I did the things they taught—go to church, obey specific commandments—it felt good. I was happy when I did them, and not so happy when I did not.

That started a pattern I have followed all my life. As I learned principles taught by the Church, I tried to live them. Each time I did, I received a feeling, a confirmation, that I had done the right thing. Often my beliefs have been challenged, by others or by circumstances. When I did not know by personal experience how to respond, I would just go forward on faith that what I had been taught by my parents, Church leaders, and others was right. Sooner or later, even after trials that seemed too hard to bear, I would emerge with those same feelings that I had learned as a youth—a quiet feeling that I was on the right path and that I was doing the right things.

I have learned to trust those quiet thoughts and feelings and have found that they permeate every part of my life. They are not restricted to religious settings. In fact, often they come when I am

doing things that would appear
to have nothing to do with my
life as a Mormon.

After being a professor
and then serving in the Federal
Reserve System, I went to work
at General Mills. I loved what I
was doing. I was traveling the
world, learning new things,
and working with a remarkable
group of people. The company
had exceptionally high standards, and I felt proud to be

part of it. While serving as president and chief operating officer, I
had the hope I would someday be appointed the company's CEO.

The decision was made that I would not be, and after much
time and careful consideration, I decided to find another opportunity. As I visited with executive recruiters, I indicated that although I
had been approached over the years to run financial firms, universities, and so on, what I really wanted to do was run a company that
made tangible products. When asked if I would like to interview
with Times Mirror—a newspaper, magazine, and professional information company—I said I would not. Printed products did not
seem very interesting to me. However, the thought kept coming that
I should at least talk with them.

So I went to Los Angeles for a series of interviews. After the first
set, I was driven to the hotel though some sections of the city that
seemed rather unappealing. It was not a positive encounter. Once
in my room, I stood for a few minutes looking out the window. A
strong impression, the same kind I had learned to pay attention to
as a youth and had felt repeatedly since then, came over me. I called
my wife, told her I had not finished the interviews and did not have

a job offer, but felt we would be moving to California. Somehow I just knew that the offer would come and that we should accept the job.

No one was more surprised than I, but I had learned to trust those feelings. That led to five of the most interesting years of my career. Providentially, those experiences also turned out to be extremely helpful for the assignment I now have with Deseret Management Company.

After Times Mirror was sold, an action that I confess greatly disappointed me, my wife and I were asked to preside over the Hawaii Honolulu Mission of The Church of Jesus Christ of Latter-day Saints. That was a huge blessing for us, and an interesting test of what I had learned to be the reality of personal revelation. Somewhere along the line, I had come to a full realization that thoughts that entered my mind and were confirmed by special, quiet feelings were really the Lord's way of giving me personal revelation, direction, and comfort.

During the three years we served in Hawaii, we supervised an average of 200 to 210 young missionaries who voluntarily spent eighteen months (young women) to two years (young men) sharing the gospel of Jesus Christ. Every six weeks, we needed to assign each missionary to a companion and to an area of service on one of the islands. We knew that the only way to make sure those assignments were optimal was to get direct inspiration from the Lord.

We would do our homework first. I would interview every missionary every six weeks. They would write letters letting me know how they were getting along with their companions, how they were progressing with their teaching, and so on. I would also collect a lot of information from reports and from discussions with local Church leaders. I would then think through, as carefully as I could, what assignments made the most sense, which missionaries were going home or arriving from the Missionary Training Center, which missionaries were ready for leadership responsibilities, who could best help train new missionaries, and who had been with a companion or in an area long enough.

Next, we would place a photograph of each missionary in the logical place on our "transfer board." That is, we would put each missionary's picture next to their recommended companion, in the area that seemed most suitable for them to serve in for the next six weeks. My wife, my assistants, and I would then kneel and pray. We asked if the assignments were correct, seeking confirmation to that effect. Every six weeks, for more than three years, we did not receive that special feeling of confirmation the first time we prayed. Knowing, therefore, that something was not in place, we would stand and look at the pictures and proposed assignments. Additional thoughts and ideas would come, and we would move a few pictures from one companion and one place to another.

When we felt we had it right, we would pray again. Thankfully, we usually received that quiet but unmistakable feeling that things were now as they should be. But a few times, after repeated efforts, we knew it was still not right without knowing why. So we would stop and wait for additional information. In every case, usually within twenty-four hours, we would get a letter or a phone call that provided just the information we needed about a particular missionary or area. We would then make a few more changes, and pray. The confirmation always came, and we gave the missionaries their new assignments.

In subsequent weeks, I often received comments or letters from missionaries indicating they knew they had been given exactly the assignments the Lord intended. This occurred frequently when missionaries were assigned to learn a new language. We taught missionary lessons in more than twenty different languages. We often needed to have missionaries learn those languages so the teaching could continue. I rarely knew the ability of a missionary to learn a new language, so such assignments were real acts of faith. Yet in almost every case, the newly assigned missionaries would initially look surprised and then burst into joyous smiles. I heard many stories about how missionaries had always wanted to learn a foreign language. Some indicated that they had been promised in a blessing by a Church official that they would serve a foreign-speaking mission and had not known until that moment why they had been called to serve in Hawaii. I did not know those promises had been made, but the Lord did, and had prompted us to make the necessary assignments so those blessings could be fulfilled.

To some, the above experiences might seem strange or unremarkable. To me, they represent parts of a succession of events in my life that began as a small stream and grew to be like a large river flowing down from the mountains. One experience after another, they have consistently and persistently answered my questions and eroded my doubt away.

Mountain streams eventually make canyons. In my case, the walls of my belief are tall and firm. Peering into my heart, I find a depth of belief and conviction I once thought impossible. Now that I have it, I wish I could speak and write with the power to crack stone and remove obstacles for others.

Yet, that is rarely the Lord's way. He does not force us. He is committed to letting us freely choose what paths to follow, using quiet thoughts and gentle feelings to nudge us along. Over time, the cumulative effect is remarkable and powerful. I may not yet have a Grand Canyon of faith and understanding, but my belief and commitment are deep and strong. Who am I? I am a Mormon!

ROBERT S. WOOD

ROBERT S. WOOD is currently president of the Boston Temple, having served for more than thirteen years as a General or Area Authority of The Church of Jesus Christ of Latter-day Saints. He previously served in many other capacities in the Church, including as a missionary in France.

A native of Idaho, he married Dixie Leigh Jones of California, who graduated from Stanford University in modern European literature. They are the parents of four daughters and have thirteen grandchildren.

President Wood is known in civic, government, and academic circles as a respected commentator and teacher on international affairs, national security policy, and strategic theory. He was dean of the Center for Naval Warfare Studies at the U.S. Naval War College, a focal point of strategic and campaign thought in the naval services and a major research group in the national security field. The Center houses the largest gaming and simulation department in the U.S. as well as departments in advanced technology, oceans law and policy, and national military strategy. He oversaw the work of the Naval War College Press. He held the Chester W. Nimitz Chair of National Security and Foreign Affairs and twice served as director of the Chief of Naval Operations' Strategic Studies

Group. He regularly provided advice to the White House, the Congress, and the Department of Defense.

A Phi Beta Kappa graduate in history with highest distinction from Stanford University, President Wood earned his AM and PhD in Political Science from Harvard. He has taught at Harvard University and Bentley College and was a professor in the Woodrow Wilson Department of Government and Foreign Affairs at the University of Virginia.

He served in the Netherlands as Fulbright-Hays Senior Professor at the University of Groningen Law School and at the University of Tilburg Department of Political Economy. He has also authored or contributed to more than two dozen books and numerous articles on public affairs, executive development, international affairs, and national security policy. He also authored *The Complete Christian* (Deseret Book, 2007).

Active in civic affairs, President Wood has served as a member of several councils of the Boy Scouts of America, the Newport Institute, the World-Scholar Athlete Games, and the Armed Services YMCA. He has also served on the boards of advisors of Salve Regina University, Southern Virginia University, and a number of other academic and professional institutions. He is a member of the International Institute for Strategic Studies.

. . .

THE STORY IS TOLD that after Napoleon's coronation, he visited a small town in France that failed to fire the requisite fusillade honoring the emperor as he entered. When Napoleon demanded to know why, the mayor replied that there were three reasons, the first of which was they had no bullets. Napoleon stated that he had no need to hear the other two.

There are several reasons why I am a Mormon, the first of which is decisive. Although I was reared as a Latter-day Saint, I knew early on that I needed to establish for myself the proposition that Jesus is the Son of God, the universal and my personal Redeemer, and that The Church of Jesus Christ of Latter-day Saints is indeed His Church. Paul said that one can only say that Jesus is the Christ by the witness of the Holy Ghost (see 1 Corinthians 12:3), and, as I had been taught, the truth of eternal things is established by the same principle (Moroni 10:4–5). As a teenager I sought this confirmation through prayer and have had it sustained through countless experiences in my life.

Like the French mayor, I could stop here. But I will take this opportunity to provide a number of reasons that reinforce that fundamental witness of my faith.

First, I find the explanation of the meaning of life provided by Mormon doctrine intellectually and emotionally compelling. Many philosophies and faiths posit a radical distinction between the Creator and the created, portraying a divine being who is self-contained, whose positive characteristics are utterly incomprehensible, and who is unaffected by the passions and actions of men. In contrast, Mormonism presents God as approachable, even desiring that we approach Him. It teaches that all people are literally spirit children of an engaged and personal Heavenly Father, and, as such, have a divine potential. Crucial to the realization of this potential is the ability to distinguish between truth and error and to choose right over wrong.

The inevitable mistakes and sins pertaining to our mortal existence require, however, that we be rescued from their consequences—alienation from our Father in Heaven and the permanency of death. A loving Father has provided such a Savior in His Firstborn in the spirit and Only Begotten in the flesh, Jesus Christ. Through faith in Him and a willingness to emulate Him, we may transcend ignorance, sin, and death and become with Him a co-heir of the glory of God.

Man is, therefore, not depraved, nor is his fate predetermined. He is endowed with moral agency and subject to the consequences of his own actions and those of others. The heavenly standard is high, and man's actions are inadequate, but through faith in Christ, men and women may eventually realize the mandate given by the mortal Messiah, "Be ye therefore perfect, even as your Father which is in heaven is perfect" (Matthew 5:48).

I find the appeal of Mormonism thus to be its cosmic optimism and its insistence that each of us is responsible for our actions. We are needy but accountable. We are heirs not only to a divine destiny but to the persistent and consistent love of a Heavenly Father and His Only Begotten Son. The universe is purposeful, and life—despite trials and misfortunes—is intended to be not only good but joyfully redemptive.

Second, the personal perspectives, aspirations, and daily habits that Mormon doctrine generates have led to a sense of joy and well-being that transcends the challenges of life. How we view life determines how each of us lives. In Mormonism, a remarkable balance exists between faith in the grace of God through Christ and appreciation of the remarkable capacities of growth within us. Some would denigrate man in order to exalt God. While declaring our fundamental dependence on divine grace to surmount sin and death and to cope with daily trials, Mormonism is nevertheless insistent that an eternal plan exists to bring to fruition the sacred attributes of our divine conception.

In large and small ways, this perspective shapes the contours of my life. As a lad I remember that whether it was a horse that had fallen on me or the triumph of a school event, my mother would always remark, "Well, that was a useful experience!" Inherent in every event, good or bad, was the potential to learn and improve as well as confidence in an outcome that would leap over the limits of time and space. Such orientation produces a remarkable society.

Third, the society of other Latter-day Saints has provided a community of friends and mutual support that has blessed me and my family in special ways. One of the greatest blessings of my life has been the opportunity to associate with wonderfully talented, energetic, and good people from many backgrounds who profess many faiths and commitments. Within that group of people I have, of course, also associated closely with numerous Mormons. I have been struck by something among Mormons that, although it is not entirely unique, exists in the LDS culture to such a degree that we stand apart—a willingness both to give of one's time, talents, and resources to good causes and to organize to achieve those purposes.

Some years ago I had lunch with a prominent humanitarian leader. He had come to the headquarters of the Church in Salt Lake City to meet with some of the leaders of The Church of Jesus Christ of Latter-day Saints to discover how the Church accomplished so effectively its many missions, particularly welfare and humanitarian assistance. One of those leaders said, "We can give you an organizational chart, but it won't do you any good. The answer to your inquiry lies over there." He pointed out the window to the Salt Lake Temple. "In there, we are taught the fundamental purpose of life and commit ourselves to give all we have to follow Christ and to bring forth a good and just society." The visitor commented that he could see that such success was not due to the organization or the resources of the Church, but to the beliefs and character of its people.

Willingness to follow the counsel of a living prophet and the sense of mission found at the very core of Mormonism make the "call to serve" a powerful incentive in the lives of both the obscure and the renowned. I have seen men and women of modest means lay aside everything to serve others and to undertake humanitarian and ecclesiastical missions in response to the call. Perhaps more remarkably, I have known those of considerable means and responsibility to be equally willing, not only to devote some time and resources to serving in the Church community, but to give all they have if called upon to do so. The invitation of Christ to the rich young man to sell all that he had, then give to the poor and follow Him, is reenacted every day. Unlike the young man in the story, I have witnessed countless individuals willingly respond.

Fourth, the character of such a community has impelled me to get out of myself and reach out to others. I recall the bishop of our congregation in the small town in Idaho where I grew up. He was a wonderful man of modest means. He worked on the railroad and lived in a small duplex. His two counselors were far more prominent, one being a banker and the other a successful businessman. I marveled at the thought that, despite their differences in worldly status, these three men were united, and the wealthier counselors supported the bishop in all things. Such has been my experience ever since. Men and women of vastly different economic means, education, and social status have cooperated with no concern for worldly distinctions—showing love for each other and concern for others.

I currently have a calling in the Church in which I work together with many men and women from throughout New England. Among that group are carpenters and plumbers, salespeople and day laborers, renowned physicians and professors, financial planners and accomplished musicians, and many representing other jobs and professions. Those of modest means often travel hours at their own expense to fulfill Church callings. All of them are prepared to give everything they have to serve the Lord. This diverse group serves without thought of reward or status.

Although, as noted earlier, such behavior is not unique to the Latter-day Saints, the scope and depth of the devotion that I daily observe have both humbled me and inspired me to do more and to do better. I have had many professional opportunities and family responsibilities that have engaged my interest and energies. I could with great satisfaction devote all my time to these enterprises. Yet the community of which I am a part constantly elicits from me a desire to reach further and include more within the circle of good works. In a remarkable way, I find that such drawing out has helped me to be a better husband, father, and professional. These associations and opportunities to serve cannot in themselves explain why I am a Mormon. But they do clarify one thing: I am a better person because I am a Mormon.

Finally, I recall an experience with my father when I was about twelve years old. He was a convert to the Church. As a young man he was an able athlete and had been asked by some Mormon friends to join a Church basketball team. While he was playing basketball, a young lady watching the games caught his eye, and that girl later became my mother. Now, some years later my father and I were at a movie together (one of the great movies of all time, *Abbott and Costello Meet Frankenstein!*). Afterward, we walked together to a favorite drugstore and had an ice-cream sundae at the soda fountain. On the way home we stopped to sit on a park bench. He turned to me and asked, "Robert, do you know why I joined the Church?" I replied, "Probably to marry Mother!" He laughed and said that it was a help, but that was not why he joined. He then bore to me his personal testimony as to the truthfulness of the restored gospel and its impact in his life.

My dad was a man of tremendous integrity, and I knew he always spoke the truth. I thought to myself, if he is willing to testify so forcefully about the truth of these things, I have an obligation to take that witness seriously and make the same effort to establish in my own life the true and the good. The Book of Mormon, the scriptures from which the nickname for The Church of Jesus Christ of Latter-day Saints is derived, begins with these words from one of its principal authors: "I, Nephi, having been born of goodly parents. . . ." Surely the trajectory of my life owes much to good, loving, and honest parents. They encouraged faith but allowed inquiry and freedom to make the faith my own.

And so I return to the decisive reason for my choice to be a Mormon. As a teenager I prayed about the truthfulness of the restored gospel of Jesus Christ and found out for myself that it is true.

STEVE YOUNG

A NATIVE OF CONNECTICUT, Steve Young is perhaps best known as the quarterback for the San Francisco 49ers who earned Most Valuable Player of Super Bowl XXIX by throwing for a Super Bowl record six touchdowns. During his fifteen-year professional football career, he also was selected as the *Sports Illustrated* and *Sporting News* Player of the Year from 1992 to 1994 and the NFL's Most Valuable Player for 1992 and 1994. In 2005, Steve was inducted into the Pro Football Hall of Fame, the first left-handed quarterback to be so honored. He is still the highest-rated quarterback in NFL history and has the distinction of  being the only signal caller in league annals to win four consecutive NFL passing titles.

Today Steve is actively involved in children's charities world-wide through the Forever Young Foundation, which he founded and chairs. He is also a former international spokesperson and the current broadcast host for the Children's Miracle Network (CMN), which has raised over one billion dollars worldwide to benefit children's hospitals.

Steve currently serves as managing director and cofounder of Huntsman Gay Global Capital and as a member of Huntsman Gay's policy and investment committee. Previously, he was a member in

Northgate Capital, LLC, the general partner of Northgate Capital Partners, L.P., and then a cofounder and managing director of Sorenson Capital, a private equity fund focused on middle market leveraged buyouts in the western United States.

Companies such as Nike, Visa, Sun Microsystems, Sprint, PowerBar, and ICON Health & Fitness have used

Photo courtesy of San Francisco 49ers

Steve as a corporate spokesperson, and he has been profiled in a variety of publications, including the *Wall Street Journal, Business Week, Worth Magazine, Sports Illustrated, People, Inside Sports,* and *GQ.*

He is a graduate of Brigham Young University, where he earned a JD degree from the J. Reuben Clark Law School as well as a BS in finance and political science. He and his wife, Barbara, are the parents of four children.

• • •

WHEN I WAS YOUNG, I had trouble leaving home to go to school. In second grade, my mom had to walk me to school and then stay in class so that I wouldn't run home. Home has always been a centerpiece in my life, both as a physical place and as a state of mind. For many years I have contemplated, even yearned, for an eternal home and have made it a quest to find it.

I was born into a long and storied genealogy of faith in The Church of Jesus Christ of Latter-day Saints, but it has become the core of who I am through the rigors of my life. Every time I have been pushed to my extremes—whether in discomfort, fatigue, depression, anxiety, frustration, or through mistreatment or resentment—in those times, I have always found a sense of home through my Savior Jesus Christ and the calming influence of the Holy Spirit. My entire life I have found comfort and peace, or at least patience and perspective, giving me strength to go forward in faith. That sense of home is never further away than an act of faith.

As a Mormon, I am inspired daily by that which is plain and simple yet incomparable in its depth and personal impact. Through the Gospel of Jesus Christ and through Christ's Atonement in Gethsemane, my sins are paid as long as I believe in Him, take His name, humble myself, and repent. And I have been repenting my whole life. Repentance is an invitation from the Creator of this earth to participate with Him in the Atonement. I believe that I need His sacrament weekly to renew myself. This constant renewing process defines my life and is the greatest gift that I have ever been given. Without it I am left to myself, alone, powerless to overcome a fallen world. In other words, I cannot get home by my own wits and guile. And I want to be home.

I have always strived to see how good I could be—whether in educational or professional endeavors. But my quest to return home also applies to the most precious and vital relationships that define me: husband, father, son, brother, or friend. I cannot embark on a quest to be my best in these roles without a Savior, without His gospel, without scripture that teaches me how the Holy Ghost works His heavenly science to wash away sins and renew me. I've always wondered how I could ever come close to fulfilling Jesus' invitation to "believe in me." Only by constant refinement, by qualifying for the Atonement through faith and obedience, can I walk that path.

I could write extensively on the day-to-day, pragmatic benefits of being Mormon, but I want to address the question at a very fundamental level that feels the truest to me. Why am I a Mormon? Why do I believe?

- Because without this heavenly plan, I cannot grow beyond myself.
- Because the Savior loved and believed in His Father and was perfect in every way—perfectly faithful and perfectly obedient—thus providing the only true way home.
- Because scripture and prophets set before me the examples I need, showing me the value of being obedient to the laws of God, of giving my behavior freely and willingly, of acting in a way to qualify for His Spirit. What am I doing here if I'm not being led by God's hand? How can I think that this short life can be defined by anything other than finding the will of God for me? He created me, and it is His eternal purpose to help me along this path.
- Because I can see no other way to qualify for His Spirit to inspire me, to give me an eternal perspective—one that informs me of things beyond mortality, seeing myself and others as He sees us, giving me insight into who I was before this life and the enormity of what I can be after it.
- Because I know that my wife is my equal, a daughter of Eve, and that our children are gifted to us as a responsibility in this life and beyond. How can I fulfill that responsibility without daily heavenly inspiration and guidance? God can qualify us to be together beyond the grave.

I've always known that heaven is close. Maybe it's my anxiety about wanting home never to be very far away, but I know this life is a pattern for the next. God is physically like me, and I have heavenly parents who bore my spirit. All of these connections are vital to me. These fundamental beliefs are my point of departure every day as I venture out into my world.

I have faith in all God's power. I carry faith's partner—hope—with me every day, and with them I can get through anything life brings. Faith and hope, carried daily and applied with thoughtful and obedient action, can bring me before my life's end to charity, the pure love of Christ, the ultimate gift from God. I want to see everyone through this eternal lens of God's, as Christ does. To have perspective beyond this life is the phenomenal gift of belief.

What trophy, award, or accomplishment could ever support the weight that belief can? Nothing I do by my own power alone, no matter how great, could ever fill my spiritual lamp with oil. Belief is the gateway to see the mysteries of God: "My thoughts are not your thoughts, neither are your ways my ways" (Isaiah 55:8).

And to not believe is death and ending, separation from home, to have only what I can see, leaving me with all the extremities of life—depression, anxiety, and catastrophe—without a context in which to define them. This is what being a Mormon gives me: context, understanding, and the peace of home. I am a Mormon because belief is life, and I don't want a life without it.